FOR THIS?

THE LIFE & TIMES OF MICHAEL OWEN   14

He's Britain's most popular footballer! **MATCH** tells you everything you ever wanted to know about the amazing life and times of Michael Owen!

THE PREMIERSHIP 100 CLUB   22

Only five strikers have scored 100 Premiership goals. We analyse just how they each got their ton – in a comprehensive strike-by-strike guide.

ALAN SHEARER	24
IAN WRIGHT	36
LES FERDINAND	50
ROBBIE FOWLER	64
ANDY COLE	76

TAKEN FROM THE PAGES OF *MATCH facts*

AROUND THE GROUNDS   30

MATCH goes behind the scenes at St James' Park, Celtic Park, White Hart Lane, Ibrox – and loads of other top grounds!

THE BEST MATCHES OF THE '90s   42

From Italia '90 to the Man. United/Arsenal thriller at the Villa, **MATCH** takes a look at the best games of the decade!

HOW TO BECOME A FOOTBALLER   56

The **MATCH** guide to the country's best football Academies.

"IF I WASN'T A FOOTBALLER…"   70

David Beckham, Julian Joachim, Phil Neville and Ian Wright tell **MATCH** what they'd do for a living if they weren't top footy stars!

GREAT BRITAIN UNITED   82

Should Britain have a united football team? **MATCH** picks its UK selection!

"MY KINDA MUSIC!"   88

Keith Gillespie, Lee Hendrie, Danny Dichio and the stars of footy pick the best sounds from their own record collections!

HOW MAN. UNITED WON THE TREBLE   94

Gary Neville and the stars of Man. United tell the story of that incredible treble year!

MATCH ANNUAL 2000 MANAGING EDITOR Chris Hunt **ART DIRECTOR** Darryl Tooth
PRODUCTION EDITOR Alistair Phillips **FEATURES EDITOR** Bev Ward **DESIGNER** Ben Bates
STAFF PHOTOGRAPHER Phil Bagnall **WRITERS** Gary Sherrard, Phil Smith, Tim Unwin
AND THE REST OF THE MATCH TEAM Paul Smith, Hugh Sleight, Kevin Hughes, Michelle Daniel,
Stewart Parkes, Kerry Craig, Richard Ecclestone, Russ Carvell & Russ Carter.

MATCH **BRITAIN'S BIGGEST SELLING FOOTBALL MAGAZINE**

Yup, I think the league will do for starters, then the double after that.

If George keeps trying to nick Leeds players, their fans will soon hate us as much as they do Man. United.

Spurs are the new Man. United!

A YEAR AGO ENGLAND DEFENDER SOL CAMPBELL stunned thousands of Tottenham fans when he announced he might have to leave the club if they didn't win honours in the foreseeable future. It wasn't exactly a surprise announcement, coming from such a top-class footballer plying his trade under the infamous Christian Gross – even though it would have meant leaving a club he loved. A season later and Sol's the happiest man in the world. **"Everything's sweet for me at the moment at Tottenham and I'm just waiting to see what happens,"** Sol says. **"I really was looking forward to playing in Europe with Tottenham this season because it's been a new experience for me. We've laid the foundations for making Tottenham great again. Winning the Worthington Cup and getting into Europe was the platform to build from – and it was a great start."**

George Graham's plans are shaping up nicely at White Hart Lane, but Sol has set high targets for his fellow team-mates if the success is to continue. **"Hopefully we can bring the right personnel into the club and keep the good players we already have at Tottenham. We need to start getting the results we want and to perform consistently well in the league. I hope that in two or three years we can achieve the kind of domination that Man. United have had in the '90s. Any longer than that won't be any good!"**

Campbell thwarts another Newcastle attacking move.

Sol loves to come forward when he gets the chance, like against Charlton last season.

Campbell wants Spurs to be as successful as Man. United have been.

There was a time when Alan Shearer would have been too much for the Spurs defence to handle.

Sol's expecting more celebrations at White Hart Lane this season.

Sol has his sights set on the top of the table with Spurs.

Sergio's getting shirty

Rangers' right-back Sergio Porrini has given himself something to do when he retires from football – he could open a footy museum! The Italian collects memorabilia from the games he's played in. **"I have a collection of over 300 football jerseys,"** Sergio tells Route 1. **"I started collecting them four years ago when I was at Juventus. I always ask for a shirt when I play against a European team. One I like is an Eric Cantona shirt, because he is retired now, but the best is a River Plate shirt I got when I played against them in the World Club Championship."** And what about all those prestigious Falkirk and Stenhousemuir shirts then Sergio?

SUPERSTITIONS

Footy stars reveal the things they do for luck.

GOT ANY SILLY HABITS SHARPEY?
"There's probably things that I do before a match, but they've become such a habit that I don't realise I'm doing them."

WAS THE NO. 7 SHIRT AT LEEDS LUCKY?
"I had disastrous luck with injuries when I started wearing the number seven shirt at Leeds, so no it wasn't."

WOULD YOU WEAR THE NO.13?
"I can't say that I'd be really pleased, but at the end of the day a shirt is a shirt."

LEE SHARPE
BRADFORD CITY

Elton's on the ball

Wonder if Elton'll lend us a few quid for some new players?

If you're a celebrity these days, you have to be seen cheering on the lads at a top football team. Liverpool have Sporty Spice to cheer them on, Newcastle have Ant and Dec on their side and Chelsea have some stuffy politicians. But Watford can beat every other club hands down by boasting the ageing, but highly successful crooner Elton John. **"Elton John is a big Watford fan,"** Hornets boss Graham Taylor tells Route 1. **"He's a very knowledgeable person if you talk to him about sport. How he finds the time to keep up with the news is beyond me. He was as excited as the next person when we got promoted through the play-offs last season."**

F.R.I.E.N.D.S

match asks the stars who's their best mate in footy?

"I've got plenty of mates here. I go out with Matt Oakley a lot and James Beattie and Jason Dodd as well. You'd probably catch us at Ocean Village, LeisureWorld or the Chicago Rock Café in town if we were having a night out."

· matt le tissier · southampton ·

high 5ive

NIGEL MARTYN
Leeds United

TOP FIVE...
DRINKS

1 John Smiths draught
2 Milk
3 Orange squash
4 Tea
5 Instant coffee

They nearly didn't make it...

Steve Harper
Newcastle United

"I was on schoolboy forms when I was at Burnley but I didn't get taken on because I was too small at the time – I was about 5ft 7ins which isn't good for a goalkeeper! I shot up a bit when I was at sixth form college and I played the occasional game for Newcastle's youth team on Saturday mornings when their normal goalkeeper got injured. I had a place at Liverpool John Moores University, but Newcastle offered me a one-year contract, so I deferred for a year and I'm still here!"

Hat-trick

MATCH asks the stars what it's really like to be a top footy player.

FRANK LAMPARD
west ham & england

AGE	21
POSITION	MIDFIELD

CLAIM TO FAME

His father, Frank Lampard Senior, is West Ham's assistant manager, his uncle Harry Redknapp is his boss and Harry's son, Liverpool's Jamie Redknapp, is his cousin!

1 ... How different is international football?
"Playing for England is a totally different class of football to playing in the Premier League. International football is much more skill-based and it isn't nearly as quick as league football is. Players take a lot more care to not get injuries as well."

2 ... What's best about being a footy player?
"Being able to go home at one o'clock, finished for the day. I like the fame as well, and there's always lots of fans here watching us train. I've got a great life! A lot of people don't make it and that's terrible and it makes you really appreciate the success even more."

3 ... How do you cope with the fame?
"It's nice to have the fame which footballers attract but it can get a bit annoying when fans won't leave you alone. I get quite a lot of fan mail – either people asking me for an autograph or girls who want me to go out with them!"

WHEN

WAS THE LAST TIME...

Jamie Pollock
manchester city

...you went to see a concert?

"That would have been Oasis at The Newcastle Arena about two years ago and the whole occasion was just tremendous. When you see them in the flesh they're just awesome."

...you missed a sitter?

"I was playing for Bolton against Man. United and the score was 0-0. With five minutes to go, a corner was swung in and I stuck my leg out but poked the ball wide. It was an open goal and I really should have scored."

...you got a dodgy hair cut?

"Today actually! I've just come back from town and my wife says it looks like a bowl cut that everyone used to have when they were little. I suppose it's an improvement on the skinhead I had at Middlesbrough."

...you paid to see a game?

"That was the FA Cup Final between Boro and Chelsea in 1996 which my old club lost 2-0. I went there with my family and although we were disappointed, it was a fantastic day. To walk down Wembley Way through a sea of red is a great experience."

...you felt like giving up?

"Last season I was sent-off three times, all for a second bookable offence, and I thought only one caution was justified. When that happens, it doesn't make you want to give the game up, but you do think enough's enough. You have to take the ups with the downs in football."

...you had a run in with the boss?

At the end of last season, I was suffering from a calf injury which had kept me out and Joe Royle left me out of the play-off final team. I was bitterly disappointed so I gave the boss a roasting!"

...you went on holiday?

"I went on a cruise around the Mediterranean last summer with my wife and kids. I left on the Friday after our play-off victory against Gillingham so it was quite a week. It was really hot but you have to be careful when you have young kids because it's important to keep them out of the sun."

ALL CHANGE AT WEMBLEY

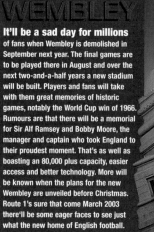

It'll be a sad day for millions of fans when Wembley is demolished in September next year. The final games are to be played there in August and over the next two-and-a-half years a new stadium will be built. Players and fans will take with them great memories of historic games, notably the World Cup win of 1966. Rumours are that there will be a memorial for Sir Alf Ramsey and Bobby Moore, the manager and captain who took England to their proudest moment. That's as well as boasting an 80,000 plus capacity, easier access and better technology. More will be known when the plans for the new Wembley are unveiled before Christmas. Route 1's sure that come March 2003 there'll be some eager faces to see just what the new home of English football.

THEY DIDN'T SEE IT COMING

> Get in! We have ze Englishmen beaten now.

This year Bayern Munich think they've won the European Cup.

JEWELL
OF THE LAUNDRY

Whatever goes on at Bradford between now and the end of the season, you can be sure their boss Paul Jewell will enjoy every minute of it. His playing career was nothing to write home about, but having started out scrubbing the pants of Liverpool's Kenny Dalglish he's learnt the tight Scotsman's darkest secret. **"I was a Liverpool nutter as a kid,"** The Bantams' boss says. **"Getting put in charge of the home dressing-room and being Dalglish's apprentice was brilliant. Not only did Kenny's boots have to be sparkling, he always wore cotton shorts. Everyone else had nylon. I always had to make sure they were ready the day before a game. If there were any problems he'd be down on me like a ton of bricks."** Yes, he'd also kill you if he found out you call him 'Scotty Skidmark' behind his back!

F.R.I.E.N.D.S
match asks the stars who's their best mate in footy?

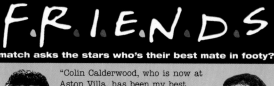

"Colin Calderwood, who is now at Aston Villa, has been my best friend for the last five years. I often go out in central London with Chris Armstrong and Darren Anderton as well. What do we get up to? Now that would be telling."

· justin edinburgh · tottenham hotspur ·

PLAYING WITH THE BIG KIDS

Darius Vassell has long been seen as Aston Villa's latest teen star. The England Under-18 striker hit the big time with two goals against Stromsgodset in last season's UEFA Cup, but has put in a lot of time on the Villa bench since then. He may not be getting the time on the pitch, but he's making the most of senior training. **"Paul Merson is always coaching me about what runs to make where,"** Darius tells Route 1. **"And Dion Dublin is always giving me advice too. Dion tells me what positions I should be in at certain times."** Darius says he's also been getting a lot of help from his boss, John Gregory. **"He's really down to earth. The players have got lot respect for him and you do what he says because you don't want to get on the wrong side of him."** You're not wrong Darius, as Dwight Yorke and Stan Collymore will tell you!

Thommo's training tips!

PRINGLE'S
SPITTING CHIPS

Most leading foreign imports come over to England laden with international caps. But some have a terrible story to tell about representing their country, like Charlton striker Martin Pringle. **"I have two full caps for Sweden,"** he tells Route 1. **"My debut was against Scotland when we won 2-0. I came on for the last 15 minutes of the game as a central midfielder, which was stupid because that is not my position. I managed to play the last four minutes of that game up front so I didn't have much of a chance to prove myself. My second game was against Japan but I got taken off with an injury in that game."** Mind you, if Andreas Andersson can get a game up front for Sweden – Route 1's sure there's a call-up in the post for Martin.

I'll just have a quick sit down if that's okay.

Alan knows it's important to rest as well as train hard.

Who said a footballer's life was

easy? It may be acceptable just to turn up in your kit for a game if you play pub football, but for the top pros training is a major part of the job. Mind you, after playing a tough game on the weekend, some players don't look forward to circuit training or doing weights on a Monday. But not Aston Villa midfielder Alan Thompson. **"I like training – even pre-season training!"** Alan told MATCH. **"It's hard after a rest, but people do keep themselves in shape over the summer. After a couple of weeks off I'm always itching to get back playing."**

There's always good and bad trainers at a club, and hard work shows on a Saturday. So who's the best players Thommo has trained with? **"Mark Bosnich used to work very hard in training. Although some people might say he came in late, he did work hard when he was there! Lee Hendrie is probably the best runner over long distances. He's only a young lad and he only weighs about three stone, so he's not got much weight to carry around!"**

HERE'S ALAN THOMPSON'S GUIDE TO A NORMAL TRAINING WEEK...

SUNDAY: "Sometimes on the day after a game, we maybe come in for a bit of a warm-down. It only lasts for half an hour or so though and then we can go back home again."

MONDAY: "We usually do a bit of five-a-side work on a Monday. Nothing too strenuous."

TUESDAY: "Everyone is given set workout programmes to follow in the gym and we are encouraged to go in to do them. It's not just aerobic exercise either, we do plenty of leg weights and if you've had an injury, you concentrate on working on that part of your body to strengthen it. I've had an ankle injury this year, so the physio points me in the right direction to work on that."

WEDNESDAY: "We have a hard physical day on a Wednesday, which involves a lot of fitness work and power running – running the length of the pitch to improve our stamina. It's tough but you have to be fit to play at the top level these days"

THURSDAY: "We sometimes have a day off on a Thursday to give our bodies a break from all the training and it prepares us for the match at the weekend."

FRIDAY: "We have a light morning on the day before a game. You might do a pattern of play on a Friday, usually playing against the youth team. We work hard on set pieces and prepare for whatever opposition tactics might crop up in the game the next day."

SATURDAY: "Sometimes we are told the match tactics as late as two o'clock on the day of the game, when the opposition have named their starting line-up. John Gregory is switched on when it comes to this sort of thing, as is his coach Steve Harrison. They watch a lot of games, so they can be sure that they get their tactics right!"

RESPECT IS DUE TO BECKHAM

David Beckham may be fast becoming a fashion model, but here at Route 1 we've found out that his greatest wish is to be respected as a role model. **"I love young players looking up to me and respecting me. That's something I always did as a youngster – look up to great players like Bryan Robson and Bobby Charlton. That's how I want to be looked at. If you go through an experience like I have, you can either crack or come out and make people eat their words, which I feel that I've done."** Good on yer, son! You can't help but warm to the guy, can you?

PAGE 3 STUNNAH!

The latest in our series of star footballers – topless!

Lorenzo, 29, Palese Italy.

WHO IS THE BEST... playmaker?

These lads are all top notch midfielders.

Leicester winger **Steve Guppy** selects the best midfielders he's faced.

DAVID BECKHAM	DAVID GINOLA	JAMIE REDKNAPP	PAUL GASCOIGNE
manchester united	tottenham hotspur	liverpool	middlesbrough
"His ability to whip a ball in under pressure is superb. He's a specialist in crossfield passing. He can play wide right or in the middle dictating play."	"He's a key man for Spurs simply because of the goals he can create by his amazing vision. He works a lot harder now than he used to as well."	"He can mix short, passes with long, ranging ones. A lot of what Liverpool do goes through him. When we play them we always mark him out as one to stop."	"He can hover in the centre circle and spray the ball around before bursting into the box – he can still do it. I'd like to see him in a Leicester shirt, that's for sure."

10 brain-bustin' facts about...

european championships

1 Frenchman, Henri Delaunay, a friend of World Cup pioneer Jules Rimet first drew up his proposal for a European Championship in the 1920s. The idea was not even discussed until UEFA was created in 1954.

2 Previously known as the European Nations Cup, the tournament was intended to bring together various regional competitions such as the British Home International Championship, the Nordic Cup and the Central European Championship.

3 Following the death of Delaunay, his son Pierre took up the quest and the UEFA executive committee took a vote on June 28, 1957 in Copenhagen. 14 out of 26 countries voted in favour.

4 On August 6, 1958, the first European Championship began and entry cost around £50. Only 17 nations competed. The trophy was named after Henri Delaunay and was hosted by France.

5 The most bizarre result in the competition came in the 1982 qualifying campaign when Spain scored nine second half goals to beat Malta 12-1 – they needed 11 goals to qualify!

6 England lost the semi-final in 1996, against Germany on penalties which means along with Italy, we hold the record for being eliminated the most times by that means.

7 Scotland qualified for their first European championships in 1992 and repeated the feat in 1996.

8 Germany won the European Championships for the third time in 1996 with Bierhoff's strike making it the first major final to be decided by the 'golden goal'.

9 Euro '96 was the biggest European tournament ever with more teams competing, higher attendances and bigger TV audiences than ever before.

10 Euro 2000 will take place in Holland and Belgium, the first time the tournament has been shared between two countries.

TOP 10

The very best of the Premiership's foreign imports of the 1990s.

1 PETER SCHMEICHEL
1991-1999

The great Dane played over 300 games for Man. United winning the European Cup, five league titles and the FA Cup three times.

2 ERIC CANTONA
1992-1997

One of the greatest foreign imports ever. He won the league five times in six seasons and the League and FA Cup double twice.

3 DENNIS BERGKAMP
1995-present day

The Dutchman was a double winner at Arsenal in 1997-98 and both Footballer and Player Of The Year in that season.

4 EMMANUEL PETIT
1997-present day

The first foreign player based in England to score in a World Cup Final. He won the double in his first season at Highbury.

5 PATRICK VIEIRA
1997-present day

Vieira and Petit are one of the strongest midfield pairings in Europe. Patrick has had two great seasons for Arsenal.

6 OLE GUNNAR SOLSKJAER
1996-present day

The scorer of the winning goal in Man. United's European Cup win, only the lack of a regular first-team place holds him back.

7 GIANFRANCO ZOLA
1996-present day

In his first two terms at Chelsea, Zola won the FA Cup, the League Cup and the European Cup Winners' Cup in which he came on to score.

8 ROBERTO DI MATTEO
1996- present day

Roberto scored twice against Middlesbrough in two cup finals and is a crucial part of the team that first Gullit, and then Vialli built.

9 DAVID GINOLA
1995-present day

Having impressed at Newcastle, David moved to Spurs where he won the League Cup in 1999 and the Footballer Of The Year.

10 JURGEN KLINSMANN
1994-1995 & 1997-1998

Jurgen's impact on English football during his first spell at Spurs sparked the influx of foreign stars that has escalated ever since.

FOOTY'S ALL WRIGHT

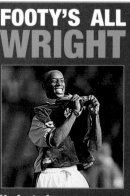

Us footy fans are passionate about the game, but can you say that most footballers love it as much? One player who can never get enough is Ian Wright. **"I cannot put into words what football means to me,"** he says. **"It is, without doubt, the most important thing in the world and you have to be that way if you want to make it to the very top.** I love scoring goals, I need that buzz I get when the ball hits the net. A tap in or a great shot from outside the box, it doesn't matter to me – they're all goals." And you've scored plenty of them Wrighty!

---

my favourite...
PLAYER OF ALL TIME

BY EFAN EKOKU
WIMBLEDON

WHO'S YOUR FAVE EVER FOOTY PLAYER?
"As a boy it was probably Kevin Keegan."
WOT, OLD PERM HEAD?!
"Yes, I'm from Liverpool and he was the best around at the time – I thought he was God."
BUT GOD HASN'T GOT A PERM HAS HE?
"He used to play up front with John Toshack and they scored goals for fun."
WHAT, GOD USED TO PLAY UP FRONT WITH JOHN TOSHACK?
"No, Keegan! He was worshipped by the whole of the red side of Merseyside. He was smaller than everyone else, the defenders used to tower over him, but he used to take the mickey out of them. I didn't model my game around his, but he was definitely a role model."

Shearer issues warning

Ronny Johnsen did nothing to improve Shearer's game in the FA Cup Final.

Dietmar Hamann impressed in his first season in England.

Few English forwards flourish in the face of Desailly.

Ever since the Premier League was born and more foreigners came over here, there has been a debate over whether there are too many overseas players and while these players have helped improve the English game. Alan Shearer is warning about such excesses. **"I think it's good if we can get high quality players here, but if you flood the country with them, that will be to the detriment of English football. I think there are a lot of foreign footballers here at the moment. It's not a problem yet but it could be if we continue to get foreigners in who aren't going to play regularly."** Shearer does agree with bringing top-quality internationals however: **"Dietmar Hamann has proved he's a quality import and can improve the English game. He's like Patrick Vieira – he's tall and has scored some important goals."**

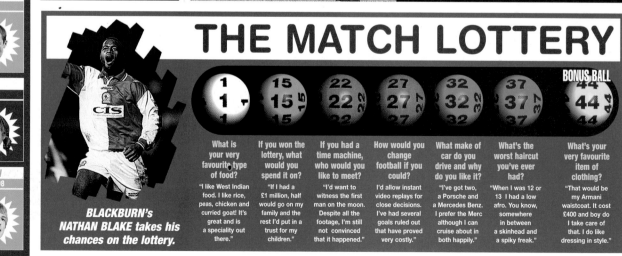

THE MATCH LOTTERY

BLACKBURN's NATHAN BLAKE takes his chances on the lottery.

1 15 22 27 32 37 **BONUS BALL** 44

What is your very favourite type of food?
"I like West Indian food. I like rice, peas, chicken and curried goat! It's great and is a speciality out there."

If you won the lottery, what would you spend it on?
"If I had a £1 million, half would go on my family and the rest I'd put in a trust for my children."

If you had a time machine, who would you like to meet?
"I'd want to witness the first man on the moon. Despite all the footage, I'm still not convinced that it happened."

How would you change football if you could?
"I'd allow instant video replays for close decisions. I've had several goals ruled out that have proved very costly."

What make of car do you drive and why do you like it?
"I've got two, a Porsche and a Mercedes Benz. I prefer the Merc although I can cruise about in both happily."

What's the worst haircut you've ever had?
"When I was 12 or 13 I had a low afro. You know, somewhere in between a skinhead and a spiky freak."

What's your very favourite item of clothing?
"That would be my Armani waistcoat. It cost £400 and boy do I take care of that. I do like dressing in style."

SOUTHGATE'S THREE SQUARE MEALS!

While you're munching over your toast and cereal in the morning, do you wonder what top footy stars eat to keep them in shape? Well, Aston Villa and England defender Gareth Southgate has told Route 1 that, although he may have advertised pizza in the past, he never touches the stuff. **"For breakfast I would have muesli and some fruit and generally stick to that throughout the week. I have lunch at the training ground, which has a canteen that is one of the best in the country. I try to have lots of potatoes and pasta. A low fat diet, high in carbohydrates is the order of the day in the evening. If you want to train properly you have to look after your body."** Not the most exciting menu, is it? Then again, it's a small price to pay for having the best job in the world.

Boateng's uncle Ron

In life, it often helps if you have friends in high places. But that isn't always the case as Coventry's George Boateng well knows. He met one of his heroes in his early days in football.

"I played against Ronald Koeman in training at Feyenoord," he told Route 1. "Once I fouled him and a penalty was given. He missed the kick and then said he would break my legs if I didn't stop laughing." It's a good job George shut up though because his former team-mate is now assistant manager of the Dutch national side. "It was only a few months before we became friends," continued Boateng. "But I did ask him what I should call him if I got a call-up for Holland. Mr Koeman? Coach? Sir? He said 'You can call me Ronald'." Ahh, all's well that ends well.

IT'S A FAMILY AFFAIR FOR BENI

What is it with footy players' women? They're always having a moan about something. Just as Zinedine Zidane's wife wanted her 'World Footballer Of The Year' husband to quit Juventus so they could live by the seaside, Olga Carbone had the final say over the career of Benito Carbone. Spectacular goals along with the club's Player of the Year award made Beni a happy chappy on the pitch last season, but at the back of his mind was his concern for his wife who has found it hard to settle in England. "That was the best season I have played in England," Carbone told Route 1. "But it's been difficult for my family, especially my wife who doesn't speak with many people in Sheffield. So I said to her that if she wanted to go then we would go. She said to me that it would be okay to stay in Sheffield and that makes me very happy with my family. Now I want her to go out and make friends." Maybe she would've done Beni if you hadn't snubbed £20 000 a week and bogged off.

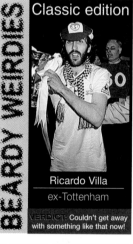

" I have this thing about the number four, my favourite used to be five and then seven. "

Paul Gascoigne **on his obsession with numbers.**

FRIENDS

match asks the stars who's their best mate in footy?

"One of my best mates in football is Steve Lomas of West Ham. We played together for Northern Ireland and a few years back at Man. City. When Steve joined City, he was a really skinny kid and weighed about six stone."

• neil lennon• leicester city •

DAN ULTIMATE PET-RESCUE

The emergence of Chelsea as top Premiership outfit has been due in no small part to Romanian star Dan Petrescu. Not only has he won several trophies during his time at The Bridge, but he's become part of MATCH folklore by having a column devoted to him. But it could have been so different as he explains. **"I was tempted to go somewhere else because I thought it wasn't the right country for me,"** recalled Dan. **"The manager of Sheffield Wednesday at that time, thought differently to me about football. Then I joined Chelsea with Glenn Hoddle before Ruud Gullit and Luca Vialli. You have to be lucky to be successful abroad. You have to have the right people around you."** What rubbish Dan. Are you saying you couldn't have had the same success with Andy Booth knocking them in alongside you?

Top foreigners have made an impact at Newcastle. Take Stephane Guivarc'h... erm maybe not.

Lebeuf's one of several World Cup winners in the Premiership.

English football made Nicolas Anelka into a sought-after star.

Shearer's glad that Laurent Charvet's in his team nowadays.

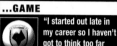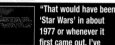

ARE ENGLAND IN GOOD SHAPE FOR THE FUTURE?

5 *Five reasons why England are on the up!*

1 Kevin Keegan is a popular manager who is respected by players, the media and fans. His enthusiasm makes his team feel like world-beaters.

2 The nation has been boosted by the European Cup triumph of Man. United and English football is now feared around the world again.

3 Many of that United team also represent England. They have a great understanding and will represent their country for the next seven or eight years.

4 With the likes of Owen, Fowler, Heskey and Jeffers around, England will be scoring plenty of goals for at least the next three major tournaments.

5 Formerly great powers like Germany and Italy are going through periods of transition and are no longer the threats they once were.

5 *Five reasons why England must improve!*

1 Keegan has never actually won anything in the big-time and England have had enough glorious failures in the past. He is not very tactically aware and admits he doesn't know about defence.

2 The Arsenal players who have formed the basis of the England defence over the years are all reaching the end of their footy careers.

3 The lack of young left-sided players in England is a concern. Both Hinchcliffe and Le Saux are thirty-something, there are doubts over Phil Neville, which only leaves Michael Gray and Michael Ball.

4 England sacked Peter Taylor, one of the most successful Under-21 managers ever, who has produced some terrific youngsters by playing attractive, flowing football.

5 Playing England at Wembley is one of the toughest fixtures in football. When it's been renovated, it won't be as intimidating for the opposition.

CONCLUSION
ONLY TIME WILL TELL

FERGIE'S FLEDGLINGS

Alex Ferguson treats all his players at Man. United like they're his kids. He takes the players from the youth team under his wing and he protects them from The Press. But even though he enjoys such a good relationship, it must be hard meeting him for the first time as a bleary-eyed, spotty school kid. **"I first met Alex Ferguson when I signed on for United as a schoolboy,"** United ace John Curtis explains. **"There is a bit of an aura about him and you do feel a little intimidated by him at first. But you soon get to know him. It's not that often that you see him around though because he doesn't really take the training sessions. He comes and watches the training sometimes, but he doesn't really take part."**

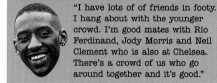

match asks the stars who's their best mate in footy?

"I have lots of of friends in footy. I hang about with the younger crowd. I'm good mates with Rio Ferdinand, Jody Morris and Neil Clement who is also at Chelsea. There's a crowd of us who go around together and it's good."

• **jason euell • wimbledon •**

URI'S HOMESICK

Ask most fans what they think the worst part of a ref's job is and they'd say the amount of stick they get. But top ref Uriah Rennie can handle that, what he's worried about is being homesick. **"The worst part about being a referee is being away from my family,"** he says. **"I've missed out on a lot of family celebrations and having to work throughout the week and then at weekends means I miss seeing my daughter growing up."** Yeah, the job may be time consuming, but the officials must get a buzz out of running on the pitch alongside Becks, Bergkamp and friends? **"The best thing is meeting people and being involved in the whole spectacle of football. There's such a great atmosphere and you can talk to the players — people's heroes — while you are doing your job."** See there is at least one good thing about being a ref!

THE MATCH OSCAR

This award goes to Man United's David May for stealing the show despite only having a walk on part.

DAVID MAY of Manchester United. When Ole Gunnar Solskjaer snatched a dramatic late winner in the Euroean Cup Final our David legged it to join in with the players who actually played, and secondly, he managed to get his ugly mug in the shot of United lifting the trophy. Quite brilliant!

THOMAS MYHRE IS…
MADE IN NORWAY, HAPPY IN ENGLAND

Thomas claims he's happy with the way things are going on the pitch. Weird!

With all the foreign players who have joined the Premiership since it began, it's only natural that a few will turn around and tear strips off English football. Remember that whinging Middlesbrough pair, Emerson and Ravanelli? They were always finding something to complain about. The weather was too cold, it got dark too early! The difference in culture made them pine for home. But one part of the world where our top-flight clubs have been more successful is Scandinavia. Everton goalkeeper Thomas Myhre is one whose move has worked out for the best and he believes the trend is no coincidence. **"When I was young I dreamed that I would play in England, so when the opportunity to play for Everton came along I was very happy,"** Myhre told Route 1. **"There is a lot of English football on TV in Norway, probably more than there is in England. The strange thing is, it's only English managers who scout in Norway. There's not many who have gone anywhere other than England."** So, with all your mates around, it can't be that hard to make the move to England then? **"Not really. If you are happy on the pitch, that can spread to your personal life and vice-versa. I am pleased to be here and have this chance."** That's okay Thomas, you're more than welcome.

A victory salute from an Everton player? Surely not!

HUCK'S THE ADRENALIN JUNKIE

You wouldn't expect a Premier League star to go thrill- seeking after all the pressure and excitement of England's top-flight, but Coventry's Darren Huckerby is no ordinary footy star. Instead of spending his spare time on the golf course or on the pool table, Hucks relaxes by riding rollercoasters! Is he showing off? Route 1 thinks so. **"Rollercoasters don't scare me, I like those kind of things,"** he said after a quick loop-the-loop. **"I even went on a bungee jump when I was at Newcastle. I liked it, but I don't think that Gordon Strachan would be too keen on me doing anything like that any more."** Okay Darren, let's get this right. You tear round gravity defying rides at 100 mph and chuck yourself off bridges, but the only thing you're scared of is little old Mr Strachan. Actually, so are we.

> The weather here is great. It's warm, light, sunny. But then I am from Norway where the weather sucks.

Thomas is happy to be playing in this country.

Even playing for Everton doesn't get him down too much.

THEY DIDN'T SEE IT COMING

> We're on our way to Wembley to win the FA Cup.

Alan Shearer anticipates FA Cup Final success.

JOB SWAP

IF I WAS ANOTHER SPORTS STAR I'D BE... NIGEL MANSELL

> Where's Michael Schumacher? I'm going to whup his butt, you wait and see.

"I really love cars, so I think if I had the chance, I would have to be a Formula One racing driver. Driving at high speed in a racing car takes a bit of nerve, but I'd love to have a go at it. If I have to choose one driver that I'd most like to be I think I'd say Nigel Mansell because of everything he achieved in the sport. He may have retired from driving now, but when he was in Formula One he was always an exciting driver to watch."

Mansell's speed was a huge asset to Celtic's title charge.

We'd all like to be famous footballers, but who do footballers dream of being? CELTIC defender ALAN STUBBS goes on a job swap for MATCH!

IF I WAS...

a Pop Star
"Probably most like to have been Elvis Presley. I'm not a big fan of his music, but he was an absolute legend."

a Soap Star
"If 'Baywatch' counts as a soap, then I would say David Hasselhoff. I think it speaks for itself really."

a Footy Legend
"I always admired Alan Hansen, so even though I'm an Everton supporter, I'd love to be as good as him."

10 REASONS WHY ENGLISH FOOTBALL IS THE BEST!

In the 1990s people have boasted that English football is far better than anywhere else in the world. So why is it better?

1 Britain is the home of football – it's where it all began. And nobody can ever take away that fact.

2 England is a great footy nation – because of its club and national sides. Every year between 1965 and 1985 an English team either won or took part in a European Final.

3 We have the best cup competition, which is watched every year by millions of people across the world.

4 Several of the 1998 French World Cup-winning side have chosen to play their football in the English Premier League.

5 The four English leagues boast a selection of internationals from Europe, as well as Australia, Peru, Brazil, China and even Thailand.

6 English clubs Arsenal, Chelsea and Man. United have all won European trophies in the 1990s, proving our top teams play a very high standard of football and can compete with Europe's best.

7 We have some great stadiums in England. Not only is there Wembley, but we've also got Old Trafford, Anfield, St James' Park and Highbury.

8 English football is entertaining and free-flowing. You don't get many stop-start diving antics like you do abroad.

9 The Premier League is the richest league in Europe. It took over from Serie A in the 1997-98 season with a turnover of £455.5m as compared to Serie A's £376.8 million.

10 It can only get better! Man. United are a great team, but face stiff competition in Arsenal, Chelsea and Leeds… then there's Liverpool and Tottenham not far behind.

CONCLUSION
IT TAKES SOME BEATING!

WHAILING WELSH

You would have thought that players would get a lot of respect for playing for their national team. Not Craig Bellamy of Wales though. He gets stick from his team-mates – and Wales supporters! "The Swansea fans don't like me because I'm from Cardiff, and the Cardiff fans don't like me because I left there to play for Norwich!" he tells Route 1. "I also get stick from my team-mates. It's good natured, but it can get a bit annoying at times. Most of the players who take the mick are English and when you take the mick back, they don't care because they don't play for their country!" It sounds like you can't win Craig!

---

my favourite... PLAYER OF ALL TIME

BY MICHAEL BALL
EVERTON

SO, WHO'S YOUR FAVOURITE FOOTY PLAYER OF ALL-TIME MICHAEL?
"Andy Hinchcliffe. Being able to work and train with him helped me a lot."

WHAT WERE HIS STRENGTHS MIKEY?
"He's great crosser of the ball."

IS HE A NICE BLOKE TOO?
"Yeah. When the England Under-18s were training at Bisham Abbey last season alongside the full England side, Andy made a point of coming over and asking me how things were going."

BUT WASN'T IT YOUR FAULT HE LEFT EVERTON?
"It was ironic really because Howards Kendall said that he was able to sell Andy because I was coming through the ranks a couple of season's ago."

SO HE HATES YOU THEN?
"No, he was great about it."

TOP 8 WAYS TO GET YOURSELF THE SACK!

1 DON'T BOTHER DOING YOUR JOB!
Talk an absurd amount of rubbish about stuff that has nothing to do with football. This can range from faith-healing to religion – anything really, so long as your team doesn't win on the pitch and you sound mad.
I'll probably come back as a lettuce.
GLENN HODDLE

2 SPLASH THE CASH ON TRASH!
Pretend you're playing the 'Championship Manager' computer game and go berserk with the dosh. Look abroad for people nobody has heard of, just like Kenny Dalglish did at Newcastle. You'll get the boot in no time.
Kenny had spotted an obscure French striker who'd never scored.

3 GO TO MANCHESTER CITY!
In the last decade, City have somehow got through seven different bosses, four of whom got the chop. It's amazing that Joe Royle has lasted this long, but if you fancy his job, just keep one eye on the 'situations vacant'!
After three days Joe was presented with a carriage clock.

4 BE TOO NICE!
Follow the example of former Liverpool boss Roy Evans by inviting in somebody you don't know to share your job at a club you have served loyally – and then be the one to leave when things go pear-shaped.
You're a lovely fella, you know that Gerard?

5 WIN THE LEAGUE CUP!
With a chairman like deadly Doug Ellis lurking in the background, nobody's job is safe. Both Big Ron and Brian Little left after enjoying League Cup glory – so John Gregory should be warned to play his weakest team in that.
Don't shoot Dion, you might score you fool.

6 BUY NEIL SHIPPERLEY!
Shortly before Dave Bassett was sacked by doomed Forest, he paid a cool £1.5 million for Neil Shipperley, maybe the unluckiest player ever who always seems to bring the threat of relegation with him.
Dave Basset couldn't remember if Shipperley was lucky or not.

7 DO WELL!
Win your club the FA Cup and guide them to second place in the Premiership with just three months of the season to go, then you'll get an untimely knock on your door from Ken Bates who'll tell you to take a hike.
Gullit was doing too well for his own good. He had to go.

8 GO MAD!
You don't have to be a gaffer to get sacked. When a player steps out of line, he's had it. If you get depressed like Stan The Man, annoy your boss by staying away from the dressing-room banter that might just cheer you up.
Man, I'm feeling really down. I can't play.

TELLY ADDICTS

NEWCASTLE UNITED & WALES star GARY SPEED tells MATCH what he enjoys sitting down to watch on the box.

'Friends'
"I know everyone likes 'Friends' but that's just because it's really funny. I used to watch 'Cheers' a few years ago when it was on Channel Four and 'Friends' is a very similar to 'Cheers'. It contains the same sort of humour. The best thing about 'Friends' is Joey and Chandler's partnership. They are the best characters on TV."
TUNE IN SKY 1 VARIOUS TIMES

'Match Of The Day'
"It's always on the TV on a Saturday night, so I have to watch it. Saturday doesn't feel right if you haven't watched 'Match Of The Day'. I like watching the analysis by Des Lynam and the rest of the team. I miss Jimmy Hill being on the programme though, it was funny watching him and Alan Hansen together."
TUNE IN BBC1 SATURDAY 10.30pm

'Coronation Street'
"I do like 'Coronation Street' because you can not watch it for a few weeks and you still know what's happening when you tune back in. I'm also a big fan of Jack Duckworth. His glasses have needed repairing for as long as I can remember but he can never be bothered to go anywhere – apart from the pub or the bookies."
TUNE IN ITV SUN/MON/WED 7.30pm

This lot will cost me my job, I swear they will. I can't watch anymore there so bad.

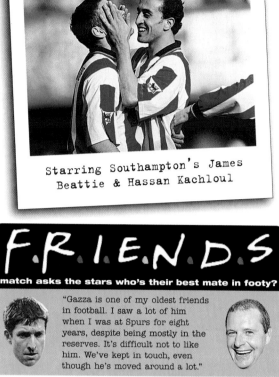

Starring Southampton's James Beattie & Hassan Kachloul

F.R.I.E.N.D.S

match asks the stars who's their best mate in footy?

"Gazza is one of my oldest friends in football. I saw a lot of him when I was at Spurs for eight years, despite being mostly in the reserves. It's difficult not to like him. We've kept in touch, even though he's moved around a lot."

• john moncur • west ham

Speak to anyone about the

player who has achieved the most over the last 12 months and inevitably they would go for a Manchester United player. One person who may not immediately spring to mind is Sunderland defender Michael Gray who made his England debut at left-back last June. Just over two years ago Gray was plying his trade as a winger, but he is full of praise for manager Peter Reid who made the decision to switch him to the back. **"The gaffer has been fantastic to me since he came to the club. He brings a lot of confidence to the squad. At first, when he started moving me back from midfield, I was disappointed. But once I'd been playing there for a few months I started to really enjoy it."** Now Gray has set his sights on a permanent place in the England set-up. **"I don't think there's a shortage at left-backs with Graeme Le Saux and Phil Neville, but there are not very many left-wingers in the country and if you get in the 22 you've always got a chance of playing."**

GRAY OF LIGHT

CZECH MATE!

This may be an uncertain

time at Liverpool, but Patrik Berger can take comfort in the knowledge that he is adored by millions of females across the country. Along with Beckham, Ginola and Redknapp, Patrik has joined the ever-growing list of pin-up footballers. Sorry to disappoint all you girls out there, but the Czech international is a devoted family man.

"It is very nice to be liked, but I do not see myself as a pin-up," he said. "I'm quite a private person and in my time away from football I am with my family. I have been married to Jarka for five years and have two children so they take up all my time. Other than that, I want to stay fit and help Liverpool win the title."

With that sort of wishful thinking from Patrik, perhaps he would be stupid enough to have a bit on the side.

BOX OFFICE

THE FILM: 'Star Wars Episode One: The Phantom Dennis'

WHO'S IN IT? Dennis Bergkamp, Arsene Wenger

THE PLOT? Emperor Wenger instructs his best pilot, Darth Bergkamp, to fly from the moon of Heathrow and bring home a European trophy. Bergkamp can't bring himself to confront his fear of the Boeing 747 and bottles it.

HOW MUCH DID IT COST? A clause-filled £7.5 million

WHEN'S IT SHOWING It's on pretty regularly during the season.

NAME	RORY DELAP
TEAM	DERBY COUNTY
AGE	23
POSITION	RIGHT WING-BACK

...you had to go in goal during a match?
"Aye, I'd have a go in goal for a laugh. I played a few times in goal when I was younger, but I always ended up getting injured. How, you ask? Well, I always used to get kicked in the head because I would come out of my goal and dive at players' feet!"

...you had the chance to star in a major movie?
"Oh, I'd have a go at that one straight away. It would have to be a violent film though – not really! But I would only have a small part. I wouldn't fancy having to learn all those lines – it would be too much like hard work for me."

...you were offered £1 million to fight Lennox Lewis?
"I think I could easily last a few rounds with Lennox Lewis. Seriously, I would fight him because a million pounds is a lot of money to turn down – even if you are a footballer. It wouldn't be any good to me if he killed me though!"

...you were asked to sing karaoke?
"I've sung karaoke in the past and the only time I would do it again was if I was really drunk! I actually won a karaoke competition a few years ago. But I was singing with my mate and he has a good voice, so it didn't have much to do with my performance."

...you were asked to present a chat show?
"Aye, I think I'd like to have a go at that. I would have to have a translator on the show though, so that everyone could understand what I was saying because of my accent. I would have Wesley Snipes on my first show as the main guest – I'd love to meet him."

...you were asked to do a bungee jump?
"I'd love to have a go at bungee jumping, but I'm not sure that my manager Jim Smith would be too happy about it. I did have a go at a similar thing called 'swing jumping' over the summer, but I couldn't really be any more daring than that while I'm still playing football. I'd get into big trouble if I did."

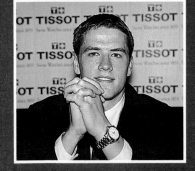

MICHAEL OWEN

> ## "That strike against Argentina changed my life. If it's the only thing I do in my career, it's not a bad thing to be remembered for."

MICHAEL OWEN SEEMS TO HAVE HAD THE PERFECT START to his football career. After all, he's gone from being totally unheard of, to being one of the most talked about players in the world within two years of his Liverpool debut. The hype after France '98 surrounding his goal against Argentina lifted Michael to superstar status across the world and you could be forgiven for thinking he'd already achieved everything there is to achieve in the game. In a short space of time, he's won the prestigious BBC Sports Personality Of The Year, the Golden Boot Award, the PFA Young Player Of the Year and the MATCH Readers' Player Of The Year.

The good news for Liverpool fans is that Michael is determined to front Liverpool's attempt to once more become Europe's most feared club. From day one, Owen has been better than everyone else because he's aimed higher than everyone else. Even in the school playground his outstanding talent shone through to leave friends and teachers amazed. His continuing hunger for success is remarkable and his appetite has only been whetted by what he's achieved so far in his career. Not only is this good news for Liverpool, but for England too because Michael plans to spearhead the nation's attack for many years to come.

But don't kid yourself. Even the flashest young striker in Britain has suffered the odd low point in his short career. Michael may have terrified defenders up and down the country but Liverpool have achieved nothing since he arrived on the scene. Whether or not he can fulfil his professional ambitions at Liverpool remains to be seen. One thing is for sure, Michael is a born winner and won't settle for second best. If he does decide to leave Anfield, there will be no shortage of top clubs fighting for his signature.

Football stardom can be frightening at first. The thought of being chased up and down the street by adoring fans may sound appealing but when you're Michael Owen, having your privacy invaded can be the norm rather than the exception and it must become a curse constantly being in the public eye. Although the fame and fortune that accompanies his lifestyle is great, he still gets the biggest buzz from going out and playing in front of 40,000 fans week in, week out.

Here MATCH takes you through the footballing life of Michael Owen, starting way back at Deeside Primary School where he first showed his incredible footballing talent.

December 1979 — A STAR IS BORN

Michael had a phenomenal scoring record even at this early age.

Michael was born on December 14, 1979 in Chester and by the age of seven he made his debut for the school's under-11 football team, scoring 36 goals in 12 games. Games teacher Hugh Dodd admitted that Michael was the only primary school player he had ever seen score with a scissor-kick from the edge of the area. Michael was lucky because his dad was a professional footballer so he had a good teacher, but he still needed to work on his natural talent.

MICHAEL SAYS: *"I was about six or seven when I first kicked a ball with my dad. Whenever I had a chance for a kickabout with friends or even on my own, I'd be out playing. My dad actually played for Everton and he was the biggest influence on my career. I'm not saying I wouldn't have become a professional footballer without him, but it's certainly been a big help having him around."*

September 1990 — RECORD BREAKER

Michael shattered schoolboy scoring records set by Ian Rush.

Michael smashed a record 92 goals in a season for Deeside Schools representative team, breaking Ian Rush's previous record mark of 72. He also broke the team's appearances record, previously held by Gary Speed. "He always had tremendous pace and even at that age his coolness in front of goal was uncanny," said Allan Beavan who was Michael's PE teacher at Hawarden High School.

MICHAEL SAYS: *"As soon as the school I was at had a team, I was playing in it. I always loved scoring goals and I was aware of Ian Rush's schools' record for goals scored in a season. Ian was a great player so to think you could be better than him at that age was something to aim for. They made quite a big deal of it in the local papers when I broke the record, so I got an early taste of what fame is all about, even though it was on a small scale."*

May 1991 — ANFIELD ARRIVAL

Michael used to go to watch Liverpool play and watch how the pros worked.

When you watch the stars in action you can see what they do to beat the best, then copy their moves and use them in your own game. That's exactly what Michael did. And every budding footy star needs to be signed up by a professional club. So where better to start than Liverpool, with a tradition of bringing youth team players up through the ranks.

MICHAEL SAYS: *"I was spotted by a Liverpool scout when I was about ten playing for Deeside, but I didn't sign until I was 11. I went to look round the club and I liked what I saw. When I was at the School Of Excellence I used to ring Steve Heighway and he'd get me tickets for games. My dad would take me to a match and I'd watch the strikers' movement and whether or not it worked. The players I saw were mainly the players around now because it was only a few years ago, people like Shearer, Sheringham and Cole."*

December 1996 — SIGNING PRO FORMS

Michael's been an England international at many levels.

Having already wowed the England schoolboy team with his cool finishing, Michael stepped up to the England Under-16 team. He made his debut away to Finland in August 1995 and scored an astonishing five times. Part of the Liverpool side which won the FA Youth Cup, Michael was then chosen to represent the England Under-18 team at the age of just 16. His debut was in Denmark and as usual, Michael scored, the equaliser in a hard-fought 1-1 draw. Soon after this Michael turned professional.

MICHAEL SAYS: *"I'd been with Liverpool for a couple of years when I went to the FA School Of Excellence at Lilleshall and so I knew what was happening. Even then I was determined to go right to the very top. I eventually signed schoolboy forms with Liverpool when I was 15 and then turned professional on my 17th birthday."*

> **"I ALWAYS LOVED SCORING GOALS. AS SOON AS THE SCHOOL HAD A TEAM, I WAS PLAYING IN IT."**

June 1997 — TAKING THE MICHAEL

Michael learned a lot from playing against people older than him.

England Under-20s was the next step for the boy wonder. At the age of only 17, he went to the FIFA World Youth Cup in Malaysia to face players up to three years older than him. His first appearance in the competition was against the Ivory Coast in a game England won 2-1. Did he score? You bet he did. It was a disappointing tournament for England overall, but Michael played four games, scoring three goals.

MICHAEL SAYS: *"I was fortunate enough to play for England from junior level against people who were quite a bit older than me and I think that helped me develop as a player. Obviously the level of experience you get changes, but you learn to adapt quickly and you become accustomed to the expectations of playing at that level. It's great because you ease your way through, rather than being thrown in at the deep end. I think that does make it slightly easier."*

August 1997 — OPENING-DAY STRIKE

Owen scored on his Liverpool debut against Wimbledon.

Michael made his first-team debut for Liverpool at the tail end of the 1996-97 season where he immediately impressed the fans after showing lightening pace to pull a goal back in a disappointing 2-1 defeat at Wimbledon. He then returned to Selhurst Park for the season's opener. The Dons took the lead, but then Liverpool won a penalty. Michael calmly stepped up to convert the spot-kick and earn a draw.

MICHAEL SAYS: *"The main thing that sticks out in my memory was taking the penalty and scoring the equalising goal. It was a decent game on a boiling hot day making it very tiring to play one of my first games for Liverpool. It was nice to get a goal on the opening day of the season even though it was a penalty. It's good when you score at any time, but in the first game of the season, it gets you off to a good start and gives you that little bit of extra confidence."*

September 1997 — EUROPEAN SCORE DRAW

Michael celebrates his first European goal against Celtic after six minutes.

With the league campaign ticking along, Liverpool turned their attention to their European campaign and it was another big step up for Michael. The draw for the first round of the UEFA Cup paired them with Celtic with the first leg at Celtic Park. Even Alan Shearer took time to adjust to European football, but Owen scored after just six minutes.

MICHAEL SAYS: *"That was one of the best atmospheres I've ever played in. A lot was made before the game of the England versus Scotland thing, so it was nice to score early on. I think the goal came after about six minutes. I don't think the players really took much notice of the England against Scotland rivalry. To us it was a big game whether we were playing a Scottish team, another English team or whoever from the other European qualifiers. We just wanted to win the game and progress to the next round."*

December 1997 — GROWING UP QUICKLY

Owen scored on his debut for England Under-21s against Greece.

After a series of impressive games for Liverpool, Michael was keeping German European Cup winner Karl-Heinz Riedle out of the side. He also stepped up a level to play for the England Under-21s and scored on his debut in a 4-2 win over Greece. England lost the tie on away goals, but Michael turned in another fine performance.

MICHAEL SAYS: *"I've scored on my debuts a number of times – for Liverpool's reserves, the A, B and full teams, and at every level for England until my full debut, so I was pleased to keep it going against Greece in my first game for the Under-21s. It was an important game for me, moving up to the Under-21s and testing myself against older players, but I think playing for England Schools' sides and the like does help you get used to the international set-up. I played quite well and it's always nice to get a goal."*

January 1998 — "MY BEST LEAGUE GOAL"

Michael's favourite goal... before the England Argentina game obviously.

The New Year got off to a flier for Michael with a starring role in the Coca-Cola Cup quarter-final. A stunning extra-time strike put Liverpool on their way to a 2-0 victory over Newcastle – a goal Michael rated as the best he'd scored at the time. The only disappointment was that The Reds were knocked out of the competition at the next stage after they were beaten by First Division Middlesbrough.

MICHAEL SAYS: *"It's always hard to choose your best league goal, but the one against Newcastle did give me a lot of pleasure at the time. It was one of my best ever, a good clean shot, so I was very pleased with it. I remember the ball dropped to me and I struck it nicely on the volley. It would have been nice to go to Wembley but we missed out on the Coca-Cola Cup through our own fault. We didn't take our chances and that was a huge disappointment for me."*

February 1998 — YOUNG GUN TAKES CHARGE

Michael became the youngest England player this century against Chile.

The Press went delirious as Glenn Hoddle made Michael the youngest international player this century to play for England. At just 18 years and 59 days he beat Duncan Edwards' record to become England's youngest player this century. Despite intense scrutiny and pressure, Michael's intelligent running and pace caused Chile a problem or two, even though they won the game, and he won the Man Of The Match award.

MICHAEL SAYS: *"I was nervous, but it didn't affect me. It was good to get a game and to be the youngest player to represent England this century was great. I'm too young to have seen Duncan Edwards play, but from what I hear, he was a great player so it was an honour to break his record. I was pleased to win the Man Of The Match award, but I was disappointed with the result. Losing 2-0 meant I couldn't be too overjoyed after the game."*

February 1998 — HITTING A HAT-TRICK

Soon after his England debut Michael notched his first Premiership hat-trick.

Just three days after his record-breaking appearance for England, Michael was back on duty for Liverpool and in scintillating form at Hillsborough. Sheffield Wednesday couldn't cope with his pace and trickery and he grabbed his first Premiership hat-trick in a 3-3 draw. Only goalscoring legends Alan Shearer and Jimmy Greaves were younger when they bagged three in a game in the top-flight.

MICHAEL SAYS: "I'd just come back from international duty so maybe a few people were looking at me for signs that it had all gone to my head. I think it could have worked one of two ways. If I'd played badly for Liverpool or not scored then everyone would have said, 'It's gone to his head,' then when I did score, everyone said, 'He's still on a high from the England game'. It was great to score a hat-trick so that no one could have too many arguments."

April 1998 — PFA YOUNG PLAYER AWARD

His fellow pros voted Michael PFA Young Player Of The Year.

A fantastic first season was rewarded when Michael was named Carling Player Of The Year and more importantly PFA Young Player Of The Year. The award is widely thought of as the highest individual honour a young player can receive. He picked up his trophy at a swish ceremony at glamorous The Grosvenor Hotel attended by his fellow professionals.

MICHAEL SAYS: "To win that poll in my first year with Liverpool was a great honour, something I'm very pleased and proud to. I think the PFA awards are the ones that mean most to players. It is true what players say about it being the most prestigious award. When you're being voted for by your fellow professionals, you must be doing something right, so I was very happy with that. It's a great achievement in my first year and I just hope that I can go on from there and keep getting even better."

April 1998 — SEEING RED AT UNITED

The big clash with Man. United in spring '98 saw Owen sent off.

With Liverpool in third position, nine points behind the leaders Man. United and still clinging to their championship dream, a win at Old Trafford was vital. United took the lead, but Owen soon levelled after taking advantage of a mix-up between Pallister and Schmeichel. With the game evenly balanced, Michael mistimed a challenge on Norwegian defender Ronny Johnsen and received a second yellow card. It was the first time he had been sent-off in his career.

MICHAEL SAYS: "It was a terrible feeling to be sent off in such a big game. I didn't go out trying to get sent-off or trying to hurt anyone, but things like that happen. It was a bad feeling walking off in front of all the United fans at Old Trafford. I'd already scored, which softened the blow, but we were playing well and believed we could have gone on to win. That was a low point."

May 1998 — THE GOLDEN TOUCH

Winning the Golden Boot in his first season was some achievement.

In his first full campaign, Michael's 18 Premiership goals put him level with Coventry's Dion Dublin and Blackburn's Chris Sutton as the leading scorer in the division and won him the Golden Boot. Having missed out on just two league games all season, it was a tough year for Michael both physically and mentally and he carried a lot of expectation with him. But Michael kept his feet firmly on the ground.

MICHAEL SAYS: "Winning the Golden Boot was obviously a great honour to get in my first season. As a striker, the main thing I will always be judged on is scoring goals. You've got to believe you're going to score in every game or you'll never make it as a striker, you'll never succeed. No matter how well I might be playing, if I'm not scoring goals people will say there's something wrong. So to score quite a fair number of goals was very important."

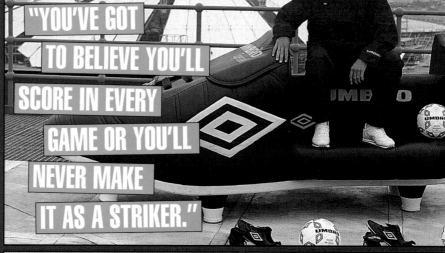

"YOU'VE GOT TO BELIEVE YOU'LL SCORE IN EVERY GAME OR YOU'LL NEVER MAKE IT AS A STRIKER."

May 1998 — HITTING THE BIG-TIME

Owen rewrites history again, becoming the youngest man ever to score for England.

In the pre-World Cup game in Morocco, Michael replaced Ian Wright after 25 minutes and grabbed the only goal of the game to become the youngest ever scorer for England in just his fourth appearance. He did enough to be selected by coach Glenn Hoddle for France '98 and grew in stature as a result.

MICHAEL SAYS: "We were a squad of 28 preparing to go to the World Cup, so there was still a lot of tension around the camp. No one knew who was going and who wasn't, but I enjoyed the time out in La Manga and playing in the tournament in Morocco. Obviously, the highlight for me was scoring a goal in the game against Morocco because that made me the youngest player ever to score for England. But the main purpose of the trip was to get to know each other as a squad, to focus on the World Cup and for the manager to choose his final 22 to go to the World Cup in France."

June 1998 — WORLD CUP HOT-SHOT

Michael celebrates the goal that made him a star worldwide.

Michael had scored in the opening round of France '98 after coming on as a substitute in the disappointing 2-1 defeat by Romania. He was in the line-up from the start for the crucial second-round clash with Argentina as England sought revenge for the Maradona 'Hand Of God' incident in 1986. Owen scored a wonder goal to signal his arrival on the world stage.

MICHAEL SAYS: "It was just an unbelievable feeling. To go to a World Cup at 18 and be widely remembered for that one goal changed my life. It is something that will be with me forever and even if it's the only thing I do in my career, it's not a bad thing to be remembered for, is it? I often wonder what would have happened if I'd have actually missed that chance. I'd have come back and found things a lot quieter that's for sure. When I came back everyone was looking at me differently and everyone wanted to talk to me."

December 1998 — TOP PERSONALITY

Winning the BBC Sports Personality Of The Year means you get to meet Des Lynam.

To cap a tremendous year for Michael, he was named BBC Sports Personality Of The Year after being voted for ahead of many other illustrious names in the world of sport. The award was a personal milestone for Owen and a great achievement for someone of such a tender age. But like the down to earth guy that he is, Michael took it all in his stride.

MICHAEL SAYS: "I have to admit I was stunned to win the BBC Sports Personality Of The Year award, but perhaps not as stunned as my mother, who got very emotional. It's an award that is really special to me because it's voted for by the public. It's nice to be appreciated by your friends, your team-mates and Liverpool fans, but when people I don't know vote for me across the country, it does mean a great deal to me. It's hard to believe how quickly things have happened for me, but I haven't finished yet."

January 1999 — MATCH WINNER

The big one. Michael captures the MATCH Readers' Poll Player Of The Year award.

One man reigned supreme in the world of football during 1998 and it was no surprise when Michael was crowned the Player Of The Year in the MATCH Readers' Poll. He also scooped the award for Best Young Gun, Best World Cup Star and Flashest Goal for his stunning effort against Argentina.

MICHAEL SAYS: *"I know that not every single MATCH reader is a Liverpool fan, but if I'd helped to entertain them during the year, that's nice and I was very proud to have won the Player Of The Year Award. When it's an award given to you by the public, the fans that watch you play week in, week out in all kinds of weather, you tend to look upon that as a bit special. I've always maintain that the first thing that strikes you when you become accepted by the public in general is the reaction of the fans. It makes me appreciate how fortunate I am to be doing all this."*

April 1999 — OUT BUT NOT DOWN

Owen's hamstring injury last season was bad news for Liverpool and England.

When Michael chased the ball on a greasy Elland Road pitch and fell to the ground clutching his right hamstring, it wasn't just Liverpool fans who looked on with anxiety. The injury was serious enough to rule him out of the rest of Liverpool's faltering season and he was sorely missed in the Euro 2000 qualifiers against Sweden and Bulgaria that were so crucial to England in their quest to qualify for the final stages.

MICHAEL SAYS: *"It's the worst injury I've ever had. I knew as soon as I did it against Leeds that it was serious. The medical people say it can be traced back something that happened in an earlier game against Derby, when I damaged a knee tendon. The torn hamstring probably occurred because I tried to compensate for the knee injury. The body has a way of warning you not to push it too hard and it pays not to ignore such a message."*

August 1999 — HAPPY TO BE HERE

Owen says he'll stay at Anfield but he wants to win trophies and soon.

Despite finishing the season on the injured list, Michael still shared the position as the Premier League's top scorer for the second year running. He proved once again what a handful he can be and that attracted interest from Lazio. A world record £30 million move to Italy was rumoured but Michael is keen to stay at Liverpool for the foreseeable future.

MICHAEL SAYS: *"If we are winning things there is no reason for me to go anywhere else. I love Liverpool, but it's important they match my ambitions. I certainly don't want to finish my career without having won something. I want all the trophies – the FA Cup, the League Cup and the Premier League. I'm not happy just to play every week and go home with my wages. I want to win things and be playing for the best team. But I can promise Liverpool fans that the reports linking me with Lazio had nothing to do with me. I'm happy right here."*

ISN'T IT ABOUT TIME...
Dave Bassett learnt how to talk properly so the good folk of Barnsley don't spend their lives trying to understand his dull Cockney moaning.

CAREER CHECK

JOHN GREGORY
aston villa manager

One of the most talented young managers in the game. Route 1 takes a look at what he's done at Villa.

THE YORKE SAGA
Never one to mince his words, Gregory said he wanted to shoot Yorke when he asked for a move. This was not the last time he publicly spoke his mind.
RATING 2

STAN COLLYMORE
Gregory went mad when Collymore claimed he was suffering from depression. Not the kind of loving support the sensitive striker needed really.
RATING 0

GARETH BARRY
Fair play to Gregory on this one. He didn't splash out on a new centre-half. He signed an unknown youngster from Brighton and got a great talent.
RATING 7

LEE HENDRIE
Probably his biggest success so far and he cost nothing. Gregory got the best out of the young midfielder and his performances earned him a full England cap.
RATING 8

ALAN THOMPSON
Looked a decent signing but when Villa began to lose it so did he. Gregory played him wide too often when he's more effective playing down the middle.
RATING 6

PAUL MERSON
No questioning his ability on the pitch and he did well when he first arrived from Boro, but his battle with the booze continues and limits his effectiveness.
RATING 5

DION DUBLIN
Money well spent. Started off in blinding form but a hernia proved too much for him and the goals began to dry up. Injury free he is a big threat though!
RATING 7

COLIN CALDERWOOD
A panic buy when Villa started leaking goals and Gregory opted for a 4-4-2 formation. An average player at best, now he's hampered by a walking stick.
RATING 2

DROP FROM THE TOP
It was an amazing achievement to lead the Premier League for so long but Gregory must take his share of the blame. Why didn't they even qualify for Europe?
RATING 5

HANDLING BOSNICH
A complete shambles! This was a saga worthy of 'EastEnders' and Gregory emerged with very little credit, while Bosnich came up with the big-money move.
RATING 1

GREGORY RATING
COULD DO BETTER

DREAM TEAM

Ole Gunnar Solskjaer manchester united & norway

"I regard Peter Schmeichel as the best goalkeeper in the world. He would definitely be between the posts in my team. Our back four at United did really well but I'd go for a more international flavour in defence. In midfield, I'd link Roy Keane and Ryan Giggs with my Norwegian team-mate Petter Rudi. Up front I'd like to play alongside two legends, Eric Cantona and Romario. With us three in attack, we wouldn't need to leave it until injury time to score! What colour strip would we play in? It's got to be red hasn't it."

Gary Neville — Manchester United
Position Full-back
Country England

Matthias Sammer — Borussia Dortmund
Position Defender
Country Germany

Peter Schmeichel — Sporting Lisbon
Position Goalkeeper
Country Denmark

Paolo Maldini — AC Milan
Position Defender
Country Italy

Roberto Carlos — Real Madrid
Position Full-back
Country Brazil

Petter Rudi — Sheffield Wednesday
Position Midfielder
Country Norway

Ole Gunnar Solskjaer — Manchester United
Position Striker
Country Norway

Roy Keane — Manchester United
Position Midfielder
Country Rep.Of Ireland

Romario — Flamengo
Position Striker
Country Brazil

Eric Cantona — Manchester United
Position Striker
Country France

Ryan Giggs — Manchester United
Position Midfielder
Country Wales

Gigi's living it up in LONDON

Pierluigi Casiraghi wasn't at Chelsea for long last season before a bad injury against West Ham put him out of football for a year. But in the short time that Gigi did live in London, he certainly made the most out of his time. **"Of course I like London, I loved living in England,"** Gigi says. **"The people are great and the nightlife is excellent there as well. However, I only lived there for two months before I got injured and had to go back to Italy for the operations and treatment on my injured leg."** And boy didn't we all just hate to see £5.4 million of Chelsea's money go down the plughole!

COCKY COLE

West Ham's new young star
Joe Cole is the most talked about teenager down the East End for a very long time! Cole is widely tipped to become one of the brightest young stars of the future and lead the charge for glory at Upton Park. And young Joe certainly isn't lacking in self-confidence. **"There's such a lot of expectation – people have been talking about me coming through for quite a while now,"** admitted Cole. **"But I've never doubted my own ability and I believe I can develop into a great player. Whether it happens next year or three years down the line I don't know – but I'm sure it will happen."** And with that sort of single-minded attitude to the game, the rest of the Premiership had better watch out!

DENNIS BERGKAMP ARSENAL

THE SUPER

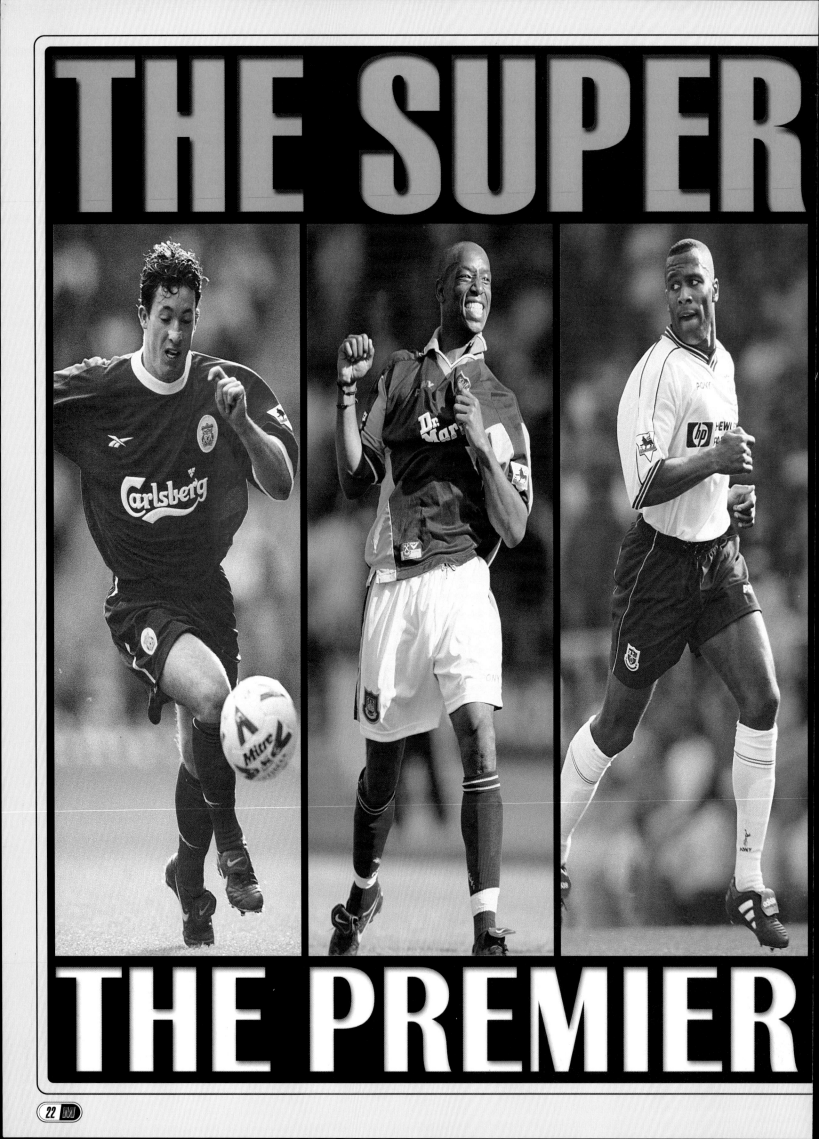

THE PREMIER

STRIKERS!

Introducing the 100 club – the five players who have scored 100 Premiership goals.

THE PREMIER LEAGUE IS NOW INTO ITS EIGHTH season and in that time it has been graced with some fine strikers – but only a talented few who have made it into the elite Premier League 100 club.

England captain Alan Shearer leads the select band of five strikers of Ian Wright, Les Ferdinand, Robbie Fowler and Andy Cole. Each one has netted more than 100 goals since the Premiership was founded. They have all been inspirational for the clubs they have played for and have all represented England at full international level during their careers. Their goal ratios are impressive, each boasting a record of scoring a goal in at least every other game – a sure sign of a truly world-class striker.

Throughout this annual, MATCH pays tribute to the country's top five strikers detailing how they scored their 100 goals and against which teams.

The Top Ten Premiership Sharpshooters!

Who's Made it!

Player	Clubs	Goals
Shearer — 216 games	Blackburn, Newcastle	153
Wright — 220 games	Arsenal, West Ham	113
Ferdinand — 216 games	QPR, Newcastle, Spurs	111
Fowler — 185 games	Liverpool	106
Cole — 195 games	Newcastle, Man. United	106

Who's Next?

Player	Clubs	Goals
Le Tissier — 237 games	Southampton	97
Sheringham — 218 games	Nott'm Forest, Spurs, Man. United	88
Sutton — 209 games	Norwich, Blackburn	80
Yorke — 211 games	Villa, Man. United	78
Dublin — 181 games	Man. United, Coventry, Villa	74

Goals Scored   0   25   50   75   100   125   150

Who's Still In The Running?

Player	Clubs	Goals
Mark Hughes	Man. United, Chelsea, Southampton	60
Tony Cottee	Everton, West Ham, Leicester	65
Stan Collymore	Nott'm Forest, Liverpool, Aston Villa	55
Chris Armstrong	Crystal Palace, Tottenham	55
Kevin Gallacher	Coventry, Blackburn	52
Efan Ekoku	Norwich, Wimbledon	52
Brian Deane	Sheff. United, Leeds, Middlesbrough	52
Dennis Bergkamp	Arsenal	51
Ryan Giggs	Man. United	48

*figures to the end of the 1998-99 season

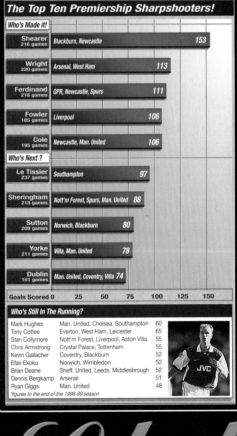

SHIP 100 *Club*

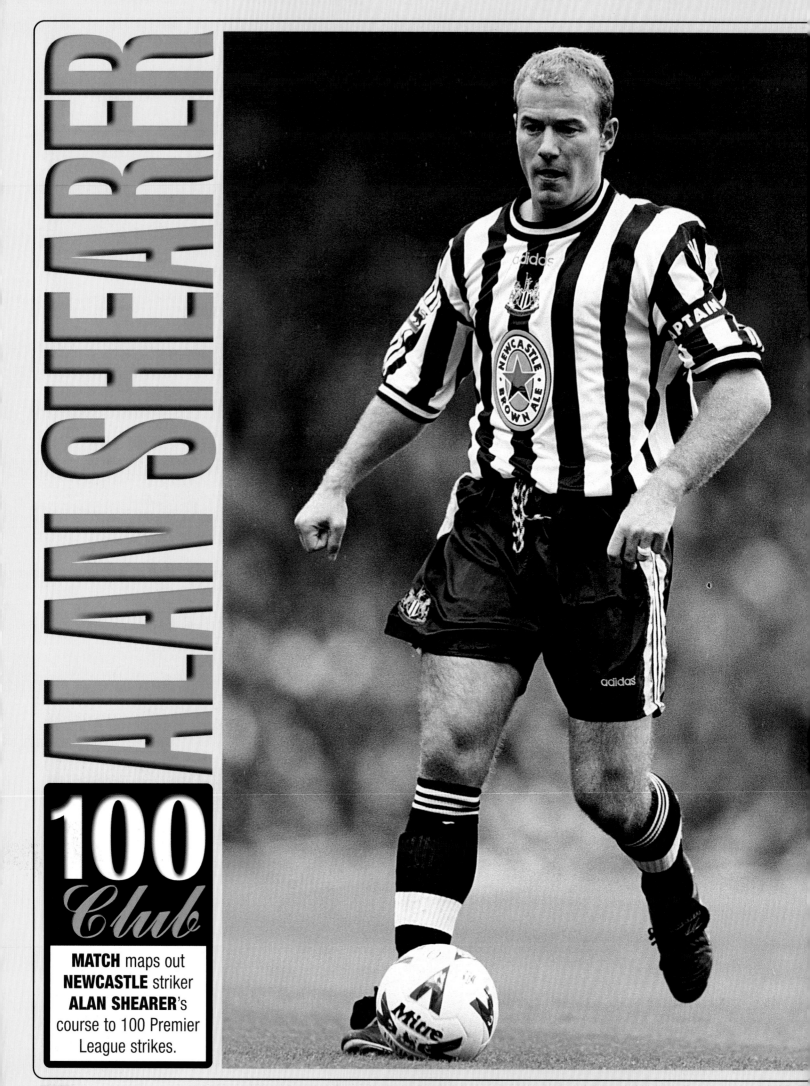

ALAN SHEARER

100 Club

MATCH maps out **NEWCASTLE** striker **ALAN SHEARER**'s course to 100 Premier League strikes.

WHEN ALAN SHEARER EXPLODED ONTO THE scene with Southampton, he showed all the potential of a future world-class striker. So much so that Blackburn were prepared to shell out £3.3 million on him.

The fee was quickly repaid when he took them to the Premiership title in the 1994-95 season becoming the first player to notch up 100 Premiership goals on the way. Now with Newcastle, Shearer carries the hopes of Tyneside on his shoulders.

Here MATCH looks in detail at how Shearer amassed his first 100 Premiership goals.

The King of Ewood Park salutes his loyal subjects.

Shearer celebrates a goal against former club Blackburn.

The King of Ewood visits the Palace and makes quite an impression.

WHERE DID HE COME FROM?

Alan began his professional career at Southampton after being rejected by his hometown club Newcastle United. He first came to the public's attention when he bagged a quickfire hat-trick for The Saints against Arsenal at The Dell in April 1988. Before long he was being watched by a number of big-money clubs and was snapped up by Blackburn for £3.3 million. In 1996 a world record £15 million transfer to Kevin Keegan's Newcastle saw him return home to Tyneside.

STRENGTHS?

He holds the ball up well, gets into the six-yard box whenever possible and use his menacing presence in the air. He also has a thunderbolt of a right foot shot which makes him a threat from distance as well.

WEAKNESSES?

Since his injury, he's possibly lost a yard of the pace which had given him that extra edge at international level. He's also weaker on his left side than his right.

STRIKE PARTNERSHIPS?

The SAS partnership with Chris Sutton helped Blackburn to the championship in 1994-95 when Alan scored 33 goals and Sutton hit 20. He's also linked up famously with Les Ferdinand for Newcastle and Teddy Sheringham for England.

BEST GOAL?

It's difficult to name one because there's been so many at every club he's played and for England, but the second goal he scored in his first game for Blackburn Rovers at Crystal Palace signalled his arrival on the big stage. The way in which he controlled a difficult shot was simply magnificent.

FINEST MOMENT?

Without a doubt, winning the Premiership title with Blackburn in the 1994-95 season. At international level, being awarded the Golden Boot at Euro '96 for finishing the tournament's top scorer must rank pretty high on his list of career achievements.

BEFORE THE PREMIERSHIP			
1987-88	Southampton	**3 goals**	Division 1
1988-89	Southampton	**0 goals**	Division 1
1989-90	Southampton	**3 goals**	Division 1
1990-91	Southampton	**4 goals**	Division 1
1991-92	Southampton	**13 goals**	Division 1

SHEARER'S PREMIERSHIP 100

BLACKBURN ROVERS

Crystal Palace 3-3 *August 15 1992*

1 **66 mins** Shearer controlled the ball and struck a superb 20-yard volley on his Blackburn debut.

2 **81 mins** A fantastic 30-yard volley inside the top far corner crowned a memorable debut.

Arsenal 1-0 *August 18 1992*

3 **84 mins** Shearer broke from just over the halfway line and his fierce shot was deflected off a defender and over goalkeeper David Seaman.

Coventry City 2-0 *August 29 1992*

4 **69 mins** (pen) Shearer was tripped from behind by McGrath but got up to convert the spot-kick.

Nottingham Forest 4-1 *September 5 1992*

5 **3 mins** Shearer was first to a knock-down and hooked the ball in from close range.

6 **59 mins** (pen) Fouled by Tiler, Shearer scored powerfully from the resulting penalty.

Everton 2-3 *September 15 1992*

7 **12 mins** (pen) After being brought down by Hinchcliffe, Shearer converted from the spot.

8 **74 mins** Shearer pounced at the near post to knock in a Jason Wilcox cross.

Wimbledon 1-1 *September 19 1992*

9 **32 mins** Shearer latched onto a through-ball and fired into the corner.

Oldham Athletic 2-0 *September 26 1992*

10 **30 mins** Raced past two defenders from a quick Stuart Ripley free-kick to strike a low drive in from 15 yards.

Norwich City 7-1 *October 3 1992*

11 **43 mins** Shearer brilliantly chipped the goalkeeper after swapping passes with Tim Sherwood.

12 **76 mins** A firm downward header from a pinpoint Alan Wright cross.

Queens Park Rangers 1-0 *November 28 1992*

13 **17 mins** Got on the end of a Wilcox free-kick to beat the 'keeper at the near post.

Liverpool 1-2 *December 13 1992*

14 **80 mins** A corner was headed into the area by Hendry and Shearer swivelled to hit a brilliant volley past Hooper.

Leeds United 3-1 *December 28 1992*

15 **45 mins** An easy tap-in from close range after a telling Jason Wilcox cross.

16 **58 mins** Another close-range finish after being picked out by Wilcox.

Newcastle United 1-1 *August 29 1993*

17 **75 mins** Shearer ran on to a superb through-ball from Tim Sherwood to slip the ball home just eight minutes after coming on as sub.

Sheffield Wednesday 1-1 *September 25 1993*

18 **81 mins** Shearer got a lucky rebound and he made the most of it with a cracking left-foot drive.

Swindon Town 3-1 *October 2 1993*

19 **15 mins** Capitalised on Fenwick's miss-kick to chase the ball and fire a low shot into the right-hand corner.

20 **90 mins** Shearer took advantage of sloppy defending to ghost past Nijholt and beat 'keeper Fraser Digby with a 15-yard shot.

Leeds United 3-3 *October 23 1993*

21 **25 mins** Tapped in after mark Beeney had saved Mike Newell's header.

22 **46 mins** Shearer finished coolly after the ball broke to him as Leeds failed to clear.

23 **75 mins** A great finish after Mike Newell's quickly-taken free-kick.

Tottenham Hotspur 1-0 *October 30 1993*

24 **15 mins** Hooked in from close range after Newell headed down Ripley's corner.

Southampton 2-0 *November 20 1993*

25 **23 mins** (pen) A perfect spot-kick after Monkou had fouled Newell.

26 **76 mins** A breathtaking volley from Gallacher's right-wing cross.

Coventry City 2-1 *November 23 1993*

27 **32 mins** Went through from Wright's pass to beat the 'keeper with a lofted shot.

28 **63 mins** Cut inside from the left to score with a low shot inside the near post.

The King of Ewood moved on and attained the status of Messiah on Tyneside.

Big Neville Southall tried every means he could think of to stop Al.

Shearer plus ball equals goal. A simple but effective equation.

Chelsea	2-0	December 5 1993

29 | **90 mins** A close-range shot finished off Stuart Ripley's cross.

Oldham Athletic	2-1	December 11 1993

30 | **27 mins** Struck from from ten yards after Oldham's defence had failed to clear a Graeme Le Saux cross.

31 | **49 mins** Slid in to produce a close-range shot after three Blackburn players broke clear to beat Oldham's offside trap.

Manchester City	2-0	December 18 1993

32 | **76 mins** Clinical finish after Gallacher miss-kicked from Batty's cross.

Everton	2-0	December 29 1993

33 | **24 mins** Buried a half-chance into the bottom corner of the net from 12 yards.

34 | **42 mins** A superb near post header from a well-worked free-kick routine.

Aston Villa	1-0	January 1 1994

35 | **38 mins** Shearer side-footed home Le Saux's pass from the byeline.

Sheffield United	2-1	January 15 1994

36 | **38 mins** Shearer's fierce shot finished off a Stuart Ripley cross.

37 | **64 mins** A simple tap-in after Alan Cork had failed to clear for Sheffield United.

Leeds United	2-1	January 23 1994

38 | **11mins** A close-range volley from a pinpoint Wilcox cross.

39 | **90 mins** A brilliant header from a Le Saux cross from wide on the left.

Wimbledon	3-0	February 5 1994

40 | **7 mins** A well-struck shot from the spot after Barton's foul on Le Saux .

Tottenham Hotspur	2-0	February 12 1994

41 | **60 mins** Shearer started and finished a great move which ended in a superb header from Ripley's cross.

Swindon Town	3-1	March 26 1994

42 | **6 mins** Cut inside from the left and unleashed a bullet of a shot from 20 yards.

43 | **82 mins** (pen) Shearer converted the spot-kick after Luc Nijholt had fouled Stuart Ripley.

Manchester United	2-0	April 2 1994

44 | **46 mins** A precision header from Tim Sherwood's right-wing cross.

45 | **76 mins** A thumping volley after latching on to Ripley's superb long ball.

Aston Villa	1-0	April 11 1994

46 | **10 mins** A fierce right-foot shot after Newell had headed down a Wilcox cross.

With Newell, Warhurst and Shearer, goals came easily for Blackburn.

How Alan Shearer scored his first 100 Premiership goals!

Goal Total | 3 | 5 | 3 | 7 | 2 | 7 | 4 | 8 | 1 | 2 | 4 | 3 | 1 | 3 | 5 | 2 | 3 | 5 | 3 | 4 | 6 | 4 | 4 | 7 | 4

Bar chart — Y-axis: Number of Goals Scored Per Game (0, 3, 6, 9, 12). Clubs along X-axis: Arsenal, Aston Villa, Chelsea, Coventry City, Crystal Palace, Everton, Ipswich Town, Leeds United, Leicester city, Liverpool, Manchester City, Manchester United, Middlesbrough, Newcastle United, Nottingham Forest, Norwich City, Oldham Athletic, Queens Park Rangers, Sheffield United, Sheffield Wednesday, Southampton, Swindon Town, Tottenham Hotspur, West Ham United, Wimbledon.

Queens Park Rangers   1-1   April 24 1994

47 — **45 mins** A quickly taken free-kick into the top corner from 25 yards.

Southampton   1-1   August 20 1994

48 — **60 mins** Latched on to Sutton's knock-down to shoot under Bruce Grobbelaar.

Leicester City   3-0   August 22 1994

49 — **73 mins** An easy tap-in after Stuart Slater's initial shot rebounded off a post.

Everton   3-0   September 10 1994

50 — **17 mins** Turned Unsworth before firing into the bottom corner from 25 yards.

51 — **60 mins** Sent Southall the wrong way after Sutton was tripped by the goalkeeper.

Aston Villa   3-1   September 24 1994

52 — **17 mins** (pen) Gave spot-kick specialist Mark Bosnich no chance with the penalty after Chris Sutton was fouled in the area by Ehiogu.

53 — **72 mins** Sutton's superb header put Shearer clear for a thumping drive.

Newcastle United   1-1   October 15 1994

54 — **58 mins** (pen) Wilcox was brought down by Srnicek and Shearer sent the 'keeper the wrong way from the penalty spot.

Sheffield Wednesday   1-0   November 2 1994

55 — **53 mins** Shearer took the ball in his stride to score from just outside the box.

Tottenham Hotspur   2-0   November 5 1994

56 — **49 mins** (pen) Beat Walker from the spot after being fouled by Edinburgh.

Ipswich Town   3-1   November 19 1994

57 — **70 mins** Netted after 'keeper Forrest had failed to hold Chris Sutton's header.

Queens Park Rangers   4-0   November 26 1994

58 — **56 mins** Ignored a defender tugging his shirt to score from eight yards.

59 — **66 mins** (pen) Perfect spot-kick after Ripley was fouled by Karl Ready.

Shearer bagged a brace in the win over Spurs to take Newcastle to the FA Cup Final.

---

60 — **85 mins** A stunning drive went in off the bar from almost 30-yards out.

Wimbledon   3-0   December 3 1994

61 — **74 mins** Tapped in from close range after Sutton had pounced on a defensive mistake.

Southampton   3-2   December 10 1994

62 — **13 mins** (pen) Followed up to fire home after his penalty was saved.

63 — **74 mins** Clinically finished after getting on the end of a low cross by Le Saux.

Manchester City   3-1   December 26 1994

64 — **9 mins** Slotted the ball home from four yards after Sutton's header from Le Saux's cross had come back off the bar.

West Ham United   4-2   January 2 1995

65 — **14 mins** (pen) Scored easily after being brought down by the goalkeeper.

66 — **75 mins** Brilliant finish after superbly controlling a pass from Jason Wilcox.

67 — **79 mins** Another good strike after Wilcox was fouled by Marc Rieper.

Ipswich Town   4-1   January 28 1995

68 — **3 mins** Shearer took the ball off Whelan to shoot low into the far corner.

69 — **29 mins** Superb swerving shot into the top corner from Sutton's flick-on.

70 — **90 mins** (pen) Scored comfortably after being fouled by Whelan.

Leeds United   1-1   February 1 1995

71 — **6 mins** (pen) Sent Lukic the wrong way after Sutton had been fouled.

Sheffield Wednesday   3-1   February 12 1995

72 — **66 mins** A precise downward header from Henning Berg's cross.

Wimbledon   2-1   February 22 1995

73 — **3 mins** A downward header after getting on the end of a cross from Henning Berg.

Arsenal   3-1   March 8 1995

74 — **4 mins** Fierce low shot on the turn from Chris Sutton's pass.

75 — **48 mins** Clinical spot-kick after Atkins was fouled by Linighan.

Coventry City   1-1   March 11 1995

76 — **87 mins** A cross from Graeme Le Saux was missed by 'keeper Gould and Shearer headed a face-saving equaliser.

Chelsea   2-1   March 16 1995

77 — **16 mins** Received a through ball from Le Saux to thunder the ball past Hitchcock.

Everton   2-1   April 1 1995

78 — **6 mins** Glorious 18-yard volley from a half clearance by an Everton defender.

Manchester City   2-3   April 15 1995

79 — **7 mins** Coton's miss-kick found him 30 yards out and he fired it straight back.

Newcastle United   1-0   May 8 1995

80 — **29 mins** Powerful downward header from Le Saux's precise cross.

Liverpool   1-2   May 14 1995

81 — **20 mins** Ran on to Ripley's right wing cross to fire low past James.

Queens Park Rangers   1-0   August 19 1995

82 — **6 mins** (pen) Sent the 'keeper the wrong way after he had been pushed by Bardsley.

Sheffield Wednesday   1-2   August 23 1995

83 — **60 mins** A deadly close-range finish after slick build-up from midfield.

Manchester United   1-2   August 28 1995

84 — **59 mins** A superbly struck left-foot shot after a corner was only half cleared.

Aston Villa   1-1   September 9 1995

85 — **52 mins** An opportunist right foot shot when the ball fell to him after an aerial challenge.

Coventry City   5-1   September 23 1995

86 — **8 mins** A close range shot from a near-post corner routine.

87 — **60 mins** An easy tap-in for Shearer after he was set-up by Mike Newell.

88 — **67 mins** A blockbusting finish after connecting with Mike Newell's flick-on.

Southampton   2-1   October 14 1995

89 — **77 mins** A 28 yard free-kick which hit the corner of the net before anyone moved.

West Ham United   1-1   October 21 1995

90 — **89 mins** Looping six-yard header after Dicks slipped challenging for Bohinen's centre.

Chelsea   3-0   October 28 1995

91 — **49 mins** Beat the offside trap to score right-footed from 10 yards.

Nottingham Forest   7-0   November 18 1995

92 — **20 mins** Right-foot shot from 10 yards after Newell headed down.

93 — **58 mins** A towering header connected with a Stuart Ripley corner.

94 — **68 mins** A well struck right foot free-kick from 25-yards out.

West Ham United   4-2   December 2 1995

95 — **3 mins** Low right foot shot from 15 yards after taking a pass from Ripley.

96 — **17 mins** Half volley from six yards after Newell flicked on a throw-in.

97 — **65 mins** Right-foot shot after he had been fouled by Julian Dicks.

Middlesbrough   1-0   December 16 1995

98 — **42 mins** Right-foot shot from 20 yards after being set up by Mike Newell.

Manchester City   2-0   December 26 1995

99 — **11 mins** Right-foot drive from 22 yards after the ball was laid off by Newell.

Tottenham Hotspur   2-1   December 30 1995

100 — **41 mins** Turned to curl a right foot shot past over Walker from 22 yards.

SINCE JOINING THE 100 CLUB

1995-96	Blackburn Rovers	13 goals	Premiership
1996-97	Newcastle United	25 goals	Premiership
1997-98	Newcastle United	2 goals	Premiership
1998-99	Newcastle United	14 goals	Premiership

Despite his best efforts Shearer has still to bring any silverware to Tyneside.

KEY HOME GAME AWAY GAME

M 27

THE FINAL WHISTLE

HOW DID YOU SCORE?
Think you're a soccer expert? There are 200 fantastic footy quiz questions in the Annual – fill in your answers on Page 108 and see how well you scored.

Michael Owen is already an established England player.

first XI

How much do you know about the international debut games of England's current crop of footballers?

1 Which striker made his international debut against Uruguay in 1995 as a Manchester United player?

2 Which defender, now with Chelsea, kicked off his England career against Denmark in 1994 as a Blackburn Rovers player?

3 Which record-breaking young striker made his debut against Chile at Wembley in 1998 as a Liverpool player?

4 Which goalkeeper played his first game for England against Saudi Arabia back in 1988 as a QPR player?

5 Which striker who moved to London in the close season, made his debut against Cameroon in 1997 as a Blackburn Rovers player?

6 Which midfielder made his debut against Moldova in 1997 as a Manchester United player?

7 Which inspirational defender debuted for England against Spain in 1987 as an Arsenal player?

8 Which famous frontman made his debut against the French in 1992 as a Southampton player but moved north soon after?

9 Which much travelled midfield playmaker made his debut against Denmark in 1989 as a Tottenham Hotspur player?

10 Which goalkeeper, currently England's second choice, made his debut against the CIS in 1992 as a Crystal Palace player?

11 Which treble-winning striker started his international career against Poland in 1993 as a Tottenham Hotspur player?

THE MEGA WORD SPOT

Can you spot the players who have been on the move in the last year in the grid below?

```
M X I S G U N N L A U G S S O N I M E
E Q Y Q R E R A R W R M Y U N A K A Q
L K M A I E D S S H E R W O O D P R Q
C C L F E R G U S O N Z J U I X A I J
H E T T S T U A R T S T O N E R H C T
I B A B C A L D E R W O O D P X A B P
O C W B H K B V O I N A C I D S R B R
T I Z I O D O N N E L L W E I R S G I
U I H P N C I N L W C Y Y S N V D X N
A Y H H E F B E W G G K T M E S I V G
R C A I D Q A S Z N C A R S L E Y H L
A D L N S J K N W O M U Q L Y B B A E
M I L E R L K A T S H L A L S P V R S
A J E D A W E J G E P C L I V X T T C
C B O Y M E K O R S T E N I P N P S O
P A L M E R F L M M N F O E E P R O T
M C M A N A M A N N G S S W H N Y N T
S L Y A B O R B O K I S P B V F O H H
B O S N I C H D C R E S S W E L L O N
```

- BAKKE
- BECK
- BORBOKIS
- BOSNICH
- CALDERWOOD
- CARSLEY
- CAMARA
- CRESSWELL
- DI CANIO
- DONNELLY
- FERGUSON
- FOE
- GUNNLAUGSSON
- HALLE
- HARTSON
- HENCHOZ
- HYPPIA
- JANSEN
- KANU
- KORSTEN
- MARIC
- MARSDEN
- McMANAMAN
- MELCHIOT
- O'DONNELL
- O'NEILL
- PAHARS
- PALMER
- PRINGLE
- SCOTT
- SHERWOOD
- SONG
- STONE
- STUART
- WEIR

What was the result?

Can you remember the results of these FA Cup semi-finals in the 1990s?

1 April 14, 1991
Nott'm Forest v West Ham

2 April 13, 1992
Sunderland v Norwich

3 April 3, 1993
Sheff. United v Sheff. Wed

4 April 9, 1994
Chelsea v Luton

5 March 31, 1996
Aston Villa v Liverpool

6 April 5, 1998
Wolves v Arsenal

ONE-O

All these games finished 1-0, but who scored the goals?

1 February 1999
Manchester United v Derby County

2 December 1998
Charlton Athletic v Arsenal

3 December 1998
Wimbledon v Liverpool

4 December 1998
Middlesbrough v West Ham

5 April 1999
Nottingham Forest v Tottenham

CIVVY STREET

Can you name this top footy star without his kit on?

WHO PLAYS WHERE?

Can you match up these teams with their home grounds?

1. Peterborough United	A. Britannia Stadium
2. Stoke City	B. Ninian Park
3. Gillingham	C. London Road
4. Hartlepool United	D. Priestfield Stadium
5. Cardiff City	E. Victoria Ground
6. Ipswich Town	F. Boundary Park
7. Oldham Athletic	G. Brunton Park
8. Carlisle United	H. Madejski Stadium
9. Reading	I. Portman Road

GUESS THE PLAYER

Can you work out who this famous footy player is?

DAVID GINOLA TOTTENHAM

"I have only been in our stands at Selhurst Park a few times," says Wimbledon striker Jason Euell, *"but it is brilliant here when there's a full house."*

"If we've won the game, the players come in here afterwards for a quick drink."

SELHURST PARK

The permanent south London home of Crystal Palace – and also the ground which Wimbledon use for their home games. It is well known for being hard to get to.

Built	1924
Capacity	26,500
Average Attendance	18,237

Greatest Moment: Wimbledon haven't had that many big moments here, but way back in 1962 the Real Madrid side, five times European champions, came to Selhurst Park to play Crystal Palace in an exhibition game. Stars such as Di Stefano, Puskas and Gento turned out for the Spanish side.

"What we want is a new ground for ourselves. It would be great for our loyal fans."

AROUND THE

THE STADIUM OF LIGHT

Sunderland boast a fantastic new stadium on the outskirts of the city centre, which is filled every week by their passionate fans, some of whom had the chance to put their names on bricks, which were incorporated in the building.

Built	1997
Capacity	41,590
Average Attendance	38,724

Greatest Moment: As the ground is only two seasons old, the greatest moment came only recently, at the end of last season in fact, when Peter Reid's outfit beat Birmingham City 2-1 and finally lifted the First Division trophy after leading the league for months.

"At 1.30pm we'll all come into the changing room and talk tactics."

"Our club shop has everything – even Sunderland beds!"

"I used to have to clean Alan Shearer's boots when I was a trainee at Southampton."

"I like to see number ten shirts with my name on," says Kevin Phillips. *"When the fans chant your name, you get a buzz."*

Welcome to **COVENTRY CITY F.C.**

GRANDSTAND RESTAURANT Hospitality Suites

MAIN STAND BLOCKS K–M

"Our supporters are fantastic and they've always been good to me. They can be really noisy."

HIGHFIELD ROAD

Since 1993 Coventry attendances have risen by 50 per cent. The club have applied for planning permission for a new 40,000-capacity stadium to be built by the summer of 2001.

Built	1899
Capacity	23,627
Average Attendance	20,805

Greatest Moment: In Division Two in 1966-67, the Sky Blues went on a 25-match unbeaten run. In a game dubbed 'the Midlands match of the century', they beat local rivals Wolves 3-1 in front of a record 51,455 crowd to lift the title.

"By the time we get to the tunnel, I just want to get on the pitch," says Darren Huckerby.

"Before a game, the boss will go through what he wants us to do."

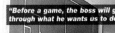

"This stadium is really quite something," says Colin Hendry. "The atmosphere is amazing when you walk on to the pitch with 50,000 fans cheering for you."

"There's a waiting list of about 10,000 to get a season ticket here."

"There's an interesting mixture of players here – in a great squad."

"A club like Rangers would fit quite easily into the Premiership."

"Because of all the success, there's always an expectancy to do well."

IBROX

Rangers' magnificent, imposing stadium has witnessed so much success in its 112 year history. It boasts an electric atmosphere and the ground is intimidating for away teams to play in.

Built	1887
Capacity	50,500
Average Attendance	46,700

Greatest Moment: There have been many great Ibrox nights, but most recently after winning nothing in 1997-98, the Rangers fans particularly enjoyed the success of last season – Dick Advocaat's side bringing back the title from the clutches of rivals Celtic.

GROUNDS

Britain's top footy stars take **MATCH** on a guided tour of some of the greatest grounds in the country.

Deon Burton is proud to play at Derby's new ground.

PRIDE PARK

Pride Park is just two miles away the site of the Baseball Ground, but the facilities are much better. The stylish entrance leads to a stunning state-of-the-art stadium.

Built	1997
Capacity	33,000
Average Attendance	29,195

Greatest Moment: In November 1997, just months after the stadium had been opened by the Queen, over 30,000 fans saw Derby beat Arsenal 3-0 in the Premier League. And Arsenal went on to do the double that season!

"We were all impressed when we first saw the new stadium."

EWOOD PARK

Jack Walker's millions have helped to redevelop Ewood Park into one of the country's great stadiums. It's unfortunate, however, that the town isn't big enough to provide a bigger crowd – as the ground is rarely full!

Built	1890
Capacity	31,367
Average Attendance	25,761

Greatest Moment: In the penultimate game of the 1994-95 season, Blackburn entertained Newcastle and an Alan Shearer goal put them within reaching distance of the Premier League title.

"Since Jack Walker arrived the ground's changed so much you can get lost!"

PLEASE KEEP OFF THE GRASS

"I think the groundsmen are trying to win an award for the best pitch," says striker Kevin Gallacher.

WELCOME TO BLACKBURN ROVERS F.C. ARTE ET LABORE

"I made my debut here when I was 18 against Chelsea. It was a full house – the atmosphere was brilliant."

GOODISON PARK

Everton's rich history and tradition echoes around Goodison Park on matchdays, with the passionate Toffees fans still getting behind the team despite years of hurt.

Built	1892
Capacity	40,200
Average Attendance	36,203

Greatest Moment: In 1985 Everton fans witnessed many thrilling games at Goodison as Howard Kendall's side overshadowed the achievements of Liverpool by winning the league title and the European Cup Winners' Cup, as well as making it to the FA Cup Final.

Toffees' defender David Unsworth tries to pass as a photographer.

"Sid is our assistant groundsman – he knows everything about Everton."

THE DELL

Southampton have had plans approved for a new stadium, which will be on the outskirts of the town and will have a bigger capacity. The Dell is small and pokey, but does provide a good atmosphere on matchdays.

Built	1898
Capacity	15,220
Average Attendance	15,139

Greatest Moment: The best year at the Dell was 1983-84. Peter Shilton was in goal and the team finished title runners-up to Liverpool and lost an FA Cup semi-final to Everton in extra time.

"I've been very impressed with the plans for our new stadium."

"Although the crowd at The Dell is small," says John Beresford, "they are as loud as any in the Premiership."

EXIT

"We have a great crowd at West Ham," says Frank. "We're just like one big happy family."

"I've always been a West Ham fan and only ever wanted to play for them," says Frank Lampard.

BOLEYN GROUND

Many people refer to the ground as 'Upton Park' – but that's the name of the district. The ground is a bit of a fortress and can be intimidating for away teams as the fans are so near to the pitch.

Built	1904
Capacity	26,054
Average Attendance	25,684

Greatest Moment: The Boleyn Ground witnessed a great performance against Real Zaragoza in the first leg of the 1965 Cup Winners' Cup semi-final. Two better performances in Spain and at Wembley saw The Hammers lift the trophy.

"Frank and me make sure the music's good. We can't listen to pop rubbish," says Rio Ferdinand.

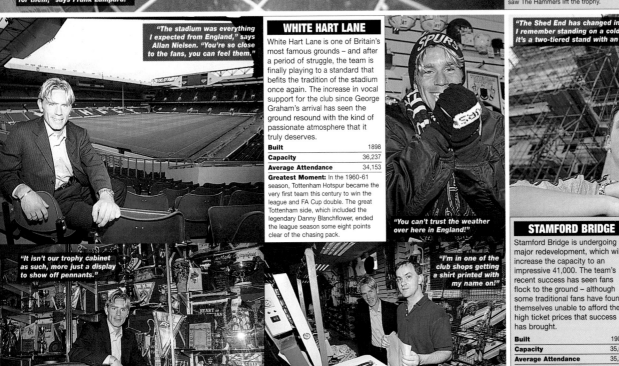

"The stadium was everything I expected from England," says Allan Nielsen. "You're so close to the fans, you can feel them."

WHITE HART LANE

White Hart Lane is one of Britain's most famous grounds – and after a period of struggle, the team is finally playing to a standard that befits the tradition of the stadium once again. The increase in vocal support for the club since George Graham's arrival has seen the ground resound with the kind of passionate atmosphere that it truly deserves.

Built	1898
Capacity	36,237
Average Attendance	34,153

Greatest Moment: In the 1960-61 season, Tottenham Hotspur became the very first team this century to win the league and FA Cup double. The great Tottenham side, which included the legendary Danny Blanchflower, ended the league season some eight points clear of the chasing pack.

"You can't trust the weather over here in England!"

"It isn't our trophy cabinet as such, more just a display to show off pennants."

"I'm in one of the club shops getting a shirt printed with my name on!"

"The Shed End has changed in the last few years. I remember standing on a cold terrace here, now it's a two-tiered stand with an executive lounge!"

STAMFORD BRIDGE

Stamford Bridge is undergoing major redevelopment, which will increase the capacity to an impressive 41,000. The team's recent success has seen fans flock to the ground – although some traditional fans have found themselves unable to afford the high ticket prices that success has brought.

Built	1905
Capacity	35,629
Average Attendance	35,278

Greatest Moment: The recent European Cup Winners' Cup semi-final 3-1 triumph over Vicenza in the home leg was a thrilling match. Chelsea came through that successfully and went on to beat Stuttgart in the Final.

"It's one of Europe's finest stadiums," says Jody Morris.

"The atmosphere in here after a game always depends on the result."

THE VALLEY

Charlton left the Valley in 1985 when derelict areas were closed, leaving the club to ground share, first with Palace and then with West Ham. They returned in '92, and the ground was redeveloped.

Built	1919
Capacity	21,046
Average Attendance	19,823

Greatest Moment: The game against Portsmouth on December 5, 1992. Charlton fans thought they would never return to The Valley, but Colin Walsh scored in front of a limited crowd of just 8,000 to make it a welcome return.

Shaun Newton isn't too sure about his new sweeper role.

"It's a real buzz running out from the tunnel and hearing the noise. I feel comfortable when I play at The Valley – we've got a good set of fans."

"This is where we come for a bit of treatment from the physio when we are injured."

"This is the tribute to Liverpool's hero Bill Shankly. Behind it is the club shop and museum."

"There is a great atmosphere at Anfield on matchdays. You really have to experience it."

ANFIELD

Anfield is one of the greatest stadiums in England, but its legendary Kop terrace was knocked down in 1994 to make way for modern seating.

Built	1880
Capacity	45,370
Average Attendance	43,321

Greatest Moment The 3-0 win over Borrussia Moenchengladbach in the 1978 European Cup semi-final was good, but possibly the 5-0 thrashing of Nottingham Forest in 1988 was the greatest moment when Aldridge, Barnes and Beardsley were in top form.

"This is the Liverpool museum, which hasn't been open that long. It's well worth coming to have a look around."

"I was given a look around Anfield when I played my first game here as a schoolboy, " says defender Jamie Carragher. "We walked on the pitch and I was really quite taken aback by it!"

"This is a drawing of Kenny Dalglish when he used to play for Celtic," says Alan Stubbs. "He was a real hero with all the fans here."

CELTIC PARK

Celtic boast by far the biggest stadium in Britain – and it is the only British club that has a higher average attendance than Man. United. A magnificent sight when there's a full house crowd in for an Old Firm derby. The imposing stadium can be seen for miles around after redevelopments.

Built	1892
Capacity	60,294
Average Attendance	59,270

Greatest Moment: The 2-0 home win over St Johnstone to clinch the league title and stopping Rangers winning record breaking ten in a row has to be right up there, but Celtic fans will remember the 5-1 stuffing of Rangers last November as their greatest game.

"This place is so intimidating. It must be well scary for the opposition running out of the tunnel here."

"You can see the ground from miles away as you drive towards it. It is certainly a daunting place."

FILBERT STREET

The ground has been redeveloped gradually over the years, which means the stands are all different heights. But this does give the place its own special character and history, rather than being a modern structure.

Built	1891
Capacity	21,500
Average Attendance	20,469

Greatest Moment: In 1928 in the record 10-0 win against Portsmouth, five Swans are said to have flown over the stadium and – as striker Arthur Chandler notched a double hat-trick– a sixth is said to have passed overhead.

"I first came to Leicester on loan from Chelsea in March 1996 and I helped them to win promotion."

The Foxes' Muzzy Izzet strikes his catalogue pose.

"I love it here and the good thing is the club is always looking to improve."

ST JAMES' PARK

The Newcastle ground is being redeveloped to house 51,000 fans, which will be ready for next season. It's slap bang in the city centre and is always booked up with season ticket holders.

Built	1880
Capacity	36,824
Average Attendance	36,682

Greatest Moment: The 3-2 win over Barcelona in 1997 and the return of idol Hughie Gallagher in 1930 (attracting 68,000 fans) are close seconds. But the fans' fave is the 7-1 thrashing of Leicester at the end of the 1992-93 season, which celebrated promotion!

"The ground has been very noisy recently because of all the building work that's being done on it," says Aaron Hughes.

"This is where all the fans come to buy their club shirts."

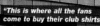

ISN'T IT ABOUT TIME...
Sir Fergie let Brian Kidd take over at Man. United to give everyone else in the Premiership a chance of winning something.

have you ever...

DEAN GORDON
middlesbrough

...PLAYED AGAINST A HERO OF YOURS?
"I've been lucky enough to play against one of my heroes in John Barnes. Unfortunately, I never had the chance to play against my other two heroes, Kenny Dalglish and the great Brazilian Zico."

...GIVEN UP ON THE TEAM YOU SUPPORTED AS A BOY?
"I grew up supporting Liverpool and I still look out for their results. But seeing as I'm a Boro player now I always want to know how the teams around us in the league have done. They're always the most important results."

...TRIED ANY DANGER SPORTS?
"I'd call swimming a danger sport because I can't swim! But apart from that I haven't done anything like skiing or bungee jumping. I'm pretty sure that the gaffer wouldn't want us doing anything like that."

...BEEN ON HOLIDAY WITH THE LADS?
"Yeah we've been away on the odd team trip. Some of us go clubbing and stay out all night. The gaffer doesn't mind that as long as we play well and work hard in training."

...GOT A ROLLICKING FROM THE MANAGER?
"Yeah, when I haven't performed well I have. But in that situation, you just have to hold your hands up and say you deserved it. But it upsets me when I get a pasting and haven't deserved it."

...HAD A TEAM-MATE PLAY A TRICK ON YOU?
"It's funny you should ask me that. One that always sticks in my mind is when I was at Palace and I've no idea who the culprit was to this day. At the end of the week someone had taken all my credit cards so I spent the weekend cancelling them only for them to reappear on Monday."

INJURY TIME

Duncan Ferguson Newcastle United

Do football stars spend more of their time on the physio's treatment table than they do on the pitch?

DOUBLE HERNIA
When? April 17, 1995
Where? Sheffield Wednesday v Everton
How? Simply by wear and tear over a period of time through excessive kicking, sprinting and stretching.
What is it? Weakened stomach muscles are breached more than once.
How long injured? Five weeks.
Does it hurt? It's pretty painful, especially as Ferguson needed a double hernia operation. It was made worse when he played from the start in the FA Cup Final when he wasn't fit to do so.
THE MATCH AGONY RATING 4

HERNIA
When? August 23, 1995
Where? Everton v Arsenal
How? Returned to first-team action too early, before a previous injury had sufficiently repaired, causing the problem to re-occur.
What is it? Stomach muscles get weak and allow other bits to bulge through.
How long injured? Two months
Does it hurt? It's not agony, it's more of a dull nagging pain that won't go away. The pain comes and goes – some days are worse than others.
THE MATCH AGONY RATING 3

GROIN STRAIN
When? December 28, 1998
Where? Liverpool v Newcastle United
How? Ferguson had an operation at a London hospital after it became clear the long-standing problem could not be solved by rest.
What is it? Muscley area where the leg connects with the body.
How long injured? Four months
Does it hurt? It's more of a hindrance than a real pain, but Ferguson was frustrated after initially being ruled out for only six weeks.
THE MATCH AGONY RATING 2

GROIN STRAIN
When? April 16, 1996
Where? Everton v Liverpool
How? After injuring his groin in training, Big Dunc insisted on playing through the pain. But he was eventually forced to sit out the end of the season after struggling through the Merseyside derby.
What is it? Muscley area where the leg connects with the body.
How long injured? Three months
Does it hurt? Not too badly, though it's important to rest and not to aggravate it even further.
THE MATCH AGONY RATING 2

CARTILAGE DAMAGE
When? September 21, 1996
Where? Blackburn Rovers v Everton
How? Suffered a nasty knock after a 50-50 challenge for the ball and the cartilage damage was discovered later.
What is it? A plastic-like shock absorber in the knee joint that stops bones rubbing together.
How long injured? Seven weeks.
Does it hurt? It's not serious, but you can't put any real weight on the joint and more often than not it needs surgery to make the problem go away.
THE MATCH AGONY RATING 6

KNEE LIGAMENT
When? September 18, 1993
Where? Rangers v Aberdeen
How? Overstretched when trying to get on the end of a cross and damaged his knee ligaments.
What is it? Fibrous tissues that hold bones together at a joint.
How long injured? Six weeks.
Does it hurt? You bet it does. Any kind of flexing of the knee results in stabbing pains around the joint. It can be cured by rest and physiotherapy, though quite often surgery is required.
THE MATCH AGONY RATING 7

THE PRICE IS WRONG!

Call it what you want, but you can't deny that David O'Leary seems to have something pretty special going on at Leeds United at the moment. Since the big Irishman took over from George Graham he's opted to snap up the best young talent in the game. But it looks as though he's inherited the tight-fisted attitude of his mentor when it comes to wheeling and dealing in the transfer market. When he swooped to sign full-back Danny Mills, David admitted he was worried about splashing the cash. **"I wanted Danny for a while and the thing that didn't help was that he was doing better all the time,"** said the O-man. **"He got into the Under-21s and it nearly killed me when he got picked for England's full team because it seemed the price was going up by a million every day."** C'mon David, be honest! You were just worried that you wouldn't have enough change left over to buy yourself a pint of Guinness later on.

At the end of each football year, it's inevitable that players will have time to kill. So, have you ever wondered what they get up to when they're not playing? Well, believe it or not, a common thing to do seems to be getting hitched. The problem for Derby left-back Stefan Schnoor when he recently wed the love his life during the close season was that he couldn't do so in his native country. **"In Germany everybody pays part of their salary towards the church – if you don't do that then it makes it difficult for you to get married there,"** he told Route 1. **"Last year the church cost me about £400 a month. But Nicole and I watched a programme about marriage and saw Las Vegas as one of the options so we decided on that. We spent four days in Las Vegas in all then four days in Honolulu, eight days in Maori and then rounded it all off with five days in New York – it was all good fun!"** A small consolation for not having to go back to Germany, eh Stefan?

GERMAN FLY OVER

DAVID BECKHAM MAN. UNITED

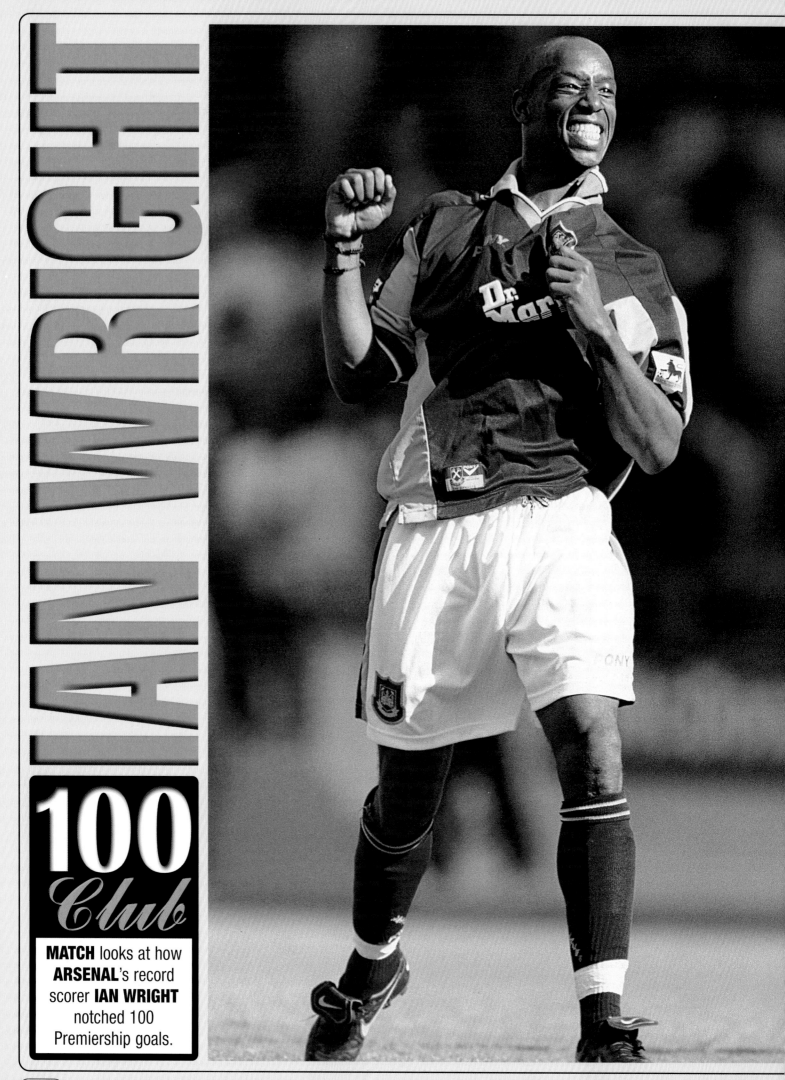

IAN WRIGHT

100 Club

MATCH looks at how **ARSENAL**'s record scorer **IAN WRIGHT** notched 100 Premiership goals.

IAN WRIGHT IS AN ARSENAL LEGEND. EVEN before the striker broke Cliff Bastin's club record of 178 career goals in a Gunners shirt, Wrighty was worshipped by the Highbury fans. The former England striker has always had a talent for scoring and his celebrations were loved as much as the success which went hand in hand with his goals.

Wright won numerous trophies with Arsenal and has featured prominently throughout his Highbury career at the top of the goalscoring charts and is one of an elite group of players to have scored over 100 Premiership goals.

Wrighy's continued his scoring ways with West Ham.

WHERE DID HE COME FROM?

Although he began his league career with Crystal Palace, Wrighty started out with non-league outfit Greenwich Borough. After six free-scoring years at Selhurst Park, Arsenal boss George Graham splashed out £2.5 million to take him to Highbury.

STRENGTHS?

Wrighty has the gift of being in the right place at the right time. He is full of confidence and will shoot from anywhere whether it's from ten yards out, or from the halfway line. He is the master of one-on-one situation and is as effective off the ball as he is on it.

WEAKNESSES?

His temperament has put him in a lot of trouble over the years. There was the well-publicised clash with Peter Schmeichel, numerous appearances before the FA on misconduct charges and many missed games through suspension. Wright has had counselling to help control his temper but it remains his major flaw.

STRIKE PARTNERS?

Wrighty's had many over the years, but his partnership with Mark Bright at Crystal Palace brought the pair over 150 league goals between them and put both of them into the spotlight. He also teamed up extremely well with Dennis Bergkamp for three years at Arsenal and together the pair netted over 100 goals.

BEST GOAL?

It came in the 90th minute, when Arsenal were already leading struggling Swindon 3-0 at the County Ground in December 1993, Wrighty picked up the ball from 35 yards out and exquisitely lobbed the stranded Fraser Digby. It wasn't his most vital strike in terms of trophies or key points, but it was done with such style.

FINEST MOMENT?

Gunners fans will always remember Wrighty's delight after he broke Cliff Bastin's club goalscoring record of 178 with his second strike in a hat-trick against Bolton in 1997. Definitely his career highlight.

Goal celebrations have always been a bit of a trademark.

So often Merson and Wright combined for Arsenal to good effect.

BEFORE THE PREMIERSHIP

1985-86	Crystal Palace	**9 goals**	Division 2
1986-87	Crystal Palace	**8 goals**	Division 2
1987-88	Crystal Palace	**20 goals**	Division 2
1988-89	Crystal Palace	**24 goals**	Division 2
1989-90	Crystal Palace	**8 goals**	Division 1
1990-91	Crystal Palace	**15 goals**	Division 1
1991-92	Crystal Palace	**5 goals**	Division 1
1991-92	Arsenal	**24 goals**	Division 1

WRIGHT'S PREMIERSHIP 100
ARSENAL

Liverpool   2-0   *August 23 1992*

1   **80 mins** Wright was put through by Ray Parlour and he sprinted away from the Liverpool defence before shooting past James.

Oldham Athletic   2-0   *August 26 1992*

2   **31 mins** Wright netted Arsenal's second goal of the game to clinch victory. He outpaced Jobson and beat 'keeper Hallworth easily.

Wimbledon   2-3   *September 5 1992*

3   **34 mins** Wright opened the scoring for Arsenal with a classy effort which left Segers stranded.

4   **82 mins** Grabbed a late consolation with a low shot past the 'keeper.

Sheffield United   1-1   *September 19 1992*

5   **85 mins** Stuck out a foot to steer Linighan's cross past the advancing Alan Kelly.

Manchester City   1-0   *September 28 1992*

6   **19 mins** Headed home a cross from strike partner Kevin Campbell.

Chelsea   2-1   *October 3 1992*

7   **85 mins** Fired in the winner past Hitchcock from an Anders Limpar cross.

Everton   2-0   *October 24 1992*

8   **5 mins** Met Paul Merson's cross with an accurate header past Southall in the Everton goal.

Crystal Palace   2-1   *November 2 1992*

9   **73 mins** Finished off from close range after great build-up play from Merson and Campbell.

Coventry City   3-0   *November 7 1992*

10   **31 mins** Collected a pass from Alan Smith and lobbed Steve Ogrizovic with ease.

Middlesbrough   1-1   *December 19 1992*

11   **81 mins** Fired in from close range past Steven Pears after Kevin Campbell's shot hit a post.

Norwich City   1-1   *March 3 1993*

12   **81 mins** Norwich's defence failed to clear a cross from Limpar and Wright took his time to shoot past Gunn.

Coventry City   2-0   *March 13 1993*

13   **29 mins** Shot the ball into an empty net after a mix-up between 'keeper Ogrizovic and Peter Atherton.

Nottingham Forest   1-1   *April 21 1993*

14   **67 mins** Broke through the Forest defence, picked up a pass from Parlour and slid the ball past Andy Marriott.

Crystal Palace   3-0   *May 8 1993*

15   **9 mins** Merson found Wright in space and he fired a shot past Nigel Martyn from close range.

Tottenham Hotspur   1-0   *August 16 1993*

16   **86 mins** Andy Linighan flicked on a corner to Wright whose header beat Eric Thorstvedt in the Spurs goal.

Sheffield Wednesday   1-0   *August 21 1993*

17   **8 mins** Kevin Campbell squared the ball to Wright, who side-footed into an empty net.

Everton   2-0   *August 28 1993*

18   **48 mins** Kevin Campbell flicked on David Seaman's long goal-kick and Wright finished emphatically.

19   **78 mins** Dispossessed Ablett on the edge of the area and lobbed the stranded Neville Southall.

Ipswich Town   4-0   *September 11 1993*

20   **30 mins** Slotted home from an acute angle after Kevin Campbell flicked the ball on into his path.

Aston Villa   1-2   *November 6 1993*

21   **58 mins** Martin Keown played the ball in to Wright who shot low past Mark Bosnich.

Chelsea   2-0   *November 20 1993*

22   **45 mins** (pen) Sent Dmitri Kharine the wrong way after he was brought down by defender David Lee.

Newcastle United   2-1   *November 27 1993*

23   **15 mins** Steve Bould got his head to a corner, flicking the ball to Wright who headed in from close range.

Scoring against Spurs meant a low key celebration from Wright.

LOVE THE LADS

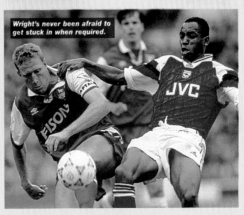

Wright's never been afraid to get stuck in when required.

Stealing a yard on Steve Yates of QPR.

Tottenham Hotspur   1-1   *December 6 1993*

24   **65 mins** Anders Limpar played the ball inside and Wright crashed home a left-foot shot from 12 yards.

Sheffield Wednesday   1-0   *December 12 1993*

25   **90 mins** Steve Morrow played a long ball forward, Alan Smith flicked on and Wright pounced at the far post.

Swindon Town   4-0   *December 27 1993*

26   **90 mins** A sublime inch-perfect 35-yard chip beat the stretching Fraser Digby in the Swindon goal.

Sheffield United   3-0   *December 29 1993*

27   **40 mins** Fired in a low shot across the goal and past 'keeper Alan Kelly following a neat pass from David Hillier.

Wimbledon   3-0   *January 1 1994*

28   **56 mins** Wright headed home after a mistake from Dons' defender Scott Fitzgerald.

Oldham Athletic   1-1   *January 22 1994*

29   **45 mins** (pen) Oldham's Mike Milligan was penalised for a handball and Wright converted the spot-kick past 'keeper John Hallworth.

Ipswich Town   5-1   *March 5 1994*

30   **18 mins** Rounded David Linighan before slotting past 'keeper Clive Baker from a narrow angle.

31   **40 mins** (pen) Fired the penalty into the roof of the net after Mick Stockwell had tripped Limpar.

32   **86 mins** Adams' through-ball was collected by Wright who beat the 'keeper to clinch his hat-trick.

Southampton   4-0   *March 19 1994*

33   **12 mins** Stooped to head in an Ian Selley cross from close range.

34   **30 mins** Limpar chipped the ball over The Saints' defence and Wright slammed a spectacular volley into the top corner.

35   **69 mins** (pen) Struck the spot-kick past Dave Beasant after Monkou had upended Limpar.

Chelsea   1-0   *April 16 1994*

36   **72 mins** Headed the match-winner past Dmitri Kharine following a cross from Lee Dixon.

Aston Villa   2-1   *April 23 1994*

37   **29 mins** (pen) Picked himself up after being brought down by Neil Cox and fired past Nigel Spink to open the scoring.

38   **90 mins** A low shot after being put through on goal by Kevin Campbell.

Manchester City   3-0   *August 20 1994*

39   **76 mins** Collected a Kevin Campbell centre and fired the ball past Tony Coton.

Newcastle United   2-3   *September 18 1994*

40   **88 mins** Fired a consolation goal past Pavel Srnicek from 20 yards after good work from Schwartz.

West Ham United   2-0   *September 25 1994*

41   **53 mins** Looped a header into the far corner following an accurate cross from Paul Merson.

Crystal Palace   1-2   *October 1 1994*

42   **72 mins** Headed in a consolation goal from Campbell's right wing cross.

Wimbledon   3-1   *October 8 1994*

43   **11 mins** Ran on to a clearance from David Seaman and drove the ball past the advancing Wimbledon 'keeper Hans Segers.

Chelsea   3-1   *October 15 1994*

44   **40 mins** Fired a shot past Dmitri Kharine after Chelsea's defence failed to clear a corner.

How Ian Wright scored his first 100 Premiership goals!

Goal Total: 7 3 3 7 7 3 2 7 8 5 2 3 3 4 4 1 2 2 2 1 2 5 5 1 4 3 6

Number of Goals Scored Per Game (y-axis: 0, 3, 6, 9, 12)

Teams (x-axis): Aston Villa, Blackburn Rovers, Bolton Wanderers, Chelsea, Coventry City, Crystal Palace, Derby County, Everton, Ipswich Town, Leeds United, Leicester City, Liverpool, Manchester City, Middlesbrough, Newcastle United, Norwich City, Nottingham Forest, Oldham Athletic, Queens Park Rangers, Sheffield United, Sheffield Wednesday, Southampton, Swindon Town, Tottenham Hotspur, West Ham United, Wimbledon

---

45 | 63 mins Nigel Winterburn advanced down the left flank and passed to Wright, who netted from 20 yards.

Coventry City 2-1 — October 23 1994

46 | 13 mins Schwarz dispossessed David Rennie and passed to Wright who fired home past Ogrizovic.

47 | 34 mins Broke free after a mistake from Steven Pressley and scored with ease.

Leicester City 1-2 — November 23 1994

48 | 19 mins (pen) Brought down in the area by Jimmy Willis but picked himself up to score from the spot past helpless 'keeper Poole.

Ipswich Town 2-0 — December 28 1994

49 | 16 mins Fired in a left-footed volley after Schwarz's corner was flicked on into his path.

Everton 1-1 — January 14 1995

50 | 4 mins Latched onto David Hillier's chipped through-ball to fire past the stranded Southall.

Ipswich Town 4-1 — April 15 1995

51 | 47 mins Fired home past Clive Baker from 12 yards after good work from Merson.

52 | 50 mins Paul Merson delivered a great crosss into the area from the byeline and Wright met the ball with a superb diving header.

53 | 56 mins Rounded the 'keeper at the second attempt and finished with ease.

Aston Villa 4-0 — April 17 1995

54 | 32 mins Raced away from the Villa defence and hammered a shot past Bosnich.

55 | 72 mins (pen) Fired in from the spot after Paul McGrath had brought him down.

Tottenham Hotspur 1-1 — April 29 1995

56 | 61 mins (pen) Brought down by Justin Edinburgh and picked himself up to fire the spot-kick past Spurs 'keeper Ian Walker.

Middlesbrough 1-1 — August 20 1995

57 | 36 mins Met Parlour's cross with a powerful header beating Alan Miller in the Boro goal.

Everton 2-2 — August 23 1995

58 | 86 mins Outpaced David Unsworth and finished neatly from an acute angle.

Manchester City 1-0 — September 10 1995

59 | 90 mins Dennis Bergkamp crossed and Wright stooped for a header six-yards out.

Wright celebrates breaking Cliff Bastin's goalscoring record.

West Ham United 1-0 — September 16 1995

60 | 75 mins (pen) Powered the penalty past Miklosko after Bergkamp was brought down by Steve Potts.

Southampton 4-2 — September 23 1995

61 | 73 mins Twisted and turned past the Southampton defence before firing a shot past Beasant.

Leeds United 3-0 — October 14 1995

62 | 86 mins Picked up a loose ball, turned Wetherall and chipped Lukic from the edge of the box.

Aston Villa 2-0 — October 21 1995

63 | 78 mins Bergkamp crossed and Wright shot left-footed past Bosnich from six-yards out.

Liverpool 1-3 — December 23 1995

64 | 8 mins (pen) Beat David James from the spot after being brought down by Mark Wright.

Queens Park Rangers 3-0 — December 26 1995

65 | 44 mins Flicked the ball in the net from close range following a superb cross from strike-partner Paul Dickov.

Wimbledon 1-3 — December 30 1995

66 | 27 mins Slotted past Segers from seven-yards out after connecting with a delightful pass from Bergkamp.

Everton 1-2 — January 20 1996

67 | 38 mins Latched onto John Jensen's pass and unleashed a powerful 25 yard shot past Southall.

Newcastle United 2-0 — March 23 1996

68 | 17 mins Winterburn robbed Barton on the right flank, crossed to the waiting Wright, who shot from five yards.

Leeds United 2-1 — April 6 1996

69 | 44 mins Fired home though a crowd of defenders from five yards.

70 | 90 mins Controlled a David Platt flick-on, turned and shot past 'keeper John Lukic.

Blackburn Rovers 1-1 — April 27 1996

71 | 75 mins (pen) Converted the penalty past Tim Flowers after Colin Hendry had brought down Ray Parlour.

Leicester City 2-0 — August 24 1996

72 | 90 mins Keller's clearance was charged and fell to Wright who shot into an empty net from 18 yards.

Chelsea 3-3 — September 4 1996

73 | 77 mins Winterburn found Wright in space and the striker lobbed Kharine in the Chelsea goal.

Sheffield Wednesday 4-1 — September 16 1996

74 | 62 mins (pen) Hit the a penalty to Pressman's left after Walker had brought down Merson.

75 | 78 mins Merson challenged for the ball in the area and broke to Wright who fired home the loose ball.

76 | 89 mins Met Winterburn's cross for the 100th league goal of his career.

Middlesbrough 2-0 — September 21 1996

77 | 27 mins Took advantage of a slip by Steve Vickers to shoot powerfully past Alan Miller.

Blackburn Rovers 2-0 — October 12 1996

78 | 3 mins John Hartson knocked the ball down to Wright who shot powerfully into the top corner past 'keeper Flowers.

---

79 | 51 mins Vieira played the ball though to Wright who beat Flowers from ten yards.

Leeds United 3-0 — October 26 1996

80 | 65 mins Beat the Leeds offside trap to meet Bergkamp's cross and score from close range.

Wimbledon 2-2 — November 2 1996

81 | 6 mins Latched on to Vieira's through ball to fire past Neil Sullivan from 25 yards.

Tottenham Hotspur 3-1 — November 24 1996

82 | 27 mins (pen) Bergkamp was brought down by defender Clive Wilson and Wright stepped up to score.

Newcastle United 2-1 — November 30 1996

83 | 59 mins Turned the ball in from close range after Merson's shot was deflected into his path.

Southampton 3-1 — December 4 1996

84 | 57 mins (pen) Merson was brought down by Lundekvam and Wright slotted the penalty low to Beasant's left.

Nottingham Forest 1-2 — December 21 1996

85 | 62 mins Crossley dropped a cross at Wright's feet who made no mistake from eight yards out.

Aston Villa 2-2 — December 28 1996

86 | 12 mins Bergkamp's pass found Wright who ran past the Villa defence and shot past Bosnich from 15 yards.

Middlesbrough 2-0 — January 1 1997

87 | 44 mins Stabbed home his 200th career goal after Beck's header fell at his feet.

West Ham United 2-1 — January 29 1997

88 | 66 mins Merson's pinpoint cross found Wright, who fired past Miklosko from ten yards.

Everton 2-0 — March 1 1997

89 | 27 mins Collected a pass from Garde and beat Southall with a shot into the corner of the net.

Liverpool 1-2 — March 24 1997

90 | 78 mins Bergkamp's header found Wright who looped the ball over James from four yards out.

Chelsea 3-0 — April 5 1997

91 | 22 mins Intercepted a misplaced pass and raced into the box to slide the ball past the advancing Grodas.

Coventry City 1-1 — April 21 1997

92 | 19 mins (pen) Ogrizovic brought Wright down inside the area and the striker fired in past the 'keeper.

Derby County 3-1 — May 11 1997

93 | 55 mins Shot past Poom after pouncing on a loose ball in the Derby box.

94 | 90 mins Met Anelka's accurate cross and finished neatly from close range.

Leeds United 1-1 — August 9 1997

95 | 5 mins Had a shot cleared by Martyn but regained possession and squeezed the ball into the far corner.

Coventry City 2-0 — August 11 1997

96 | 29 mins Reacted fastest to poke the ball past Ogrizovic from four yards, after he failed to hold Vieira's shot.

97 | 47 mins Curled the ball right-footed over the onrushing Ogrizovic.

Bolton Wanderers 4-1 — September 13 1997

98 | 20 mins Received a Dennis Bergkamp pass and fired across a diving Keith Branagan from 15 yards.

99 | 25 mins Struck the ball into the net from just three yards to break Cliff Bastin's Arsenal goalscoring record.

100 | 81 mins Platt lifted a pass over the defence leaving Wright to guide the ball in from yards.

SINCE JOINING THE 100 CLUB

1997-98	Arsenal	4 goals	Premiership
1998-99	West Ham	9 goals	Premiership

Dixon and Wright celebrate more Arsenal success.

FOOTY MAD!

There is always room for a laugh at someone's expense as this selection of last season's **MATCH** pics shows.

THEY SAID WHAT!

MATCH finds stars who say something more memorable than 'sick as a parrot'…

"I hadn't scored in my new boots so I sold them for charity. This guy bought them and he scored a hat-trick. I asked for them back and wore them for the Leeds game, which I scored in." Andy Booth of Sheffield Wednesday on his magic boots.

"I give 100 per cent and I want to win every time I play. I am that way when I am playing with my daughter at home." Paolo Di Canio explains why his competitive nature is taken to extremes at times.

"I used to draw diagrams of my goals because I didn't have a video and I wanted a record of every goal." Tony Cottee of Leicester remembers his poorer days as a footy pro.

"People think I am always looking at myself in the mirror. But that is rubbish. When my daughter looks at me and says, 'Daddy, you're beautiful', I go red and feel really pleased. When others say it, I don't care." David Ginola on why he's not vain… sure Dave, whatever you say.

"I want it from Stephen Glass the same way I want it from Alan Shearer. At first they found it odd because it wasn't what they were used to. But they are all adults and I want them all to take responsibility." Ruud Gullitt explains how he introduced a new way of playing at Newcastle…er, we hope.

"After training, some of the lads do the full monty. Even when the laundry ladies are around they just strip off." Ian Harte reveals the naked truth about life at Elland Road

"In some parts of the world, if you beat three pub teams then you're in the World Cup finals." Neville Southall gets screwed up about never playing in the World Cup Finals with Wales.

Not only had dear old Ray Wilkins lost all his hair, but he was starting to go a bit deaf as well.

Dennis hadn't realised that he was this week's lottery jackpot winner.

Merse saw a flying pig that did not bode well for the start of England's Euro 2000 campaign.

Some were unsure about the man being groomed to replace Fergie at the helm.

Marian Pahars waits his turn for an audience with LeTiss.

Big girlie foreign stars hugging and wearing woolly jumpers under their shirts.

The velcro on the front of the shirt trick proved a winner once again.

"Aw! is poor little Stanny a tired bunnykins?" John Gregory before he got tough with Collymore.

The tout's prices were too high for Incey.

Hamilton was pleased with the inflatable sofa he'd bought from the Leeds club shop.

Things went so badly at Palace last season, Tel took to applauding the arrival of the fizzy pop.

The carrots were coming along a treat but the early frost had ruined the brussel sprouts.

Mikael Forssell and Dave Beasant walked away with first prize in the dance-off.

Wimbledon's Mick Harford tries to attract the attention of a passing taxi.

Changing ends at half time continued to confuse Razor.

Ginola takes a sneaky peek while he's 'it' during a game of hide and seek.

The ref found that shutting his eyes meant he made more correct decisions than normal.

Tension turned to anger as the half-time biscuits began to run out.

The Boro boys react to the news that Mikkel Beck had joined Derby.

Dave couldn't believe the public reaction to the birth of baby Brooklyn.

Albert and Jesper's form suffered when they were stricken with a frightening limb-straightening disease.

Keith Flint of The Prodigy was having an impressive debut for Leicester.

Ref David Elleray's cunning disguise wasn't fooling anyone.

40 M

JAMIE REDKNAPP LIVERPOOL

From the pages of the *MATCH facts* results service, we bring you the...

10 GREATEST GAMES OF THE '90s

EVERY SEASON THROWS UP ITS FAIR SHARE OF GREAT MATCHES AND last season, with Man. United doing the treble, again provided several to choose from. Throughout the 1990s there have been countless matches, from famous cup giant-killings to momentous World Cup showdowns, which have taken the breath of many a football fan away. Whether the teams we support were involved in the games or whether we watched them as neutrals, there is no doubt that these ten matches have entertained us for every second of the ninety, or so, minutes that they lasted.

The games have included a whole catalogue of nail-biting moments, from penalty shoot-outs to great goals, close action, great saves, near misses, dismissals – and above all, really high quality entertaining football. They're the stuff footy fans' dreams are made of.

So as we enter the Millennium, MATCH looks back on the ten most exciting matches of the 1990s and finds out what the players who played in them thought. Sit back and relive these never to be forgotten games.

10

"The Italians could only watch as Ireland outplayed them."

Republic of Ireland 1 Italy 0

WHEN? June 18, 1994 **WHERE?** New York

WHO SCORED? Republic of Ireland Houghton 11

WHY IMPORTANT? The Republic Of Ireland's first game of the 1994 World Cup Finals

WHAT HAPPENED? Jack Charlton's Irish heroes won the hearts of the world by beating, out-playing and out-thinking stunned eventual finalists Italy. Ray Houghton surprised everyone with a superb 11th minute strike from 25 yards to put the Irish in front, sending the 73,000 New Jersey crowd into a frenzy! While Houghton ultimately won the match, Paul McGrath and Phil Babb shone at the heart of the Irish defence, making their world-class opposite numbers of Baresi and Costacurta look rather ordinary.

TEAMS IRELAND: Bonner 7, Irwin 8, Phelan 7, Babb 8, **McGrath 9*** (sub 68 mins McAteer 7), Keane 7, Townsend 8, Sheridan 8, Coyne 8 (sub 90 mins Aldridge). **ITALY:** Pagliuca 7, Tassotti 6, Maldini 6, Baresi 6, Costacurta 6, Albertini 6, **D Baggio 8***, Donadoni 7, R Baggio 7, Signori 7 (sub 84 mins Berti, Evani 6 (sub 45 mins Massaro 6).

9

Wright came off the bench to equalise and put Palace ahead with this goal in extra-time.

Crystal Palace 3 Man. United 3

WHEN? May 12, 1990 **WHERE?** Wembley

WHO SCORED? Palace O'Reilly 19, Wright 72, 97;
Man. United Robson 35, Hughes 62, 113.

WHY IMPORTANT? FA Cup Final

WHAT HAPPENED? A Mark Hughes goal late in extra-time saved Man. United from Cup Final humiliation, forcing a replay. But at one stage it had all seemed so different as Fergie's men looked to be cruising towards victory – until supersub Ian Wright joined the game. The Final was fast and frantic from the off, with Palace's Gary O'Reilly heading home a Pemberton free-kick after just 19 minutes. Captain Bryan Robson nodded in to equalise, before Mark Hughes put United ahead. Wrighty came on to bring Palace back into it, but then Hughes chased a Wallace through-ball to give United a second chance five days later.

TEAMS CRYSTAL PALACE: Martyn 7, Pemberton 7, Shaw 7, **Gray 8*** (sub 118 mins Madden 7), O'Reilly 6, Thorn 6, Barber 6 (sub 69 mins Wright 7), Thomas 7, Bright 7, Salako 7, Pardew 7. **MAN. UNITED:** Leighton 5, Ince 7, Martin 6 (sub 88 mins Blackmore 6), Bruce 6, Phelan 6, Pallister 5 (sub 93 mins Robins), Robson 7, Webb 5, McClair 5, **Hughes 8***, Wallace 5.

8

Clive Mendonca was a hat-trick hero for Charlton.

Sunderland 4 Charlton 4 Charlton win 7-6 pens

WHEN? May 25, 1998 **WHERE?** Wembley

WHO SCORED? Charlton Mendonca 24, 72, 104, Rufus 86
Sunderland Quinn 50, 74, Phillips 58, Summerbee 99

WHY IMPORTANT? Division One Play-Off Final

WHAT HAPPENED? In a thrilling end-to-end play-off final, Charlton eventually saw off the challenge of Sunderland to clinch promotion to the top flight for the first time in their history. In front of a record crowd of 77,739, Clive Mendonca became the first player to score a hat-trick in a play-off final as the balance of play shifted between the two sides. They were inseparable after 90 minutes – and extra-time. The first 13 penalties failed to settle the matter until Charlton 'keeper Sasa Ilic saved Michael Gray's effort to win promotion.

TEAMS CHARLTON: Ilic 8, Mills 7 (sub 77 mins Robinson 8), Bowen 7, K Jones 7, Rufus 8, Youds 7, Newton 7, Kinsella 7, Bright 6 (sub 94 mins Brown 7), **Mendonca 9***, Heaney 6 (sub 65 mins S Jones 8) **SUNDERLAND:** Perez 7, Holloway 6 (sub 46 mins Makin 6), Gray 6, **Clark 8*** (sub 100 mins Rae 6), Craddock 6, Williams 6, Summerbee 7, Ball 7, Quinn 8, Phillips 7 (sub 75 mins Dichio 5), Johnston 6.

7

Edwin Van der Sar found himself on the floor several times during the match.

England 4 Holland 1

WHEN? June 18, 1996 **WHERE?** Wembley

WHO SCORED? England Shearer 23 pen, 56, Sheringham 51, 62
Holland Kluivert 78

WHY IMPORTANT? Group stages of Euro '96

WHAT HAPPENED? England had their dream of qualification for USA '94 ended by Holland – and now they wanted revenge! The small fact that England hadn't beaten them in 14 years was conveniently forgotten in the patriotic fervour of Euro '96, but when Terry Venables' first XI set about destroying the mighty Dutch, it really did seem like anything was possible! With the SAS attack firing the team ahead, Paul Gascoigne led the charge from midfield as England played football with a passion not seen in recent Wembley memory. Shearer and Sheringham were a class apart, and the defence, marshalled by Tony Adams, didn't let anything get by until Kluivert's consolation goal 12 minutes from time. As the final whistle blew, the sound of 'Three Lions' boomed around the stadium as a jam-packed Wembley turned into the best and biggest street party of the year!

TEAMS HOLLAND: van der Sar 6, Reiziger 6, Blind 6, Seedorf 6, de Boer 6 (sub 71 mins Cocu 6), **Bergkamp 8***, Hoekstra 5 (sub 71 mins Kluivert 6), Winter 6, Witschge 5 (sub 46 mins de Kock 5), Bogarde 6, Cruyff 6. **ENGLAND:** Seaman 8, G Neville 7, Pearce 7, Ince 7 (sub 67 mins Platt 6), Adams 7, Southgate 7, Gascoigne 7, Shearer 8 (sub 75 mins Barmby), **Sheringham 9*** (sub 75 mins Fowler), Anderton 6, McManaman 7.

6

Ferdinand and Collymore were just two of the on-form strikers playing that day.

Liverpool 4 Newcastle 3

WHEN? April 3, 1996 **WHERE?** Anfield

WHO SCORED? Liverpool Fowler 2, 57, Collymore 63, 90; **Newcastle** Ferdinand 10, Ginola 14, Asprilla 60

WHY IMPORTANT? Premier League showdown

WHAT HAPPENED? The Magpies had won 14 matches out of 19 in the run up to Christmas and at one stage had led the Premiership by a remarkable 12 point-margin. Under Kevin Keegan, Newcastle played exciting, attacking football, and with Les Ferdinand putting the ball in the net on a regular basis, the title looked to be heading for St James' Park. But suddenly it all started to go wrong.

Having just been knocked off the top of the table by Manchester United for the first time, Newcastle faced a testing trip to Liverpool. And in an epic see-saw encounter, the two teams staged the most amazing match of the season. After some great attacking football from both sides, which produced plenty of chances, the Merseyside club came from behind to snatch a last-minute winner. Stan Collymore was the Liverpool hero that night and, with only a few seconds left on the clock, he fired home a powerful left-foot shot past goalkeeper Pavel Srnicek. The expression on Keegan's face when Collymore scored told its own story, while in the post-match TV interview, the Newcastle boss famously lost his cool as he screamed that he: "would love it, just love it" if his team beat Alex Ferguson's Manchester United to the title – but by then it was too late and The Red Devils ended up with another championship.

TEAMS LIVERPOOL: James 7, Jones 7 (sub 85 mins Rush), Wright 6 (sub 46 mins Harkness 7), Ruddock 6, McAteer 7, Barnes 7, Redknapp 7, Scales 7, **McManaman 9***, Collymore 7, Fowler 8. **NEWCASTLE:** Srnicek 7, Watson 7, Howey 6 (sub 81 mins Peacock), Albert 7, Beresford 7, Beardsley 6, Lee 7, Batty 6, Ginola 7, Asprilla 7, **Ferdinand 8***.

WHAT THEY SAID!

Rob Jones: "It was a big game for both teams and I think that match, along with the 3-3 draw we fought out with Manchester United a couple of years earlier, was the best game I've ever played in. The score was up and down throughout the match and it was a big relief to all the Liverpool players when Stan Collymore popped up to score the winner with just a minute to go. It is always a great feeling for your team to get a winner so late on in the game when it looks like it's going to end as a draw and it's especially good coming after such a tense encounter like that. I remember feeling sorry for them though. They had played just as well as us, but were the unlucky ones who went home with nothing. They really needed the points as well because they were chasing the title. I can still remember our fans going mad at the end – I guess it was one of the best games they had seen too."

5

Heartbreak for England as David Batty's penalty is saved.

England 2 Argentina 2 *Argentina win 4-3 on pens*

WHEN? June 30, 1998 **WHERE?** St Etienne, France

WHO SCORED? England Shearer 10 (pen), Owen 16; **Argentina** Batistuta 6 (pen), Zanetti 45

WHY IMPORTANT? World Cup second round

WHAT HAPPENED? After a brilliant performance against Colombia, England fans in France and at home were confident of beating Argentina. But hopes were dashed after 6 minutes when a Seaman foul allowed Batistuta to open the scoring with a penalty, but minutes later the fans were in thunderous song as Shearer put away a penalty.

A truly remarkable goal from Michael Owen put England ahead, but Zanetti's equaliser made it an even more tense game. The deciding moment came when David Beckham kicked out at Diego Simeone and was shown the red card. England rallied and, with captain Shearer in great form, desperately held on to a scrappy draw through extra time. Sol Campbell had a goal disallowed, which meant it was all down to penalties. England's curse came to the fore again though as Paul Ince and David Batty's misses booked the team an early flight home. Their tears echoed a nation's.

WHAT THEY SAID!

David Seaman: "We did what we could and it was a performance in itself to have played with a man down for such a long time. It was a shame it had to go down to penalties and worse still that, once again, it knocked us out of the tournament."

David Batty: "After the game everyone just kept to themselves. You can dwell on the miss and get upset, but I knew I couldn't have done any better. It doesn't matter how many times I've gone over it in my head since – nothing changes."

TEAMS ENGLAND: Seaman 8, Campbell 9, Le Saux 7 (sub 71 mins Southgate 7), Adams 9, Neville, G 8, **Ince 9***, Beckham 7, Anderton 7 (sub 97 mins Batty 8), Scholes 7 (sub 79 mins Merson 7), Shearer 7, Owen 8. **ARGENTINA:** Roa 7, Ayala 7, Chamot 7, Vivas 7, Zanetti 8, Almeyda 7, Simeone 7 (sub 92 mins Berti 7), **Ortega 9***, Veron 8, Lopez, C 6 (sub 69 mins Gallardo 7), Batistuta 8 (sub 69 mins Crespo 7).

Barcelona 3 Man. United 3

WHEN? November 25, 1998 **WHERE?** Nou Camp

WHO SCORED? Man. United Yorke 25, 68, Cole 53; **Barcelona** Anderson 1, Rivaldo 57, 73

WHY IMPORTANT? Champions League group stage

WHAT HAPPENED? No-one thought that the rivetting 3-3 tie at Old Trafford earlier in the campaign could be bettered, but the return fixture proved to be undoubtedly the most outstanding Champions League game of the season.

Realising that only victory would be good enough for them progress further in the competition, Barcelona attempted to outscore and outplay Manchester United from the start. In an amazing match filled with defensive errors and chances galore, the two European giants produced another six-goal thriller, but the score could easily have been much higher. With the exceptional Rivaldo producing the performance of a lifetime for Barça, and with Peter Schmeichel playing the role of both hero and villain with an incredible display of eccentric goalkeeping, there was very little that this match lacked in terms of class, style and pure entertainment value. Andy Cole and Dwight Yorke combined to produce arguably their best performance in Europe – and maybe even their best game together so far, as both of them scored memorable goals. This was the game that proved that Manchester United's attack could, on its day, destroy any defence in Europe, home or away and sent a chilling warning to Europe's other super powers that they really meant business.

4

Andy Cole gave one of his best performances in Europe that season.

WHAT THEY SAID!

Dwight Yorke: "European nights are always the best and there was a buzz about the side following our draw in Barcelona. People talk about how me and Andy played well in that game, but the whole team played well. It was a great performance and a great result."

TEAMS MAN. UNITED: Schmeichel 9, G Neville 8, Irwin 6, Stam 7, Beckham 8 (sub 81 mins Butt), Brown 7, Blomqvist 7, Keane 8, Cole 8, **Yorke 9***, Scholes 7. **BARCELONA:** Hesp 7, Celades 7, Okunowo 6, Reiziger 7, Figo 8, Sergi 7, Giovanni 7, **Rivaldo 10***, Xavi 8, Zenden 7, Anderson 8.

Liverpool 3 Manchester United 3

WHEN? January 4, 1994 **WHERE?** Anfield

WHO SCORED? **Liverpool** Clough 25, 38, Ruddock 79
Man. United Bruce 8, Giggs 20, Irwin 23

WHY IMPORTANT? Premier League showdown

WHAT HAPPENED? An amazing fight-back by Liverpool prevented Man. United striding further towards the title in a six-goal thriller that was described at the time as 'the match of the century'. The struggling Merseyside club were 21 points behind United and went 3-0 down inside the first 23 minutes. But Clough's rasping right-foot shot signalled the start of their fightback, while his second strike just before half-time brought The Kop back to life and suddenly United were under the cosh.

Urged on by a deafening roar, the second-half began with constant pressure from Liverpool. Chances went begging as they threw men forward in search of an equaliser, but this left gaping holes at the back, which United threatened to exploit. But Liverpool continued to press and Ruddock deservedly levelled with a powerful header on 79 minutes. Phew! What a game!

WHAT THEY SAID!

Nigel Clough: "We went three-nil down early in the first half, after making a couple of mistakes at the back. Graeme Souness wasn't very happy with the score at half-time, but we managed to get back into it. Our fans wanted us to go on to win the game, but the players were happy enough with the result! On a personal note, it was good to score two goals at the Kop end and to beat Peter Schmeichel from 20-yards out! I will remember it as one of the best matches I played in particularly because of the rivalry which exists between the two clubs."

TEAMS LIVERPOOL: Grobelaar 7, Jones 5, Wright 6, Ruddock 6, Dicks 6, McManaman 6 (sub 77 mins Bjornebye), Redknapp 6, **Clough 8***, Barnes 7, Fowler 6, Rush 6. **MAN. UNITED:** Schmeichel 8*, Parker 6, Bruce 6, Pallister 6, Irwin 7, Kanchelskis 6, Keane 5, Ince 6, McClair 6, Giggs 7, Cantona 7.

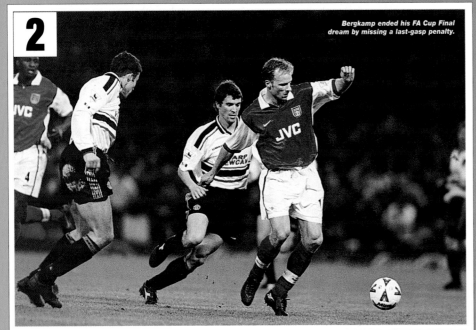

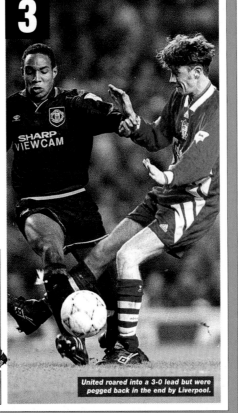

United roared into a 3-0 lead but were pegged back in the end by Liverpool.

Bergkamp ended his FA Cup Final dream by missing a last-gasp penalty.

Manchester United 2 Arsenal 1

WHEN? April 14, 1999 **WHERE?** Villa Park

WHY IMPORTANT? FA Cup semi-final replay

WHO SCORED? **Man. United** Beckham 17, Giggs 109
Arsenal Bergkamp 68

WHAT HAPPENED? Days after fighting out a close but uninspiring 0-0 draw, Fergie stunned fans arriving for the replay by leaving Dwight Yorke, Andy Cole and Ryan Giggs on the bench. Emmanuel Petit returned in midfield for Arsenal, combining well with Vieira to play some great football in the middle of the park, but Roy Keane and David Beckham matched their creativity. At 1-0 up after Beckham's great strike, United thought they had the upper-hand but then Keane was sent-off for a second bookable offence and Arsenal rallied, equalising with a 25-yard volley from Bergkamp in the 68th minute. Then the Dutch striker dramatically missed a penalty in injury-time and the game went into extra-time. With just 11 minutes of the extended period remaining, however, Ryan Giggs turned this extraordinary game on its head again. Picking up the ball inside his own half, Giggs ran from the halfway line, shrugging off challenges from Vieira, Keown, Dixon and Adams, before smashing the ball into the back of the net to settle the game with what people dubbed 'the goal of the century'.

TEAMS MAN. UNITED: Schmeichel 7, G Neville 6, Johnsen 6, Stam 6, P Neville 6, Keane 7, **Beckham 8***, Butt 7, Blomqvist 6 (sub 62 mins Giggs 7), Sheringham 6 (sub 75 mins Scholes 8), Solskjaer 6 (sub 91 mins Yorke 6). **ARSENAL:** Seaman 6, Dixon 6, Adams 6, Keown 6, Winterburn 6, Petit 7 (sub 118 mins Bould), Parlour 7 (sub 104 mins Kanu), Vieira 6, Ljungberg 6 (sub 62 mins Overmars 7), Anelka 7, **Bergkamp 8***.

WHAT THEY SAID!

Ryan Giggs: "What a great game – and what a goal! It was definitely one of the best I've ever scored. Once I started on the run towards their goal, I just couldn't stop. As I got closer to the Arsenal penalty area I just kept thinking to myself, 'you can go all the way here'. When it went past David Seaman and into the roof of the net I was off. The celebration afterwards wasn't pre-planned – I just took my shirt off instinctively. I didn't know what I was doing. It is only when I've seen the goal on TV since I've thought, 'did I really do that?'."

Right-back Paul Parker had a brilliant World Cup.

Lineker's strike puts England level with just 10 minutes of normal time left.

West Germany 1 England 1 West Germany win 4-3 on pens

WHEN? July 4, 1990 **WHERE?** Rome

WHO SCORED? West Germany Brehme 59

England Lineker 80

WHY IMPORTANT? World Cup semi-final

WHAT HAPPENED? After scraping through the earlier games at Italia '90, Bobby Robson's England found West Germany standing between themselves and a place in the World Cup Final. With the nation expecting, England went on the offensive – and a Paul Gascoigne volley early on tested German 'keeper Bodo Illgner. England had the better first half chances, but in the second period England 'keeper Peter Shilton had to be in top-form. Shilton was finally beaten by a deflected 59th minute Andreas Brehme free-kick, but Gary Lineker equalised on 80 minutes. Gazza ran tirelessly, but a rash challenge on Berthold brought a booking which meant that if England reached the Final, Gazza would play no part. Extra-time failed to separate the teams despite both sides hitting the post and the game went to penalties. Lineker, Platt and Beardsley all hit the target, but Stuart Pearce's powerful strike cannoned off Illgner's legs, giving the Germans an advantage. Chris Waddle stepped up, but his shot flew over the bar. Germany were through, England were heartbroken.

WHAT THEY SAID!

Gary Lineker: "What a dramatic way to settle such an important football match – you can't get much more pressure than a penalty shoot-out in the World Cup semi-final. I'm sure it was great to watch for the general public around the world, but it was certainly very nerve-wracking for those of us who were involved. As the regular penalty taker I was asked to take the first one to get us off to a good start. I hit it in the corner, much to my relief, but then Stuart Pearce and Chris Waddle had the misfortune to miss theirs. In a game so tense, you're bound to be devastated if you miss. I don't think anyone in the squad or in the country blamed them for missing, but it was an awful weight for the players to carry around."

David Platt was part of the devastated England team.

TEAMS ENGLAND Shilton 8, Parker 8, Pearce 8, Walker 8, Wright 8, Butcher 6 (sub 70 mins Steven 8), Platt 7, **Gascoigne 9***, Waddle 8, Beardsley 6, Lineker 8. **WEST GERMANY** Illgner 7, Berthold 7, Brehme 7, Augenthaler 6, Kohler 6, Hassler 6 (sub 68 mins Reuter), Buchwald 7, **Thon 8***, Voeller 7 (sub 39 mins Riedle 6), Matthaus 6, Klinsmann 6.

MATCHfacts Throughout the 1990s MATCHfacts has provided you with all the info on the games that matter. Remember, each player is rated out of ten and the top-rated player in each team has their name printed in bold.

second XI

Exactly how much can you really remember about football in the top flight during the 1990s?

1 Name the championship winning Leeds United player who finished as the top scorer in the old First Division in 1990-91.

2 True or false? In the same season, Crystal Palace finished the season in third position in Division One.

3 How much did French star Eric Cantona cost Manchester United when they signed him from Leeds in November 1992?

4 In which season did Norwich City finish high enough in the league to qualify for the next season's UEFA Cup?

5 For how many seasons did Oldham Athletic feature in the top flight during the 1990s?

6 True or false? Queens Park Rangers finished as the top London club in the Premiership in 1992-93.

7 Who was the Arsenal defender who scored in the last minute of extra-time to defeat Sheffield Wednesday in the 1993 FA Cup Final replay?

8 Name the former England assistant manager who failed to save Swindon Town from relegation to Division One in the 1993-94 season.

9 Which club have suffered relegation from the top division the most times in the last ten years?

10 What is the record number of points achieved by a Premiership club to win the league championship in the 1990s?

11 What is the lowest position that Man. United have finished in the top flight during the 1990s?

United have had a lot to celebrate in the 1990s.

THE ANFIELD QUIZ

Everyone knows Anfield is Liverpool's ground but how much do you know about the stadium?

1 In what year did Liverpool play their first game at Anfield?

2 What is the name of the park between Anfield and Goodison?

3 What words are written on the famous Shankly gates?

4 When was the famous Kop terrace knocked down?

5 What does the famous sign above the players' tunnel say?

6 True or False? Anfield hosted a World Cup finals game once.

7 Who did Liverpool beat 11-0 in their record Anfield win?

8 Which other two sports have been played at the ground?

9 What is the eternal flame next to the gates in memory of?

10 Which famous racecourse is near the ground?

11 Which Euro '96 quarter-final took place at Anfield?

12 What is Anfield's capacity to the nearest thousand?

connections...

What links Arsenal's Dutch striker Dennis Bergkamp with John Beresford of Southampton?

former clubs

Name their teams before joining their current club?

1 matt jansen
blackburn rovers

2 emmanuel petit
arsenal

3 didier deschamps
chelsea

4 peter atherton
sheffield wednesday

5 mark draper
aston villa

sol campbell quiz

Five tough tacklin' questions about the Tottenham and England defender.

1 What is the name 'Sol' short for?

2 True or false? Campbell scored on his Tottenham debut back in 1992.

3 What was the first domestic trophy that Sol won?

4 How many goals did Campbell score for Tottenham last season?

5 Which country provided the opposition when Sol made his first appearance for England?

NAME THE CLUB!

Whose recent league record is this?

	Prem			Div 1	Div 2
POSITION	16th	17th	18th	14th	3rd
				22nd	
SEASON	'94	'95	'96	'97 '98	'99

GUESS THE YEAR

In what year were these players born?

1 Carlton Palmer
Nottingham Forest

2 Emerson Thome
Sheffield Wednesday

3 Steve Froggatt
Coventry City

4 Steve Staunton
Liverpool

5 Mark Bosnich
Manchester United

GIANFRANCO ZOLA CHELSEA

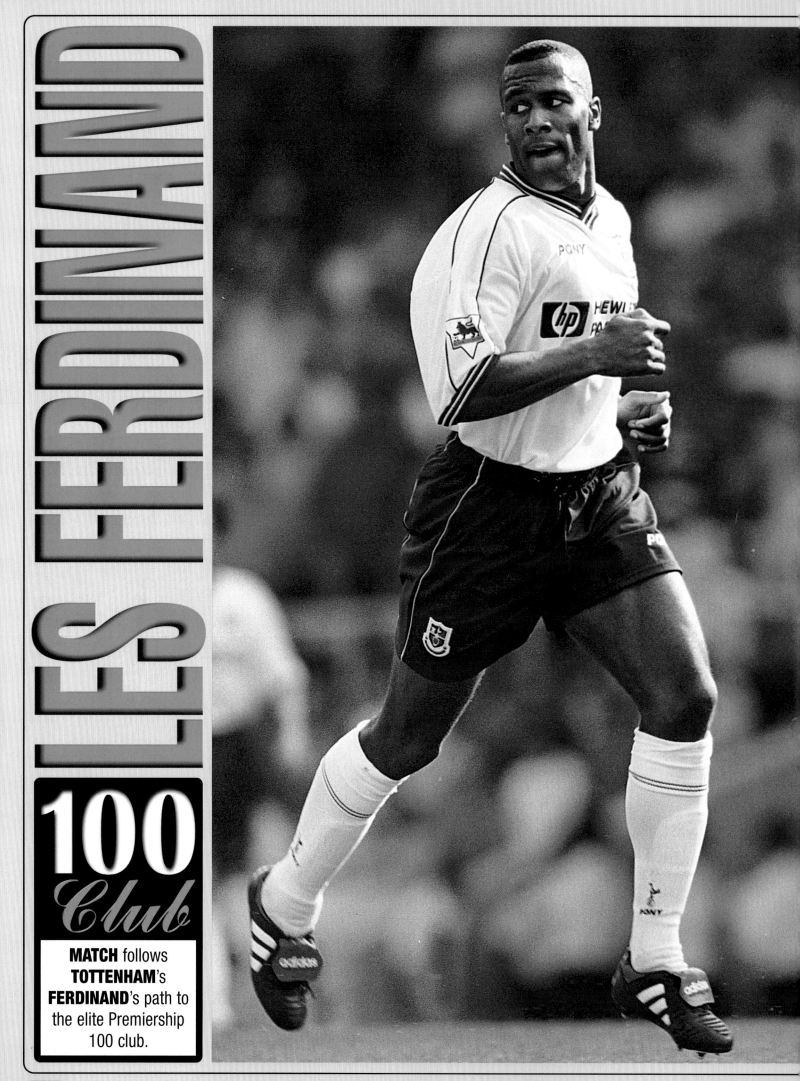

LES FERDINAND

100 *Club*

MATCH follows **TOTTENHAM**'s **FERDINAND**'s path to the elite Premiership 100 club.

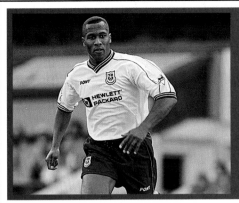

LES FERDINAND MAY HAVE HAD A COUPLE of less than prolific years at Spurs, but he has over the years, been one of the country's top marksmen. Having made a late start in the professional game with Queens Park Rangers, he made up for lost time banging in thirty goals in two years. Les was called up for England against San Marino in the 1993 World Cup qualifiers and scored on his debut.

Whether it was with QPR, Newcastle or Spurs, goals have always seemed follow Ferdinand. Here MATCH takes a look at Ferdinand's first 100 Premier League goals.

Ferdinand salutes the Toon Army after another goal.

WHERE DID HE COME FROM?

Queens Park Rangers picked him up from non-league Hayes before sending him out on loan to Brentford and Turkish side Besiktas. On his return he started knocking in the goals for QPR and earned himself a big-money move to Newcastle where he became a hero with the Toon Army, before a move back to London to join Tottenham.

STRENGTHS?

Although he is a good all-round striker, Les's biggest asset is his heading ability. Not many defenders can stop him in the air, strike-partners feed off him and crosses seem to find their way onto his forehead.

WEAKNESSES?

The injuries he has suffered over the past few seasons have affected his game. Since moving to Tottenham he seems to have lost a little of his deadliness in front of goal, which in turn has resulted in him losing his place in the England squad.

STRIKE PARTNERS?

Bradley Allen knocked in the goals alongside Les in their early days at QPR, helping the Loftus Road side to sixth in the table in 1993. Shearer and Ferdinand hit 44 goals between them in their only season together at Newcastle. Ferdinand has yet to find a regular strike-partner at Spurs.

BEST GOAL?

It came against Bolton Wanderers in only his second league game for Newcastle and was described by the man himself as: "a typical Ferdy goal". He beat two Bolton players on a powerful run and fired in an unstoppable shot past goalkeeper Keith Branagan.

BEST MOMENT?

Earning a £5 million move to Newcastle United on the back of three high-scoring seasons at Loftus Road. Les became an instant hit on Tyneside, but really hit the heights after Alan Shearer returned from injury and the two linked up to form a lethal partnership.

He's yet to find a regular strike partner at White Hart Lane.

Sir Les and Big Al were unstoppable together.

There have been some frustrating times at Spurs.

It's a good feeling to score against The Arse, eh Les?)

BEFORE THE PREMIERSHIP			
1988-89	Beskitas (loan)	**14 goals**	Division 1
1989-90	QPR	**2 goals**	Division 1
1990-91	QPR	**8 goals**	Division 1
1991-92	QPR	**10 goals**	Division 1

FERDINAND'S PREMIERSHIP 100

QUEENS PARK RANGERS

Southampton 3-1 *August 19 1992*

1 **59 mins** Ferdinand netted QPR's equaliser past Flowers after Le Tissier has opened the scoring for The Saints

2 **88 mins** Flowers had no chance with Ferdinand's effort as he sealed a win for Rangers.

Sheffield United 3-2 *August 22 1992*

3 **2 mins** Ferdinand opened the scoring with his first touch of the game, slotting the ball neatly past Tracey.

Middlesbrough 3-3 *September 19 1992*

4 **57 mins** Sinton crossed the ball from the left and Ferdinand rose to plant a fine header past Horne.

Leeds United 2-1 *October 24 1992*

5 **85 mins** Beat John Lukic to a loose ball and tapped home from close range.

Oldham Athletic 3-2 *December 5 1992*

6 **26 mins** Cashed in on a mistake by Pointon to leave debutante keeper Gerrard, no chance.

7 **52 mins** Notced hius second of the day after another error, this time by Nick Henry, let him in.

Middlesbrough 1-0 *January 9 1993*

8 **72 mins** Struck a fierce shot past Stephen Pears after a good cross by Bradley Allen.

Norwich City 3-1 *March 6 1993*

9 **18 mins** Headed home past Bryan Gunn following good work by Alan McDonald.

10 **34 mins** Ran from the halfway line and shot powerfully past Gunn.

Wimbledon 1-2 *March 13 1993*

11 **3 mins** Netted an early goal from close range after good work from Bradley Allen.

Nottingham Forest 4-3 *April 10 1993*

12 **35 mins** Latched onto a through ball, beat two Forest defenders and beat Crossley with a low shot.

13 **69 mins** Wilkins put Ferdinand clean through and he finished well past the Forest 'keeper.

14 **74 mins** A superb diving header to grab an impressive hat-trick.

Everton 5-3 *April 12 1993*

15 **38 mins** A neat through-ball from Sinton gave Ferdinand a chance from close range that he couldn't miss.

16 **46 mins** Southall dropped Impey's cross and Ferdinand stroked the ball into the empty net.

17 **51 mins** Played a neat one-two with Bradley Allen before shooting past the diving Southall.

Leeds United 1-1 *May 1 1993*

18 **15 mins** Wilkins fired in an accurate free-kick and Ferdinand met it with a diving header.

Aston Villa 2-1 *May 9 1993*

19 **67 mins** Latched onto McDonald's through ball and finished well past Mark Bosnich.

Sheffield Wednesday 3-1 *May 11 1993*

20 **67 mins** Clive Wilson sent in a pinpoint cross and Ferdinand met it with a superb header.

Aston Villa 1-4 *August 14 1993*

21 **44 mins** Ferdinand struck home a brilliant volley from outside the area.

West Ham United 4-0 *August 28 1993*

22 **47 mins** Ferdinand beat the static Hammers defence before unleashing a shot past Miklosko.

23 **71 mins** Beat Colin Foster for pace, outwitted Miklosko and fired home.

Norwich City 2-2 *September 18 1993*

24 **83 mins** Fired in a superb shot that deceived Gunn in the Norwich goal.

Newcastle United 2-1 *October 16 1993*

25 **10 mins** Latched onto a Wilkins' pass and his shot hit both posts before going into the net.

Coventry City 5-1 *October 23 1993*

26 **15 mins** Hit a superb half-volley on the turn beating Gould in the Coventry net.

Tottenham Hotspur 1-1 *November 27 1993*

27 **1 min** Headed powerfully past Eric Thorstvedt direct from a corner.

Liverpool 2-3 *December 8 1993*

28 **10 mins** Grobbelaar's clearance was intercepted by Ferdinand who coolly slotted home the loose ball.

After a long wait in the wings Sir Les became a Loftus Road legend.

Southampton	1-0	December 11 1993

29 **2 mins** Dave Beasant could only palm away Monkou's terrible back-pass and Ferdinand pounced to fire in from close range.

Sheffield Wednesday	1-2	January 1 1994

30 **70 mins** Meaker's shot was blocked and Ferdinand nipped in to score from an acute angle.

Manchester United	2-3	February 5 1994

31 **69 mins** A low shot from outside the box which left United 'keeper Schmeichel no chance.

Ipswich Town	3-1	March 26 1994

32 **70 mins** Held off Whelan and beat Baker at the near post with a deflection.

Oldham Athletic	1-4	April 2 1994

33 **35 mins** Beat Oldham 'keeper Hallworth with a snap shot from ten-yards out.

Chelsea	1-1	April 13 1994

34 **66 mins** Fellow striker Devon White flicked the ball on and Ferdinand was on hand to scramble the ball home from close range.

Everton	2-1	April 16 1994

35 **87 mins** A powerful shot past Neville Southall from outside the penalty area.

Swindon Town	1-3	April 30 1994

36 **71 mins** Ray Wilkins took a quick free-kick and Ferdinand pounced to tuck the ball past Hammond.

Sheffield Wednesday	3-2	August 24 1994

37 **22mins** Ferdinand bundled the ball past Kevin Pressman after Wednesday had failed to clear a corner.

Ipswich Town	1-2	August 27 1994

38 **90 mins** Scored from close range after good work from Kevin Gallen.

Everton	2-2	September 17 1994

39 **4 mins** Neatly looped a header over Southall after a good cross from Holloway.

40 **47 mins** Raced onto a Bardsley long ball and coolly slotted past Southall.

Nottingham Forest	2-3	October 2 1994

41 **54 mins** Cooper slipped up at the back and Ferdinand's shot went in off Crossley.

Liverpool	2-1	October 31 1994

42 **85 mins** Clive Wilson launched a long-ball forward which Ferdinand met on the outside of the area and fired past David James.

Leeds United	3-2	November 19 1994

43 **30 mins** Ferdinand shot powerfully home from 15 yards. leaving the 'keeper no chance.

44 **39 mins** Gallen fired in a cross and Ferdinand hooked home a shot into the roof of the net.

Vinnie Jones looks on as another Ferdy strike heads golawards

How Les Ferdinand scored his first 100 Premiership goals!

Number of Goals Scored Per Game vs. opponents

Goal Total: 1 6 1 2 3 2 1 10 3 5 4 4 4 5 3 4 5 3 1 1 5 5 1 1 8 4 8

Teams (left to right): Arsenal, Aston Villa, Blackburn Rovers, Bolton Wanderers, Chelsea, Coventry City, Derby County, Everton, Ipswich Town, Leeds United, Liverpool, Manchester City, Manchester United, Middlesbrough, Newcastle United, Norwich City, Nottingham Forest, Oldham Athletic, Queens Park Rangers, Sheffield United, Sheffield Wednesday, Southampton, Sunderland, Swindon Town, Tottenham Hotspur, West Ham United, Wimbledon

---

West Ham United   2-1   December 4 1994

45 — 2 mins Ferdinand was on hand to head home Simon Barker's cross from six yards.

Manchester United   2-3   December 10 1994

46 — 24 mins A spectacular effort from 30-yard out which gave Walsh no chance.

47 — 64 mins Ferdinand met a deep cross with a header into the roof of the net.

Sheffield Wednesday   2-0   December 17 1994

48 — 84 mins Beat three defenders before shooting past Nigel Pressman.

Newcastle United   3-0   February 4 1995

49 — 4 mins Rounded Hooper in the Newcastle goal and finished from an acute angle.

50 — 7 mins A shot, which went through the legs of Hooper into the net.

Wimbledon   3-1   March 4 1995

51 — 24 mins Ferdinand drove home a well-worked free-kick from 25 yards.

52 — 60 mins Beat two defenders before scoring with a low shot into the corner of the net.

Norwich City   2-0   March 15 1995

53 — 66 mins Trevor Sinclair drilled in a cross from the right and Ferdinand popped up to tap the ball home from close range.

Everton   2-3   March 18 1995

54 — 36 mins A shot from the edge of the box left the Everton 'keeper stranded.

Ipswich Town   1-0   April 11 1995

55 — 68 mins Ferdinand collected a pass from Sinclair and turned to shoot left-footed past Forrest.

Southampton   1-2   April 15 1995

56 — 63 mins Powered past Saints defender Richard Hall to finish clinically past Roberts.

Tottenham Hotspur   2-1   May 6 1995

57 — 64 mins Scored from 12 yards after being put through by Trevor Sinclair.

58 — 75 mins First to react after a goalmouth scramble, he fired in past Ian Walker.

Manchester City   3-2   May 14 1995

59 — 13 mins Gallen fired in a cross from the left and Ferdinand headed home past Burridge.

60 — 89 mins Pounced to score the winner after Kernaghan failed to cut out Brevett's cross.

NEWCASTLE UNITED

Coventry City   3-0   August 19 1995

61 — 83 mins Lee slotted through a fine though-ball and Ferdinand drew the 'keeper and shot into an empty net.

Bolton Wanderers   3-1   August 22 1995

62 — 17 mins Met David Ginola's cross with a superb glancing header.

63 — 84 mins Rode two Bolton tackles before drilling home an angled right-footed shot.

Middlesbrough   1-0   August 30 1995

64 — 70 mins Ginola crossed from the left and Ferdinand scored with an easy header.

Manchester City   3-1   September 16 1995

65 — 38 mins Ferdinand was on hand to fire home a header from close-range.

66 — 59 mins Met the cross into the area with a superb diving header.

Chelsea   2-0   September 24 1995

67 — 41 mins Gillespie's cross was missed by Fox and Ferdinand lashed it into the net.

68 — 57 mins Kharine's clearance hit Ferdinand and fortunately rebounded into the net.

Everton   3-1   October 1 1995

69 — 20 mins Turned Dave Watson and fired a superb shot past Neville Southall.

Queens Park Rangers   3-2   October 14 1995

70 — 57 mins Powered through the middle and beat Jurgen Sommer with a powerful shot from 20 yards.

Wimbledon   6-1   October 21 1995

71 — 35 mins Ginola put in a superb left wing cross and Ferdinand headed in from close range.

72 — 41 mins Gillespie fired in a cross that deflected off Ferdinand's shoulder and into the net.

73 — 63 mins Lee nodded the ball down in the area and Ferdinand scrambled it in from six yards.

Liverpool   2-1   November 4 1995

74 — 3 mins Keith Gillespie put the ball in from the right and Ferdinand slid the ball in from six yards.

Aston Villa   1-1   November 18 1995

75 — 58 mins Shaka Hislop's clearance was met by Ferdinand who shrugged off two tackles before firing in from 12 yards.

Wimbledon   3-3   December 3 1995

76 — 8 mins Slotted home a close-range effort that would have been difficult to miss.

77 — 29 mins Ginola's cross from the left was fumbled by 'keeper Paul Heald and Ferdinand fired in the loose ball.

Everton   1-0   December 16 1995

78 — 17 mins Beardsley put through a neat through ball and Ferdinand shot past Southall from six yards.

Arsenal   2-0   January 2 1996

79 — 46 mins Barton put through a long ball and Ferdinand latched onto it, scoring from eight yards.

Sheffield Wednesday   2-0   February 3 1996

80 — 54 mins Albert flicked on a Gillespie corner and Ferdinand headed in.

Middlesbrough   2-1   February 10 1996

81 — 78 mins Beardsley found Ferdinand in space and the England striker fired past Walsh from 18 yards.

West Ham United   3-0   March 18 1996

82 — 65 mins Howey flicked on a Ginola corner and Ferdinand turned the ball in from close-range.

Liverpool   3-4   April 3 1996

83 — 10 mins Asprilla wriggled past Ruddock and fed Ferdinand who fired past James from six yards.

Aston Villa   1-0   April 14 1996

84 — 64 mins Beardsley put in a ball from the right and Ferdinand rose to head in.

Tottenham Hotspur   1-1   May 5 1996

85 — 71 mins Asprilla drifted wide and crossed for Ferdinand to stab home past Ian Walker.

Sunderland   2-1   September 4 1996

86 — 62 mins Ferdinand outjumped the Sunderland defence to power home a header from a corner.

Tottenham Hotspur   2-1   September 7 1996

87 — 36 mins Scrambled the ball in at the second attempt after Shearer's shot had been saved.

88 — 60 mins Rob Lee crossed first time to Ferdinand whose shot beat Ian Walker in the Spurs' goal.

Blackburn Rovers   2-1   September 14 1996

89 — 60 mins Fired in past Flowers after Shearer had knocked down a Ginola corner.

Aston Villa   4-3   September 30 1996

90 — 5 mins Alan Shearer turner Villa defender Ehiogu and fed the ball through to Ferdinand who beat 'keeper Michael Oakes from close range.

91 — 22 mins Gillespie crossed and Ferdinand finished with a superb diving header.

Manchester United   5-0   October 20 1996

92 — 62 mins A header, which crossed the line via the crossbar.

Tottenham Hotspur   7-1   December 28 1996

93 — 22 mins Beardsley's shot on goal was saved by the 'keeper and Ferdinand pounced to score from six yards.

94 — 58 mins Ferdinand met Beresford's cross with a fierce volley that gave Walker no chance.

Leeds United   3-0   January 1 1997

95 — 87 mins Lee cut the ball back inside from the byeline and Ferdinand stabbed the ball home past Nigel Martyn.

Southampton   2-2   January 18 1997

96 — 13 mins Scored at the second attempt after Taylor saved his original shot.

Everton   4-1   January 29 1997

97 — 74 mins Shearer flicked on an Elliott free-kick and Ferdinand beat Gerrard with a powerful shot.

Middlesbrough   1-0   February 22 1997

98 — 8 mins Picked up a pass from Rob Lee and his shot went in off the post past Roberts.

Derby County   3-1   April 19 1997

99 — 51 mins Elliott crossed for Ferdinand to head sweetly past the diving Russell Hoult.

Nottingham Forest   5-0   May 11 1997

100 — 23 mins Ferdinand fell over as he rounded Fettis but picked himself up to squeeze the ball home.

SINCE JOINING THE 100 CLUB

Season	Club	Goals	Competition
1996-97	Newcastle	1 goal	Premiership
1997-98	Tottenham	5 goals	Premiership
1998-99	Tottenham	5 goals	Premiership

Les was part of the most exciting attacking team in the land at Newcastle.

Ferdinand always provides a big threat in the air.

ISN'T IT ABOUT TIME...
Chelsea's controversial chairman Ken Bates shaved that stupid beard of his off because it's got lots of bits of food in it.

The KNOWLEDGE

10 brain-bustin' facts about...

weird stuff

1 When Celtic won the European Cup in 1967 when they beat Inter Milan 2-1 in Lisbon, many Celtic fans missed out because they flew to Milan by mistake.

2 In October 1954, when Crystal Palace drew 1-1 with Reading at Selhurst Park, one home supporter yawned so wide that he had to be taken to hospital and treated for lockjaw.

3 Until they built the Eric Miller Stand at Craven Cottage, Fulham fans could swap ends during a match by walking along the Riverside terrace.

4 The only referee to score a goal in a first-class game was Ivan Robinson in 1968. He deflected a Plymouth cross past the Barrow 'keeper. It turned out to be the winner!

5 The fastest ever own goal was scored by Torquay's Pat Kruse who headed past his own 'keeper after six seconds against Cambridge United on January 3, 1977.

6 The lowest league attendance for a senior game in Britain was for the game between East Stirling and Leigh on April 15, 1939 when only 32 spectators turned up.

7 Tony Cascarino was once transferred from Crockenhill to Gillingham in exchange for a set of tracksuits!

8 Exeter boss Brian Godfrey was so appalled by his team's 5-1 defeat by Millwall in 1982 that he made them play Millwall's reserves the next day. They lost 1-0.

9 Peterborough striker Paul Culpin looked over his shoulder when playing Cardiff on May 4, 1991 to see 30 Welsh fans chasing him. He then shot from 25 yards and scored!

10 In early 1993, Hartlepool shattered the record for the longest spell without a goal. They went 13 matches, that's 1,221 minutes without scoring.

WILL YOU SPONSOR ME?
David Beckham Manchester United

If you're a top footy star you can make yourself more dosh off the pitch than you can on it. Take David Beckham...

ADIDAS PREDATOR BOOTS

WHEN? October 1996
NICE LITTLE EARNER? £350,000 a year
David was already with Adidas when he scored his halfway-line goal against Wimbledon in 1996 and his market value soared. They gave him a huge pay rise to endorse Predator boots, which he still wears.

BRYLCREEM PART 1

WHEN? July 1997
NICE LITTLE EARNER? £1 million a year
At the launch of this deal Dave claimed to wear wet-look gel for training, extra-hold gel for playing, and modelling gel for going out. Saying this meant Dave not only gets free gel for life but he gets paid a fat wedge too.

JAGUAR

WHEN? August 1998
NICE LITTLE EARNER? £100,000 a year
David gets a free car whenever he wants. He picked up a £56,000 black Jaguar XK8 with a personalised number plate. This he took home to sit next to his £70,000 Range Rover and his Porsche Carrera.

PEPSI

WHEN? October 1998
NICE LITTLE EARNER? £500,000 a year
David followed the example of fiancée Posh Spice and teamed up with Pepsi to advertise the soft drink doing a TV ad with United. Now David has signed an individual contract with the soft drinks giant.

SONDICO SHINGUARD

WHEN? April 1997
NICE LITTLE EARNER? £150,000 a year
To make a shinguard a cast was made of Dave's shin to make sure it would fit and all the data was stored on computer. Dave wore the shinguard when playing for United and England but the contract has now ended.

BRYLCREEM PART 2

WHEN? September 1998
NICE LITTLE EARNER? £1 million a year
His lucrative deal with Brylcreem gave the company a high-profile lift and he was soon promoting a new high performance range of hair gel, wax and styling cream. He even made his first TV commercial as a result.

THE PARKHEAD RAP

Having played for Kenny Dalglish at both Liverpool and Newcastle, it would be easy for new Celtic head coach John Barnes to try to copy the awkward style of his old boss when dealing with the Press. And with Dalglish his partner at Parkhead, Barnsey has already started talking a load of rubbish. **"I have thought about the way the game should be played from an early age,"** he said. **"You have to find a right way to play and stick by it and if you lose you don't necessarily change it."** What are you going on about Barnsey? **"My vision of the game is a simple one in terms of the way you move – and you don't have to be the best people to do it."** Oh, you're making yourself abundantly clear now. You're not bothered about football, you just want the boyz to get some rappin' going on and storm up the charts.

Aye! De ye ken what aam talken' aboot John?

John had enough trouble understanding Scousers and Geordies, how would he fare in Glasgow?

IT'S ALL PANTS!
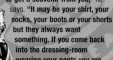

Rangers' stalwart Lorenzo Amoruso couldn't believe his luck when he charged up the tunnel clutching the Premier League trophy. He was doubly chuffed because he actually managed to keep his kit on. Confused? Let Lorenzo explain. **"When you win a trophy in Italy, the fans come charging on to the park to get a souvenir from you,"** he says. **"It may be your shirt, your socks, your boots or your shorts but they always want something. If you come back into the dressing-room wearing your pants you are doing well – I've not always been that lucky."** So there you have it, the naked truth from the Rangers captain himself!

ROD WALLACE RANGERS

How to become a

"I wish I'd had this MATCH guide when I was a nipper," says Michael.

Here's the MATCH guide to making it in football, starting with getting that first trial.

JUST OVER A YEAR AGO ONE OF FOOTBALL'S most-respected establishments – the FA's National Centre Of Excellence at Lilleshall – closed down. Following proposals from the former FA technical director, Howard Wilkinson, 34 football academies opened at clubs across England. These academies were created to offer a high standard of coaching and top class facilities to more young players on a regional scale. Liverpool is a fine example of the money being pumped into youth development – they spent around £10 million on a purpose-built academy earlier this year.

There are now hundreds of scouts out there searching for the next David Beckham or Michael Owen. Remember Beckham, Owen, Lampard and Scholes all came through the youth team once – and just like you they were out there waiting to be spotted when they were at a young age. Even Aussie star Harry Kewell was noticed and came over to play in the Leeds youth team at just 16.

Over the page MATCH gives you the lowdown on how the new academies work, tells you where EVERY academy looks for talent and reveals how you can boost your chances of getting a trial. But first some of the country's hot young stars share their stories, explaining how they made it through their club's youth system.

FOOTBALLER

GET SPOTTED

Players often get spotted when they don't know that they are being watched by a scout, as Villa striker Darius Vassell found.

DARIUS VASSELL SAYS: "I was playing Sunday league for a team called Romulous and we had a friendly match over at Villa's training ground. A guy called Stan James, who was a scout at Villa at the time, spotted me and asked me to sign on for them. I was 12 at the time and I'd played for Birmingham City, but I was out of contract. There are always scouts from clubs looking at you, so you don't have to worry about being spotted."

CHOOSE THE RIGHT CLUB

The academy system only allows you to join local teams, but you could still have a choice to make, as Joe Cole found.

JOE COLE SAYS: "There were a few clubs from the London area interested in me and also a few northern clubs, but West Ham just appealed to me when I went there for a look. I went to Manchester United, which is a great club, but I think the overall set-up at West Ham is the best. You see people like Frank Lampard and Rio Ferdinand coming through the system and you know that what they're doing works."

LISTEN TO ADVICE

Academies offer expert advice from experienced coaches that you just can't get from anywhere else.

FRANK LAMPARD SAYS: "I've had a lot of advice from my cousin Jamie Redknapp and what I would say is just practise, practise, practise. There aren't many people who make it in football and you've got to make sure that you're one of them. You must train hard, but you've also got to be able to take rejection. A friend of mine was released and he's still looking for a club. You've just got to put your head down and keep working hard."

"Beckham, Owen, Lampard & Scholes all came through the youth team!"

DON'T BE AFRAID TO CHANGE

You may already be in the youth system at a club, but if it's not going well you can change clubs if you want to.

PAUL SCHOLES SAYS: "I was at the Oldham School Of Excellence when I was about 12. Then I went for a trial at Manchester United and I wanted to go to United so I signed for them. Brian Kidd showed me and another lad from my school around the ground, the museum and everything. It was great, but we knew what a big club it was anyway. We couldn't wait to sign and I realise now that it was one of the best decisions I have ever made."

COPE WITH REJECTION

Football can be tough, but Leeds wing-back Danny Granville knew exactly what to do when he was turned away by Spurs.

DANNY GRANVILLE SAYS: "I was at Charlton as a boy and I was offered a YTS place there, but the coach who offered it to me went to Tottenham. I went to Tottenham too, but it was late on and they had all the Lilleshall boys there so I didn't get a YTS contract. I didn't think about it too much and soon I went to Cambridge, who were then in the First Division. I got offered a professional contract at Cambridge and went on to play 110 games for them."

ABOVE ALL ENJOY YOURSELF

Football is a fun game and you should make the most of it. Whatever happens you should enjoy playing the game.

MICHAEL OWEN SAYS: "When I was younger I used to enjoy playing and watching football and I think that is really important. I used to go down the local park with my dad and my two brothers to have a kick-about. You shouldn't forget that side of football. Everyone knows that football is a big business these days and it can be tough, but if you really want to be a footballer, I think it's crucial that you enjoy playing the game."

HOW TO BECOME A TOP FOOTBALLER

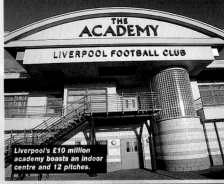

Liverpool's £10 million academy boasts an indoor centre and 12 pitches.

HOW ACADEMIES WORK

WHAT IS AN ACADEMY?

Basically it's a school for football. That doesn't sound too bad, does it? Promising young players are selected by scouts to go for a trial at the club. After four weeks, if you've impressed you will join the club for training with top coaches. In return the club hopes that you will become one of their future stars. In fact, when it comes to youth development in football this country is just catching up. Big foreign clubs like Ajax, Barcelona and Sao Paolo have been doing it this way for years.

WHO HAS THEM?

Every Premier League club is required by the FA to have an academy (although newly-promoted teams like Bradford get two years to build an academy). Football league clubs can also apply for official academy accreditation if their coaching and facilities reach the standards required. The 15 current football league academies are: Barnsley, Blackburn, Bolton, Bristol City, Charlton, Crewe, Crystal Palace, Fulham, Ipswich, Man. City, Millwall, Norwich, Nott'm Forest, Peterborough and QPR.

HOW DO THEY WORK?

Boys are divided into different age groups: 9-11 years, 12-16 years, 17-19 year-olds on scholarships and under-21s. Run by a director, they provide education for the boys as well as technical and dietary training. Scholarship lads get 12 hours teaching per week, working towards GNVQs, BTECs and A-levels. See, it's not all play!

CAN ANYONE JOIN?

First of all you've got to be good enough, but even then there are restrictions. FA rules state that clubs can only look for boys within certain distances of the club, calculated in driving time. For 9-12 years olds it's one hour's drive time rising to one and a half hours for those aged 12-16. That means you can only join an academy in your local area. So if you're living in Carlisle, don't expect to be joining Tottenham. In some ways that's unfair – London clubs face tough competition as there are 21 other clubs competing to sign the same players, whereas Southampton are virtually unchallenged in their area.

HOW DO THEY TAKE ON BOYS?

Each club has its own system for spotting talent, checking out local schools, county representative sides and league football, but a good way to get spotted is through the clubs' football in the community schemes. That's where clubs run skills coaching sessions after school and in holidays and anyone can go along.

Boys are taken into academies from the age of nine for top coaching.

Academy boys are given the training to develop into fine athletes.

There are still school lessons. You just get taught table tennis!

Classroom 1

Even in Australia Leeds spotted 16-year-old Harry Kewell!

YOUR GUIDE TO ENGLISH FOOTBALL ACADEMIES!

Here the academy directors give **MATCH** readers advice on how to get a trial at their clubs.

ARSENAL

Arsenal's academy director is Gunners' legend Liam Brady. Tony Adams, Ray Parlour and Andy Cole have all come through the youth system at Highbury. Boys in the academy train at the club's training ground in St Albans and at the JVC centre at Highbury.

How can I get spotted? Arsenal concentrate on footballers between the ages of eight and ten. They run a big operation in London and watch youth league and district matches all over the city.

What's their advice? Liam Brady says: "Get yourself playing for a good club and play for your school team. There are always scouts around watching and if you are of a certain standard, you will be spotted."

Insider's tip: Arsenal do take more notice of recommendation letters from team managers and school teachers. Make sure you're playing for a Sunday youth team in London.

ASTON VILLA

Villa have an extensive scouting network. They took on eight new lads last season, who will be hoping to follow in the footsteps of Lee Hendrie and Darius Vassell. Academy lads currently train at the club's Bodymoor Heath training ground.

How can I get spotted? Villa concentrate on watching football in schools from under-10s and upwards. The football in the community scheme, which runs in 60 local schools, makes recommendations.

What's their advice? "Start playing for your school and fight for your place in the district side because that's where most boys are picked up from now," says academy director Brian Jones.

Insider's tip: Watch the local and club press for details of the football in the community scheme. Make sure your school send their fixtures to the club's academy.

CHELSEA

Despite the foreign legion, top players like Craig Burley, Neil Shipperley and Jody Morris have come through the youth system. The academy is based at their Harlington training ground.

How can I get spotted? Chelsea have centres in Dagenham and Loughton and plan to run a coaching scheme in Canterbury for young lads not signed on schoolboy forms. Through football in the community they scout local schools and the Slough, Berkshire, Kent and Surrey councils recommend players.

What's their advice? Academy director Gwyn Williams says: "At eight or nine, don't think, 'I've got to join Chelsea', it's not serious until you're 15 or 16. It's vital to have fun and enjoy football, you're too young to worry. If you're being watched, just play your natural game."

Insider's tip: If you're good, you'll be seen. "We knew about Michael Owen as a ten-year-old and we're a London club," says Williams.

COVENTRY CITY

With 50 youth staff, Coventry run a big operation. Current player Marcus Hall was a youth product, as was former Barnsley player John Hendrie. The academy is based at the club's training ground in Coventry.

How can I get spotted? The football in the community scheme goes into local primary and secondary schools, from which talented boys are often recommended. Scouts also watch local youth league matches.

What's their advice? "Make sure you're playing regular football. We're looking at boys between the ages of six to nine and they should be able to control the ball well," says academy director Richard Money.

Insider's tip: Fight for your place in the school team and make sure they are part of the football in the community scheme run in conjunction with the club. For details of the scheme watch the local press.

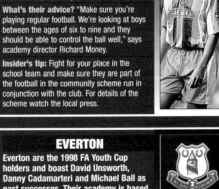

DERBY COUNTY

Dean Sturridge is one of the best products the Derby youth system has produced in the last ten years and the club is hopeful of more success in the future. Derby's academy is based at the club's Raynesway training ground.

How can I get spotted? Derby's scouts watch local school, youth league, district and county matches. They try to cover all the teams, but some can slip through unseen.

What's their advice? Academy director John Peacock says: "Keep practising with coaches at your local club and, if you're good enough, you'll get noticed. There are always scouts around watching games or getting tip-offs about talented players."

Insider's tip: Your team should have been watched by the club at some stage, but if you're in any doubt, get your school manager to send your coming fixtures to Derby County's academy director.

EVERTON

Everton are the 1998 FA Youth Cup holders and boast David Unsworth, Danny Cadamarteri and Michael Ball as past successes. Their academy is based at Bellefield, the first team training ground in Liverpool.

How can I get spotted? Everton's football in the community scheme reaches as far afield as Shropshire, Cumbria and the Greater Manchester area. They look out for talented seven to nine year olds there and watch youth league games for older lads.

What's their advice? "To succeed the boys need to be outstanding footballers. They must have a presence on the pitch and have some sort of outstanding skill," says Everton academy director Ray Hall.

Insider's tip: If you're young, get involved in your local football in the community scheme. If you're older make sure that you're playing for a good, local youth team.

LEEDS UNITED

Leeds now have one of the most successful youth policies – current players Alan Smith and Jon Woodgate were found by their team of 35 scouts. Boys in the Leeds academy train at the Thorpe Arch training ground in Leeds.

How can I get spotted? Leeds have an unbelievable 15 development centres across Yorkshire to make sure they find all the local talent. They also run a mini soccer league with local club Rothwell Town.

What's their advice? Alan Hill, the academy director at Leeds, says: "Obviously, if a local young boy hasn't been invited for a trial by scouts, write to me with your details and fixtures and I will answer all the letters."

Insider's tip: Get involved in the coaching at one of the 15 development centres and in the mini soccer league. And if you are going to write in, make sure you live within the Leeds catchment area. They can't see you otherwise!

LEICESTER CITY

City currently have around 120 boys on their books so they are carefully vetting who they let into the academy at their training ground in Aylestone. Past successes include Emile Heskey and Aston Villa striker Julian Joachim!

How can I get spotted? City hold trials in school holidays for those talented boys spotted playing school, youth league and district football, as well as those on City's community and inner-city schemes.

What's their advice? "There are lots of talented boys around and some excellent boys' Sunday teams. Get yourself playing for a good team and play at the highest level possible and we will spot you," says academy director David Nish.

Insider's tip: Get involved in City's football in the community and inner-city schemes, as well as playing on a Sunday side. The more chances to be seen the better your chance.

LIVERPOOL

First team regulars Michael Owen, Robbie Fowler and Jamie Carragher are youth products – Owen's youth side won the 1996 FA Youth Cup. Their £10 million purpose-built academy is in Kirkby, to the north of the city.

How can I get spotted? Liverpool's 40-50 scouts look at Sunday youth league matches and work closely with schools in Merseyside. They watch lots of youngsters on summer football programmes, as well as running their own skills courses.

What's their advice? Academy director Steve Heighway says: "To become a top player is not easy. It takes outstanding natural talent, but also a tremendous amount of hard work."

Insider's tip: Play for your school side and a local Sunday league side. Also try to get involved in any summer football coaching programme in Liverpool's catchment area, which ranges from Crewe to Cheshire.

MANCHESTER UNITED

United boast the most successful youth system in recent years which has brought in David Beckham, Ryan Giggs and Gary Neville – from the 1992 FA Youth Cup winning side. Young hopefuls are coached at The Cliff training ground.

How can I get spotted? United have an extensive network of scouts who watch recommended games. United may hold open trials for specific age groups in the future.

What's their advice? "Our advice to all aspiring Manchester United players is to become involved in football at the highest level commensurate with their school status and they will be automatically scouted," says academy director Les Kershaw.

Insider's tip: United's reputation is such that they don't miss players. Your best bet is to make sure you're playing for one of the best local youth teams or your county side because they will be watched more often.

MIDDLESBROUGH

Boro's youth system has spawned Colin Cooper and Southampton winger Stuart Ripley, but watch out for their latest products Robbie Stockdale and Craig Harrison. The academy is based at the first team's training ground in Hurworth.

How can I get spotted? The staff watch certain youth league games and school matches. If they are unsure about a player, they watch them a few times and then approach them for a trial.

What's their advice? Dave Parnaby of Boro's academy says: "You've got to enjoy what you're doing and play with enthusiasm. You must have some ability and you must practise, practise, practise."

Insider's tip: Play for your school team and try to get involved with a team in a local youth league. Check your local press for details of local clubs who want new players or ask your teacher because they may be able to help.

NEWCASTLE UNITED

How's this for a youth product portfolio? Steve Watson, Lee Clark, Paul Gascoigne and new boy Aaron Hughes were all on The Magpies' youth books. The academy is based at the Maiden Castle sports centre in Durham, but they'll be moving to a purpose-built centre in Newcastle in the future.

How can I get spotted? Newcastle's scouts watch international, county, boys league and school matches. They also spot boys playing for local football training schemes.

What's their advice? "You've got to be playing regular football to get noticed. Young lads need to show good ball control and natural skill – don't worry about the tactical side," says academy director Alan Irvine.

Insider's tip: Make sure you're playing for a good league team and if you're very talented and think you've been overlooked, send your details in to the club.

SHEFFIELD WEDNESDAY

Ten scouts watch youth games around Sheffield for young talent. Previous successes include Kevin Pressman and Richie Humphreys. Wednesday's academy is based at the first team training ground on Middlewood Road.

How can I get spotted? Scouts cover every junior league team and school in their area. Exceptional boys taking part on the football in the community scheme are recommended to the academy for a trial.

What's their advice? Clive Baker, the academy director, says: "Sometimes the boys who come in for a trial are a bit scared about people watching them and don't perform as well as they might. It's not a one-off trial – we bring you in for a few weeks, so relax!"

Insider's tip: Get yourself playing for a local team or get involved in the football in the community scheme - there will be details in the local Sheffield press.

SOUTHAMPTON

Southampton reach a wide area, ranging from Brighton to Cardiff. This is the club which found Alan Shearer, Matt Le Tissier and Dennis Wise. The academy boys train at King Edward's School in Southampton, as well as at two satellite centres in Bath and Slough.

How can I get spotted? Scouts watch selected matches in the local Tyro Sunday league. The Saints can also pick up players from further away because their catchment area is restricted by the sea on one side!

What's their advice? "Don't give up!" says John Sinty, the academy director. "And you must always play well, as you could be very talented but not play well on the day you're being watched by one of our scouts."

Insider's tip: Join a team in Southampton's Tyro youth league or get your football manager or school teacher to write and recommend you to the club's academy.

SUNDERLAND

Boasting Michael Gray and Michael Bridges as two of their recent successes, Sunderland's academy, based at the club's training ground, is run by ex-Southampton manager Ian Branfoot. They are planning to build their own complex in the future.

How can I get spotted? Sunderland's scouts watch as many local games as possible, that's both school and league games. Sometimes players are recommended from the community coaching programme.

What's their advice? "There's no better advice than to practise, practise, practise. If you're on your own, practise the old way by kicking a ball against a wall to improve your control, passing and shooting."

Insider's tip: Sunderland reckon the level of talent is decreasing – so they advise to get out there and play football instead of playing on your computers. You heard them!

TOTTENHAM HOTSPUR

Sol Campbell, Ian Walker, Nick Barmby and Luke Young have graced the Tottenham youth team in recent years. It's easy to be spotted in the London area and if you get in at Tottenham you will train at the Spurs Lodge first team training facility in Chigwell.

How can I get spotted? Tottenham target primary school boys through their community football scheme. Others are spotted playing youth league and school games.

What's their advice? Academy director Colin Murphy says: "You need to have plenty of enthusiasm, desire and commitment. If you add those qualities to the right technical attributes, you've got an excellent opportunity to fulfil your dream."

Insider's tip: Make sure your school is involved in Tottenham's football in the community scheme and go along for training whenever you get the chance.

WATFORD

Graham Taylor is very proud of the youth system at Watford, which they rely on to bring quality players into the first team. Gifton Noel-Williams is the recent star of the academy, which is based at the club's training ground.

How can I get spotted? Watford concentrate on picking up talent from their immediate area, before looking further afield. They are more interested in looking at nine-year-olds because," Older boys will have been snapped up by other clubs if they are good enough.

What's their advice? Academy director Gary Johnson says: "Enjoy your football and if you are good there are enough scouts out there to spot you. If you are a really top player and you haven't been spotted yet, then ring me!"

Insider's tip: Make sure you are playing for a local team in Watford and get involved in any local 5-a-side leagues during school holidays because Watford's scouts will be there."

WEST HAM UNITED

With 45 staff based in London, West Ham boast a successful youth team. Rio Ferdinand and Frank Lampard are two successes, as well as Joe Cole. The academy boys are coached at the first team's Chadwell Heath training ground in Romford, Essex.

How can I get spotted? West Ham watch most teams which play in their catchment area, from under-nines to non-league football. But there are 21 other London clubs which operate within the catchment area.

What's their advice? "Stay on at school and do your A-levels as well as working hard on your football. Education is the future and if you don't make it, you can fall back on that," says The Hammers' academy director Tony Carr.

Insider's tip: If you're not already attached to one, join a local youth league team. If The Hammers miss you, don't give up. There are 21 other teams who might want your services.

WIMBLEDON

Wimbledon set much store by their youth system. They have relied on many youth products in the past, like Chris Perry, Neil Sullivan and Jason Euell. The Dons' academy is based at the club's training ground in Wimbledon.

How can I get spotted? Wimbledon's scouts are based in different areas of London and they are instructed to watch certain youth league and school matches, upon receiving recommendation about boys.

What's their advice? Terry Burton, Wimbledon's academy director, says: "You must not give up, even in adversity when someone has told you that you are too small or too slow. Some boys will develop into good players at a later date."

Insider's tip: Get an unbiased manager or school teacher to write in to Wimbledon, detailing your football background and fixtures for when you'll be playing.

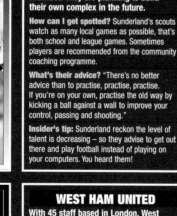

To be spotted by United make sure you're playing for one of the best local youth teams!

THE LEAGUE ACADEMIES...

BARNSLEY
Based near Oakwell, Barnsley coaches find talent in local primary schools. **"You should join an academy early because that's the way forward. Two or three years more experience early on could mean a big difference,"** says Peter Gasken, the academy director.

BLACKBURN ROVERS
Jack Walker has pledged £7 million for their training-ground-based football academy. Rovers have an extensive scouting system, watching youth league and school matches. Bobby Downs says: **"Succeeding is not just down to how skilful you are, it's also about your strength."**

BOLTON WANDERERS
Bolton work closely with local schools and teachers are encouraged to talent spot. **"You'll be given a fair chance at Bolton,"** says Martin Dobson. **"We have gifted coaches who have played at the highest level."** Ask your PE teacher to contact Bolton with your details.

BRISTOL CITY
The club runs centres of excellence from which talented boys are recommended. **"Someone who impresses us has natural technical and physical ability, as well as knowing what they're doing on the ball,"** says David Burnside. See local press for details.

CHARLTON ATHLETIC
Based in New Eltham, scouts watch local school and youth matches. **"If you want to be a footballer you've got to work exceptionally hard and improve your basic skills,"** says Mick Browne. Get your youth team manager or teacher to recommend you to Charlton.

CREWE ALEXANDRA
Crewe's famous academy is based at their training ground and they work closely with schools to identify talent. Steve Holland says: **"There's no secret formula for making it. Years ago players would slip through the system unspotted but that doesn't happen today."**

CRYSTAL PALACE
Palace reply to every letter and their scouts watch school, county and youth matches. John Cartwright says: **"Youngsters need to be capable of treating the ball as their friend and not be afraid to try in tough situations."** Write to Tony Linton at the club with your details.

FULHAM
Based at their training ground, the Fulham Academy get 200 letters a week. They have links with local schools and county team managers. **"If you are good enough you'll be spotted by our scouts. Keep yourself fit and keep practising all the time,"** says Alan Smith.

IPSWICH TOWN
With many community schemes around Norfolk, Ipswich's academy is based at the ground. **"You should practise often and enjoy your football. We are in an area where not a lot of clubs compete with us so we can offer playing opportunities,"** says Brian Cluj.

MANCHESTER CITY
Manchester City have scouts looking locally, as well as in Scotland and Ireland. **"We have the best coaching available,"** says Jim Cassell. **"We have excellent welfare and education – and we are the only club offering a place to our boys in a local school."**

MILLWALL
The older boys in Millwall's academy train at the club's training ground in Bromley, whereas the younger boys train at local schools. The club run satellite centres across London and their scouting network watch all matches in their catchment area.

NORWICH CITY
Norwich use the 'TIPS' scheme: that's Technique, Intelligence, Personality and Speed – if you've got all of these skills, then you're in! Sammy Morgan says: **"We're looking for youngsters to have the desire to play and you must have a great love of the game."**

NOTTINGHAM FOREST
Forest have many scouts in both the East Midlands and across Europe. **"Nobody's working the academy system better than Forest, so if you're good enough, we'll bring you in,"** says Paul Hart. Contact Mel Hackett on 0115 9824301 to join the grass roots training sessions.

PETERBOROUGH UNITED
Posh's academy, based at the Woodlands training ground, has brought through current players Simon Davies and Matthew Etherington. Their academy director Kit Carson has an extensive network of scouts who watch school, youth league and county games for talent.

QUEENS PARK RANGERS
Based at their Ealing training ground, QPR look for talent within the M25. **"If you haven't been spotted already, write in to me with a reference from a school sports teacher or your club manager and I promise we will answer all the letters,"** says Chris Gieler.

THE FINAL WHISTLE

HOW DID YOU SCORE?
Think you're a soccer expert? There are 200 fantastic footy quiz questions in the Annual – fill in your answers on Page 108 and see how well you scored.

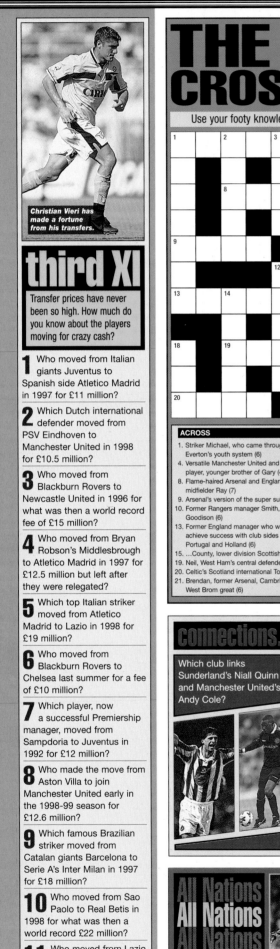

Christian Vieri has made a fortune from his transfers.

third XI

Transfer prices have never been so high. How much do you know about the players moving for crazy cash?

1 Who moved from Italian giants Juventus to Spanish side Atletico Madrid in 1997 for £11 million?

2 Which Dutch international defender moved from PSV Eindhoven to Manchester United in 1998 for £10.5 million?

3 Who moved from Blackburn Rovers to Newcastle United in 1996 for what was then a world record fee of £15 million?

4 Who moved from Bryan Robson's Middlesbrough to Atletico Madrid in 1997 for £12.5 million but left after they were relegated?

5 Which top Italian striker moved from Atletico Madrid to Lazio in 1998 for £19 million?

6 Who moved from Blackburn Rovers to Chelsea last summer for a fee of £10 million?

7 Which player, now a successful Premiership manager, moved from Sampdoria to Juventus in 1992 for £12 million?

8 Who made the move from Aston Villa to join Manchester United early in the 1998-99 season for £12.6 million?

9 Which famous Brazilian striker moved from Catalan giants Barcelona to Serie A's Inter Milan in 1997 for £18 million?

10 Who moved from Sao Paolo to Real Betis in 1998 for what was then a world record £22 million?

11 Who moved from Lazio to Italian giants Inter Milan in the summer of 1999 for an astonishing world record fee of £32 million?

THE MEGA CROSSWORD

Use your footy knowledge to solve the crossword below!

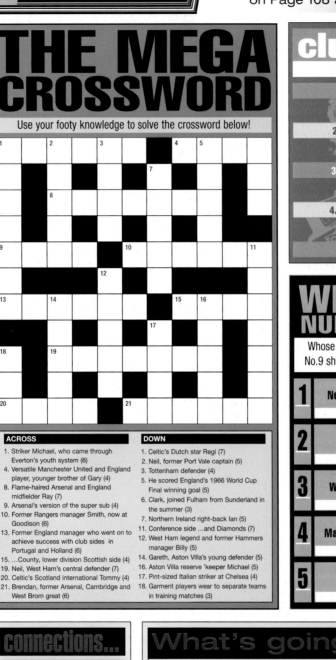

ACROSS
1. Striker Michael, who came through Everton's youth system (6)
4. Versatile Manchester United and England player, younger brother of Gary (4)
5. Flame-haired Arsenal and England midfielder Ray (7)
9. Arsenal's version of the super sub (4)
10. Former Rangers manager Smith, now at Goodison (6)
13. Former England manager who went on to achieve success with club sides in Portugal and Holland (6)
15. ...County, lower division Scottish side (4)
19. Neil, West Ham's central defender (7)
20. Celtic's Scotland international Tommy (4)
21. Brendan, former Arsenal, Cambridge and West Brom great (6)

DOWN
1. Celtic's Dutch star Regi (7)
2. Neil, former Port Vale captain (5)
3. Tottenham defender (4)
5. He scored England's 1966 World Cup Final winning goal (5)
6. Clark, joined Fulham from Sunderland in the summer (3)
7. Northern Ireland right-back Ian (5)
11. Conference side ...and Diamonds (7)
12. West Ham legend and former Hammers manager Billy (5)
14. Gareth, Aston Villa's young defender (5)
16. Aston Villa reserve 'keeper Michael (5)
17. Pint-sized Italian striker at Chelsea (4)
18. Garment players wear to separate teams in training matches (3)

club nicknames

Can you match these nicknames with these clubs?

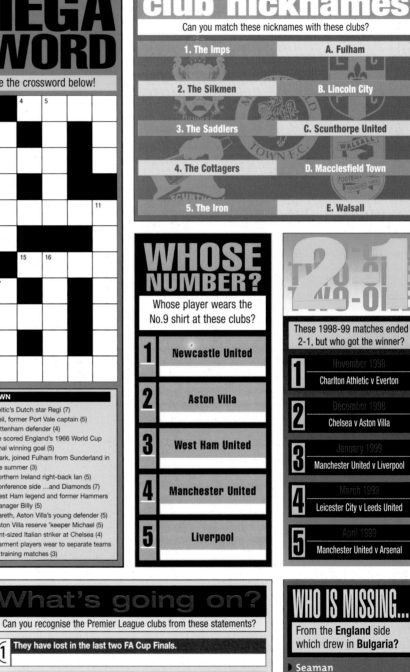

1. The Imps		A. Fulham
2. The Silkmen		B. Lincoln City
3. The Saddlers		C. Scunthorpe United
4. The Cottagers		D. Macclesfield Town
5. The Iron		E. Walsall

WHOSE NUMBER?

Whose player wears the No.9 shirt at these clubs?

1 Newcastle United

2 Aston Villa

3 West Ham United

4 Manchester United

5 Liverpool

2-1 TWO-1

These 1998-99 matches ended 2-1, but who got the winner?

1 November 1998
Charlton Athletic v Everton

2 December 1998
Chelsea v Aston Villa

3 January 1999
Manchester United v Liverpool

4 March 1999
Leicester City v Leeds United

5 April 1999
Manchester United v Arsenal

connections...

Which club links Sunderland's Niall Quinn and Manchester United's Andy Cole?

What's going on?

Can you recognise the Premier League clubs from these statements?

1 They have lost in the last two FA Cup Finals.

2 Their boss played for Liverpool, Wigan, Bradford and Grimsby.

3 They paid a club record fee in 1996 to Juve for an Italian striker.

4 The last time they were out of the top flight was in 1919.

5 Their boss used to manage an England youth and an Italian side.

WHO IS MISSING...

From the **England** side which drew in **Bulgaria?**

▶ Seaman
▶ P Neville
▶ Gray
▶ Southgate
▶ ....
▶ Campbell
▶ Batty
▶ Redknapp
▶ Sheringham
▶ Shearer
▶ ....

All Nations

Where do these Blues stars come from?

1 Marcel Desailly   **2** Pierluigi Casiraghi   **3** Bernard Lambourde   **4** Mikael Forssell   **5** Celestine Babayaro

DUNCAN FERGUSON NEWCASTLE

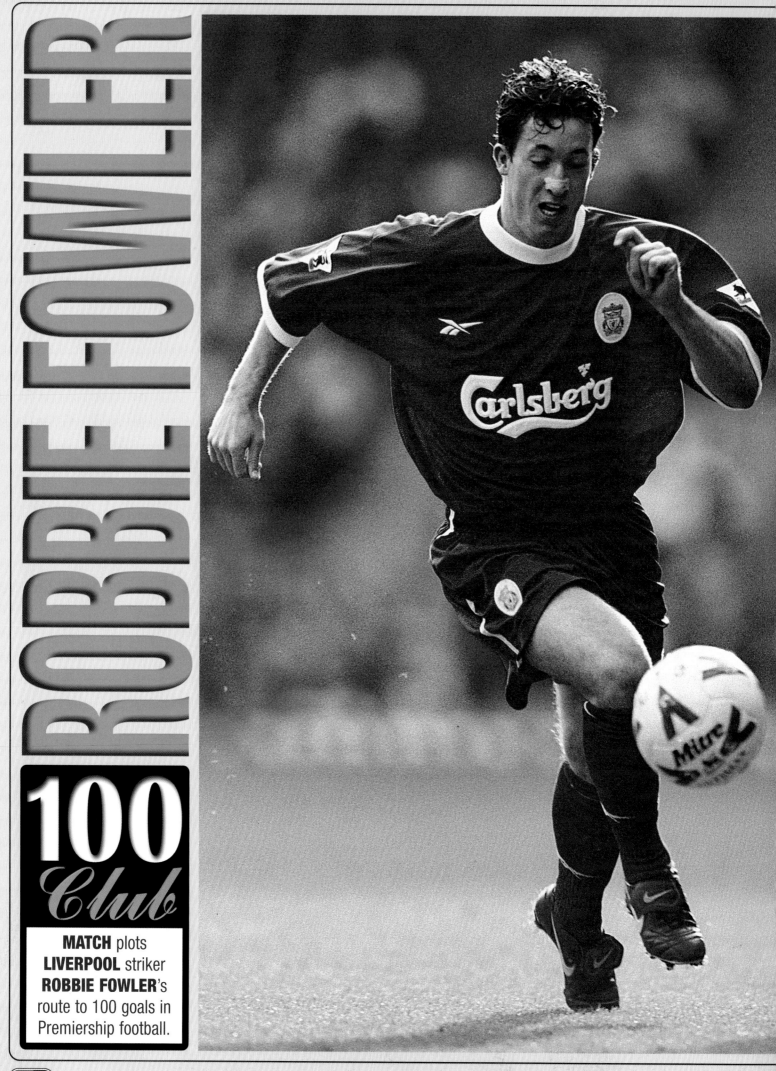

ROBBIE FOWLER

100 Club

MATCH plots **LIVERPOOL** striker **ROBBIE FOWLER**'s route to 100 goals in Premiership football.

LIVERPOOL HAVE A THING ABOUT PROLIFIC strikers. Kevin Keegan, Kenny Dalglish, Ian Rush and John Aldridge came and went, each one becoming an Anfield legend. Then came Robbie Fowler. Just 23, Fowler has already joined the elite list of all time great Liverpool strikers and has become one of just a handful of players to score 100 Premiership goals.

Fowler scored his first goals in the 1993-94 season and spearheaded Liverpool's victorious 1995 League Cup triumph.

Here MATCH looks in detail at Robbie's first 100 Premier League strikes.

Fowler's is physically strong for a small player.

WHERE DID HE COME FROM?

Born in Toxteth, Robbie grew up an Everton fan before switching his allegiance when he joined Liverpool on schoolboy terms. He made his name playing for England Under-18s in the summer of 1993, prompting Graeme Souness to give him his first-team chance.

STRENGTHS?

He has got an amazing left foot, which matches his appetite for goals. Robbie's not afraid to run around to get the ball, he has plenty of strength for a small player, great pace and is the king of the penalty area. He has a natural gift in front of goal.

WEAKNESSES?

Robbie is well known for his fragile temperament, which has got him into trouble with referees and the FA. Last season he had a bust-up with Chelsea's Graeme Le Saux during a match and that, coupled with his line-sniffing goal celebration, earned him a six-match ban at the end of the season.

STRIKE PARTNERSHIPS?

At first, Robbie formed a successful partnership with Ian Rush, who taught the youngster a lot. Then followed a less successful link with Stan Collymore. After returning from injury last season, Robbie surprised many people by the way he successfully paired up with Michael Owen.

BEST GOAL?

As with all prolific strikers there are plenty, but in September 1996 against Manchester United Robbie produced a real gem. Running at full tilt he managed to deftly lob the ball over the awesome figure of Peter Schmeichel without breaking his stride.

FINEST MOMENT?

Possibly Robbie's finest moment was when he made his debut at Fulham in the League Cup and then his Anfield debut in the second leg a few days later. Robbie scored at Craven Cottage and then bagged five in the return match at Anfield. A star was born.

One of the more familiar sights to Liverpool fans.

Robbie leaves Blackburn's Colin Hendry in his wake.

FOWLER'S PREMIERSHIP 100

LIVERPOOL

| Oldham Athletic | 2-1 | October 16 1993 |

1 — **87 mins** Notched Liverpool's first league goal in ten hours of play to equalise and open his Premiership goalscoring account for The Reds.

| Southampton | 4-2 | October 30 1993 |

2 — **14 mins** Fowler glanced the ball home with a header from a Rob Jones cross.

3 — **29 mins** Controlled a long Neil Ruddock ball on his chest and fired home.

4 — **85 mins** A fluke free-kick straight past Saints 'keeper Tim Flowers.

| Aston Villa | 2-1 | November 28 1993 |

5 — **45 mins** Fowler arrived in the area to glance home Dominic Matteo's right-wing cross with a header from close range.

| Sheffield Wednesday | 1-3 | December 4 1993 |

6 — **37 mins** A shot from 15 yards out for Fowler's 12th goal in just 13 games.

| Tottenham Hotspur | 3-3 | December 18 1993 |

7 — **48 mins** Fowler went past Tottenham defender Colin Calderwood and went on to give the goalkeeper no chance.

8 — **54 mins** (pen) Slotted home after Ian Rush was pulled down in the area.

| Oldham Athletic | 3-0 | January 15 1994 |

9 — **54 mins** Fowler shrugged off a Richard Jobson challenge before racing clear to fire past 'keeper Hallworth.

| Everton | 2-1 | March 13 1994 |

10 — **44 mins** Fed in by John Barnes, Fowler drilled a low, left-foot shot into the corner of the net.

| West Ham United | 2-1 | April 23 1994 |

11 — **10 mins** Side-footed in off the bar after Barnes crossed into six-yard box.

| Aston Villa | 1-2 | May 7 1994 |

12 — **17 mins** Exchanged passes with Ian Rush and stroked home his 18th goal of the season.

| Crystal Palace | 6-1 | August 20 1994 |

13 — **44 mins** Driven in from 18 yards following Pitcher's misplaced back-pass.

| Arsenal | 3-0 | August 28 1994 |

14 — **26 mins** Hit home the loose ball after the ball broke to him from Jamie Redknapp's free-kick.

15 — **29 mins** Took McManaman's pass to drill an angled shot in off the far post.

16 — **31 mins** Latched on to Barnes' through-ball to beat Seaman at the second attempt.

| Southampton | 2-0 | August 31 1994 |

17 — **21 mins** Ran on to control Steve McManaman's through-pass and took the ball on to score his fifth goal in three matches.

| Aston Villa | 3-2 | October 8 1994 |

18 — **26 mins** Pounced on to a loose ball to crash an angled drive past Mark Bosnich.

19 — **57 mins** Beat Bosnich at his near post with a powerful low drive.

| Blackburn Rovers | 2-3 | October 15 1994 |

20 — **29 mins** His shot looped up and over Tim Flowers, who was left helpless by a deflection.

| Wimbledon | 3-0 | October 22 1994 |

21 — **35 mins** Beat Hans Segers with a low drive following McManaman's run.

| Ipswich Town | 3-1 | October 29 1994 |

22 — **56 mins** Netted the rebound after a shot from Rush had been blocked following a spectacular run by McManaman.

23 — **60 mins** Popped up to score from an opening made by Bjornebye.

| Nottingham Forest | 1-0 | November 5 1994 |

24 — **14 mins** Flicked a Redknapp shot past Crossley from 12 yards.

| Chelsea | 3-1 | November 9 1994 |

25 — **8 mins** Latched on to Jan Molby's pass to thump the ball past Kevin Hitchcock.

26 — **9 mins** Headed home a right-wing cross from Rob Jones

| Tottenham Hotspur | 1-1 | November 26 1994 |

27 — **39 mins** (pen) Beat Walker after Campbell had fouled McManaman.

| Leicester City | 2-1 | December 26 1994 |

28 — **67 mins** (pen) Mysterious decision by the referee who awarded a foul for the use of an elbow to give Liverpool a spot-kick which Fowler stepped up to confidently blast the ball home.

Robbie combines, pace, trickery and a knack for goals.

Fowler's partnership with Owen has been a big success.

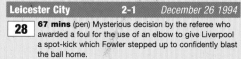

Seaman's protests precede a rare Fowler penalty miss.

Manchester City	2-0	December 28 1994

29 | **82 mins** Unleashed a rocket of a left-foot shot from fully 25-yards out.

Leeds United	2-0	December 31 1994

30 | **75 mins** Fowler kept his head to finish coolly after a terrible back-pass by Leeds defender David Wetherall had put him in on goal.

Norwich City	4-0	January 2 1995

31 | **38 mins** Powered home a shot after Rush's effort had been deflected.

32 | **47 mins** Seized on to David James' long clearance to fire left-footed past Marshall.

Nottingham Forest	1-1	February 4 1995

33 | **90 mins** A well-struck drive past Nottingham Forest goalkeeper Mark Crossley after McManaman had played the ball into his path.

Newcastle United	2-0	March 4 1995

34 | **57 mins** Reacted first after Jamie Redknapp's shot had hit the post.

Southampton	3-1	April 5 1995

35 | **71 mins** (pen) Scored from the spot following Dodd's trip on Walters.

Arsenal	1-0	April 12 1995

36 | **90 mins** Had an easy tap-in from just six yards to score the last-minute winner for The Reds after a brilliant run by Steve McManaman.

Leicester City	2-0	April 17 1995

37 | **74 mins** Took Barnes' pass to thump a 20-yarder past 'keeper Poole.

Tottenham Hotspur	3-1	August 26 1995

38 | **55 mins** Fowler struck with a good volley after another sweet passing move.

Blackburn Rovers	3-0	September 16 1995

39 | **22 mins** A diving header from Rob Jones' right-wing cross into the area.

Bolton Wanderers	5-2	September 23 1995

40 | **12 mins** Ran on to Redknapp's pass to slot the ball under Keith Branagan.

41 | **30 mins** Fowler raced clear to score from David James' long clearance.

42 | **47 mins** Thumped home a loose ball which broke to him inside the box.

43 | **65 mins** Rounded off a great move with a left-foot shot into the net.

Manchester United	2-2	October 1 1995

44 | **32 mins** A tremendous shot from the left edge of United box after being put away by Jason McAteer's pass.

Fowler gives Everton's Dave Watson a torrid time.

How Robbie Fowler scored his first 100 Premiership goals!

Goal Total 7 | 12 | 2 | 5 | 2 | 5 | 1 | 1 | 4 | 4 | 2 | 7 | 2 | 3 | 5 | 5 | 6 | 2 | 6 | 2 | 1 | 1 | 7 | 1 | 4 | 2 | 1

Number of Goals Scored Per Game																										
3																										
3	3																									
	1																									
	1																									
3	2		1		1						1				1							2				
1	2				1			1			2			2	2		1					2				
1	2	1	4	2	1	1	1	2	1	2	2	1	4	1	1	2	1	1	1	1	1	3	1	1	1	1
3	1	1		2	1			2			2	1		1		1	1		1				1	2	1	

Teams (columns): Arsenal, Aston Villa, Blackburn Rovers, Bolton Wanderers, Charlton Athletic, Chelsea, Coventry City, Crystal Palace, Derby County, Everton, Ipswich Town, Leeds United, Leicester City, Manchester City, Manchester United, Middlesbrough, Newcastle United, Norwich City, Nottingham Forest, Oldham Athletic, Queens Park Rangers, Sheffield Wednesday, Southampton, Sunderland, Tottenham Hotspur, West Ham United, Wimbledon

---

45 | 53 mins A superb chip from the left side of the United penalty area after beating Gary Neville to Thomas's excellent through-ball.

Manchester City 6-0 October 28 1995
46 | 47 mins Dummied Brightwell and Symons before firing home right-footed from inside the box.
47 | 60 mins Hooked the ball home with a left-foot shot from McAteer's cross.

Everton 1-2 November 18 1995
48 | 88 mins Beat Neville Southall with a left-foot drive from 16 yards out.

Manchester United 2-0 December 17 1995
49 | 44 mins Curled home a left-foot free-kick from 25 yards.
50 | 87 mins Took McManaman's pass, beat Beckham and scored right-footed from close range.

Arsenal 3-1 December 23 1995
51 | 40 mins Beat Seaman with a rising right-foot shot from 18 yards.
52 | 59 mins Raced on to Stan Collymore's header to hit a left-foot drive from the edge of the box.
53 | 78 mins Headed Collymore's cross past Seaman from six yards.

Nottingham Forest 4-2 January 1 1996
54 | 31 mins Nodded in Stan Collymore's cross from six yards.
55 | 40 mins Headed in another Collymore ball eight yards from goal.

Leeds United 5-0 January 20 1996
56 | 60 mins (pen) Thumped a left-foot shot past 'keeper Mark Beeney after Gary Kelly had fouled Rob Jones.
57 | 67 mins Tapped in a right-foot shot from two yards from a Collymore cross.

Aston Villa 2-0 January 31 1996
58 | 65 mins Steve McManaman and Jason McAteer combined to set Fowler free and he raced unchallenged to the edge of the Villa area before scoring with a left-foot drive.

Queens Park Rangers 2-1 February 11 1996
59 | 30 mins Stan Collymore hit a long ball down the centre, beating Maddix, which fell right into Fowler's path. Fowler clipped the ball past the onrushing 'keeper Jurgen Sommer and made certain by following the ball into the net.

Aston Villa 3-0 March 3 1996
60 | 5 mins Fowler turned Staunton and beat Bosnich with a superb 30-yarder.
61 | 8 mins Fowler raced on to Jones' pass and fired home low from 12 yards.

Chelsea 2-0 March 16 1996
62 | 62 mins A glancing header from a right-wing centre from McAteer.

Newcastle United 4-3 April 3 1996
63 | 2 mins Headed home Collymore's left-wing cross from close range.
64 | 57 mins Fired a first time shot past Pavel Srnicek from a McManaman centre.

Everton 1-1 April 16 1996
65 | 87 mins Close-range volley from Collymore's left-wing cross.

Middlesbrough 3-3 August 17 1996
66 | 65 mins Fired in a right-footer from a deep Bjornebye cross to the far post.

Chelsea 5-1 September 21 1996
67 | 15 mins Headed into the roof of the net from Stig Bjornebye's swerving cross from the left.

Derby County 2-1 October 27 1996
68 | 47 mins Followed up a low drive from Berger that was too hot for Hoult to hold and slid the ball home left-footed under the 'keeper.
69 | 51 mins Outjumped defender Rowett to head Scales' cross into the corner of the net to the 'keeper's left.

Everton 1-1 November 20 1996
70 | 30 mins Powerfully headed home Jamie Redknapp's cross into the roof of the net at The Kop End past a stranded Neville Southall.

Middlesbrough 5-1 December 14 1996
71 | 1 min Rifled the ball low into the net after Collymore's shot had been diverted into his path by midfielder Emerson.
72 | 28 mins Scored his 100th and possibly his easiest goal for Liverpool when he tapped into an empty net after Collymore's shot had come back off the post.
73 | 77 mins Completed his hat-trick with a low left-footed drive following an excellent through-ball from McManaman.
74 | 85 mins Drifted away from two defenders and clipped a shot beyond Walsh into the corner of the net.

Nottingham Forest 4-2 December 17 1996
75 | 27 mins Headed Collymore's cross from the byeline firmly into the back of the net.

Newcastle United 4-3 December 23 1996
76 | 45 mins Peeled off intelligently when McManaman cut the ball back from the left-hand side to turn in a left-foot shot.

Aston Villa 3-0 January 18 1997
77 | 63 mins Lifted the ball over Bosnich after the Villa goalkeeper had saved Redknapp's low shot.

Leeds United 4-0 February 19 1997
78 | 21 mins Collymore, set free down the left wing by Bjornebye, outpaced the defence and whipped in a low cross for Fowler to slot home.

Newcastle United 4-3 March 10 1997
79 | 42 mins Redknapp won the ball in midfield and played a glorious through-ball to Fowler, who outpaced the defence and slotted home.
80 | 90 mins Dominic Matteo played Bjornebye in to space down Liverpool's left wing and his pinpoint cross was headed home by Fowler.

Nottingham Forest 1-1 March 15 1997
81 | 4 mins McAteer took the ball past Woan up the right wing, moved into the box and made a good pass to Fowler, who rolled it past Crossley.

Coventry City 1-2 April 6 1997
82 | 52 mins Right-footed volley into the roof of the net after a through-ball from Barnes.

Sunderland 2-1 April 13 1997
83 | 33 mins Bjornebye's cross was knocked down by Wright, and Fowler made no mistake from close range.

Aston Villa 3-0 September 22 1997
84 | 56 mins (pen) Owen turned and stumbled under challenge from Southgate. Fowler drove penalty left-footed to the 'keeper's left with Bosnich guessing the wrong way.

West Ham United 1-2 September 27 1997
85 | 52 mins Fowler acrobatically volleyed 20-yarder past Miklosko after Unsworth only half-headed clear.

Chelsea 4-2 October 5 1997
86 | 64 mins Hat-trick hero Berger turned provider to feed Fowler and the England star struck a powerful deflected left-foot shot into the far corner.

Derby County 4-0 October 25 1997
87 | 27 mins Michael Owen slipped past several defenders before feeding Fowler who shot left-footed in off the post from 12 yards.
88 | 84 mins Fowler had time to control a McManaman cutback before firing home left-footed from nine yards.

Bolton Wanderers 1-1 November 1 1997
89 | 1 min Low cross from McManaman found the striker who made himself space to place a shot to the right of the 'keeper.

Manchester United 1-3 December 6 1997
90 | 60 mins (pen) Fired home low to Peter Schmeichel's left as the 'keeper dived the wrong way after Owen was adjudged to have been brought down by a combination of Pallister and Berg.

Leeds United 3-1 December 26 1997
91 | 79 mins Goalkeeper James set McManaman free and he raced 40 yards into the Leeds half before squaring to Fowler, who fired home left-footed across Nigel Martyn from the edge of the area.
92 | 83 mins Owen took on three defenders and got to the bye-line before crossing to Fowler, who scored with a simple tap-in from two yards.

Charlton Athletic 3-3 September 19 1998
93 | 33 mins (pen) Struck his penalty kick left-footed to Ilic's left with the 'keeper going the wrong way.
94 | 82 mins Poked home his second goal of the game from two yards after Sasa Ilic had dropped Owen's cross at the striker's feet.

Leeds United 1-3 November 14 1998
95 | 68 mins (pen) Broke the deadlock from the penalty spot, placing the ball to Nigel Martyn's left with the 'keeper going the opposite way after the Leeds No.1 had upended Karlheinz Riedle.

Aston Villa 4-2 November 21 1998
96 | 7 mins Redknapp's right-wing cross was curled into the danger area and the striker got between two defenders to steer home a wonderful low header from eight yards.
97 | 58 mins Collected the ball 25 yards from goal and ran towards the edge of the area before beating Oakes at his near post with a perfectly-placed right-footed drive.
98 | 66 mins Fowler found himself unmarked in the six-yard box following a cross from Owen and had time to control the ball before scooping it into the unguarded net to grab a hat-trick.

Southampton 7-1 January 16 1999
99 | 21 mins Fowler tapped the ball in from five yards after Saints 'keeper Paul Jones had dropped Bjornebye's right-wing corner.
100 | 36 mins Fowler blasted home from eight yards following a neat one-two with strike partner Owen.

SINCE JOINING THE 100 CLUB

1998-99 Liverpool | **6 goals** Premiership

Robbie rarely misses from that sort of range.

KEY | HOME GAME | AWAY GAME

FOOTY MAD!

There is always room for a laugh at someone else's expense – as this selection of last season's **MATCH** pics shows.

THEY SAID WHAT!

MATCH finds managers who say more than than 'over the moon'…

"*Andy Cole should be scoring from those distances, but I'm not going to single him out.*" Manchester United's Alex Ferguson does a less than impressive job of deflecting criticism away from striker Andy Cole.

"*I think in international football you have to be able to handle the ball.*" Ex-England manager Glenn Hoddle with another of his rather baffling opinions on the game.

"*We reckon Carlton covers every blade of grass during the course of a game – but then you have to if your first touch is that crap.*" Manager Dave Jones sings the praises of his then Southampton midfielder Carlton Palmer.

"*We're going to start the game at nil-nil and go out and try to get some goals.*" Boro manager Bryan Robson on his revolutionary tactical approach.

"*Maybe someone is talking, maybe somebody is throwing a fish for the sharks.*" Ruud Gullit reads from Eric Cantona's book of 'Bizarre Fish-Related Sayings.'

"*We have faced African teams before, we have faced English teams before – so we are ready to face Scotland because we know what their play will be like.*" Brazil national manager Mario Zagallo explains how his team has prepared to take on the might of Scotland.

"*The only way that Dennis Bergkamp will fly is if he turns into a pigeon.*" Arsenal manager Arsene Wenger remains hopeful about getting his flight-shy super-striker to overcome his little problem.

"*If the ball had gone in, it would have been a goal.*" Joe Royle, manager of Man. City, demonstrates his superb knowledge of the rules of football.

"*I'm a firm believer that if the other side scores first you have to score twice to win.*" England technical director Howard Wilkinson outdoes Royle with a moment of inspiration.

It worried Michael that his feet were so small compared to everyone else.

The search for his replacement continues as David Seaman celebrates his 50th birthday!

"I warned you son, get lippy with me and I'll smack you again."

Everyone mucked in together to try and find the missing contact lens.

Nobody had told Robbie but the bloke who puts the names on the back of the shirts had got it all wrong.

Andre was already regretting last night's chicken Madras.

"The Dog and Duck? Yeah left at the mini roundabout, through the traffic lights..."

"Ha! Now I've got you my lovely, come here and give us a snog."

Becks had a contract with a rival drinks company that meant he couldn't drink the half time lemonade"

Danny Wilson was concerned that his new striker lacked a little mobility.

"Whaddya mean it was never offside. How dare you question my authority. Now take a hike!"

"Teem you 'ave taken my parking space you stupeed man."

The floodlights had failed but club officials just couldn't think who to ring for help.

Philips Lighting The Worlds No' 1 floodlighting Supplier

The copious supply of bandages failed to stem the flow of blood.

Neil Redfearn knew which way Charlton were heading last season.

George just couldn't get rid of that bit of spinach.

"Blimey Sparky, you wanna wear some of the those special insoles, your feet don't half whiff."

Walter Smith was worried that some of his players were starting the game in a negative frame of mind.

Post-match gob clearing up is one of footy's less glamorous jobs.

Robbie remembered the time he played up front with Sean Dundee.

A gust of wind blew big Dave Watson clean off his feet and gave Coley a terrible fright.

It was a strange time for Francesco Baiano to be plucking his eyebrows, but it had to be done.

Just as an experiment Fergie decided he'd partner Yorkie up front.

RYAN GIGGS MAN. UNITED

If I wasn't a foo

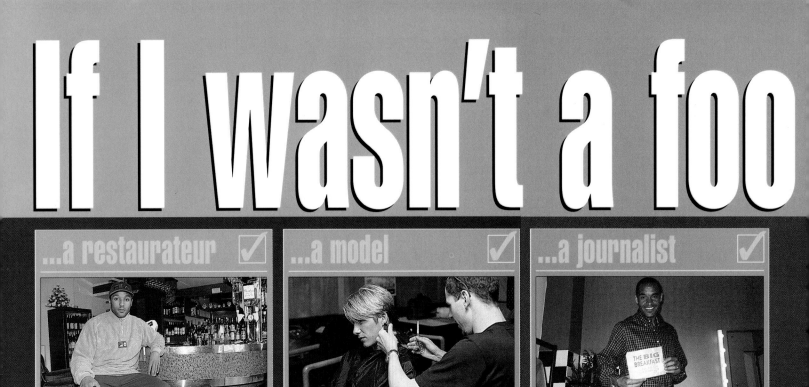

MATCH takes a look at the footballers who could earn a living in a different profession if they decided to quit football tomorrow.

FOOTBALL IS BIG BUSINESS. THERE'S LOADS OF MONEY TO BE MADE BY THE TOP PLAYERS IN wages alone, let alone the sponsorship deals and appearance money. However, for some it's just not enough and they start up an alternative job – it's an investment in their future, giving them a career to go into after they retire from football. For others, it gives them something to do on their many afternoons off! Ex-Wimbledon star Vinnie Jones has gone off to Hollywood in search of an acting career after his big break in 'Lock, Stock And Two Smoking Barrels'. Then there are players like Julian Dicks, who retired from playing for West Ham at the end of the season and is now looking ahead to a career as a professional golfer. Some players are such naturally gifted sportsmen, that they could quite easily have made it right to the very top in another sport. Here MATCH looks at what some top players would be if they weren't a footballer...

...a cricketer ✓

PHIL NEVILLE

If things had been different, the Man. United ace could easily be playing cricket for England now.

PHIL SAYS: "I was an opening batsman and I played cricket to a decent level. I played for England at Under-14 and Under-15 level, but my father quite rightly insisted that I kept up with my studies instead – he told me I had to stop playing cricket and do some more homework... and that's what I did. I'd still love to play now, even if it was just for my club side in Bury, but football commitments mean that I can't."

ANY OTHERS?

Veteran Coventry keeper **Steve Ogrizovic** represented Shropshire and **Andy Goram** played cricket for Scotland until he joined Rangers and the club made him stop.

"If those Bayern fans come after me wanting their European Cup back, I'll send them packing."

tballer, I'd be...

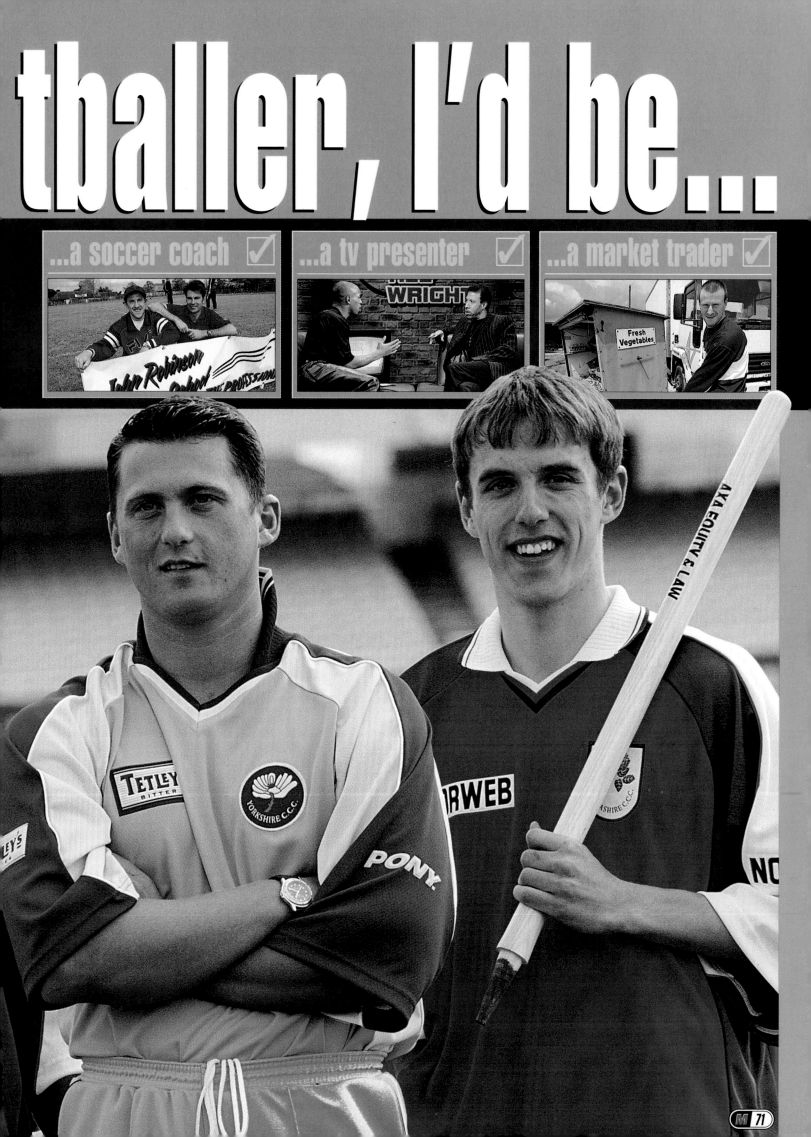

...a restaurateur ✓

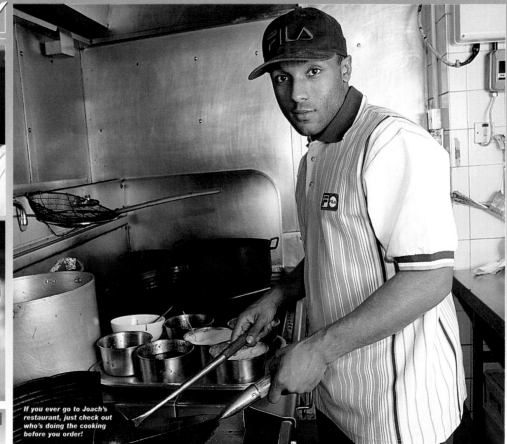

JULIAN JOACHIM

The Aston Villa striker set up his own business as a sideline and he gets free food out of it!

JULIAN SAYS: "I've always enjoyed eating Chinese food and my business partner David asked me if I'd be interested in going into business 50-50 with him a few years ago. We thought we'd give it a go and it's going well. I pop down quite often to check everything is all right. I'm still young at 24, but it might be something to consider later on – hopefully I'll have a chain of Chinese restaurants!"

ANY OTHERS?

Chelsea's Italian midfielder **Roberto Di Matteo** owns his own restaurant in a fashionable area of London. And former Leeds striker **Lee Chapman** has his own restaurant and bar.

If you ever go to Joach's restaurant, just check out who's doing the cooking before you order!

Becks tries not to raise a smile while Brooklyn breaks wind in the background.

...a journalist ✓

MARK BRIGHT

Brighty began his journalism career on MATCH before moving on to television.

MARK SAYS: "You might think that I just turn up and do my spot on 'The Big Breakfast', but I have to research my material. The secret to doing well on TV is research. I sometimes to get my mates on MATCH to help me with that. On set anything can happen and one thing I've learnt is to be ready for the unexpected. I write my own script for the voice-overs and I get input into what goes in my part of the show."

ANY OTHERS?

Gareth Southgate has always said if he hadn't been a footy star he'd like to have been a journalist and **Graeme Le Saux** has been involved in researching and presenting youth television.

...a model ✓

DAVID BECKHAM

Becks' modelling career took off with a Brylcreem contract and he hasn't looked back.

DAVID SAYS: "I work with Brylcreem to help promote their styling range. I've done some pictures, style and fashion led, for their packaging. I like to bring along my own clothes for the shoots because I am comfortable in them. When you're in front of the camera for hours on end you have to look the part. It doesn't bother me that I am seen as a fashion icon. I just wear what I think looks good with what."

ANY OTHERS?

David James was once the face of flash fashion giants Armani, while **Jamie Redknapp** and **Dean Holdsworth** had to settle for Top Man! **David Ginola** also promoted L'Oreal's shampoo.

Brighty's good work on MATCH caught the eye of the people at 'The Big Breakfast'.

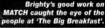

"Right lads, this is how you do the Aylesbury ducks waddle celebration," explains Charlton's John Robinson.

...a soccer coach

JOHN ROBINSON

The Charlton star set up his very own coaching school to pass his skills on to some kids.

JOHN SAYS: "I always thought I'd like to do some coaching, but because I wanted to set up my own coaching school I had to make sure I had the right people to work with and the right sponsors behind me. In the future I'm looking to do more coaching in the Eastbourne and Hailsham area, where I live and Brighton and Lancing in Sussex. It would certainly make a nice career for me to go into after football."

ANY OTHERS?

Bradford's **Peter Beagrie** and Aston Villa's **Steve Stone** both do soccer coaching when they're not playing or training, but there are lots of other footballers who run their own coaching schools.

...a market trader

STEVE CLARIDGE

The striker opened his own fruit and veg stall to bring in more money – and he loved it!

STEVE SAYS: "Early in my career when I was playing part-time, I had a lot of free-time. My dad grew vegetables, so starting a roadside Fruit & Veg stall seemed a perfect answer. I kept it going when I was at Aldershot – it was a good job too because they went bankrupt! I used to take some there and sell it after the games. Obviously if we lost I had to sell a bit more to make up for not getting my bonus."

ANY OTHERS?

Are you being serious? Footballers giving up their afternoon shopping to offload bags of sprouts on the M62? Other than **Giggsy** doing it for a Reebok ad, we don't think it'll happen...

"Take the skin off these love and you'll certainly see my eyes water!" Steve goes on the big sell.

...a tv presenter

IAN WRIGHT

Wrighty has always been an extrovert and his TV shows have been a big success so far.

IAN SAYS: "I certainly like the idea of working in TV and I really see myself as the next Arsenio Hall. He's laid back and really funny. What I want to do most is to develop my TV career as much as possible over the next few years and I couldn't have got off a better start than fronting my own chat show. I realise that I still have a lot to learn about the business and I'm keen to make this work for me."

ANY OTHERS?

There have been plenty of footballers who have gone on to present TV shows. **Gary Lineker** fronts BBC 1's 'Football Focus' and **Barry Venison** co-presents the ITV footy show 'On The Ball'.

Wrighty uses his famous name to attract top stars like Naz onto his show.

ISN'T IT ABOUT TIME...
Some big-wig at FIFA introduced a new law saying football should be played all year round because it don't half get boring in the summer.

---

do you remember your FIRST...

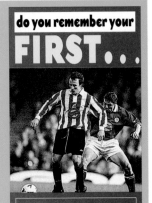

Sunderland winger Nicky Summerbee takes a stroll down memory lane with MATCH!

...KISS

"Last week! No, that's rubbish. I can't say who it was because she wasn't the best looking girl, but it was at the local youth club and I was 13-year-old."

...JOB

"I didn't become a footballer straight away after leaving school, I had a job as a window cleaner. I got £60 a week."

...CAR

"That was a beige Fiesta with a 950-litre engine. I saved up for it myself and I paid something like £1500 for it which I thought was quite reasonable."

...GAME AS A FAN

"It was definitely at Old Trafford in the late 1970s. I can remember Jimmy Greenhoff celebrating after scoring a goal."

...FOOTBALL KIT

"That would have been an old United shirt. It was made by Admiral and if you look at it today you think it must have been well uncomfortable."

...PRO GAME

"It was playing for Swindon against Wolves at the County Ground. I can't remember the score but I was very nervous and I had all my family in the stand watching me."

...FOOTBALL BOOTS

"When I was playing for my school team I wore just about anything on my feet so long as I could kick the ball. Actually, the first pair I had as a professional were made by Asics."

...HONOUR

"That was in the First Division Play-Off Final for Swindon against Leicester and we won 4-3. It was a dramatic game. The next time I played at Wembley was for Sunderland and that was a cracking match but this time I was on the losing side."

Looking around the streets and motorways of the flash country that we call England, you'll find dozens of makes of motors. From the Ford to the Ferrari, Vauxhall to Volvo, there is something out there for everyone. So, why is it that when footballers set out to buy a new set of wheels, they never get further than the local BMW dealer? MATCH takes a look at some of football's top stars and their obsession with the German engineering experience known as the 'Beamer'.

LORD WON'T YOU BUY ME A... BMW!

DANIELE DICHIO
The Sunderland striker may be one of the most chilled-out footballers, but just take a gander at Danny's wheels. Only a few years ago at QPR, he was driving a battered old Beamer.

KEITH GILLESPIE
The controversial Irishman's career has taken more turns than the Monaco Grand Prix. One thing in his life has always stayed the same though – his love of Beamers!

NOEL WHELAN
The Coventry frontman has a reputation as a bit of a lad, so he's bound to have a flash motor. Oh! Noel went down the same road as his mates, picking up this little 325 convertible.

LEE HENDRIE
Lee's a bit spesh. He's a Villa regular and has won a full England cap aged just 21. He must be our saviour. Yikes! he's just become the sixteenth 'Beamer' owner at Villa Park.

MATTHEW OAKLEY
Matt was supposed to go out and get something sensible when he went out to buy a new car. What a mouthful he got from his Mum when he brought back this little monster.

DOUGIE FREEDMAN
Dougie has had to make his way into the top-flight the hard way. He's bound to have an economical little runaround. Wrong again, it's a 300 series for the wee Scot.

MARK DRAPER
'Drapes' joined Aston Villa from Leicester after just one season in the top flight. To celebrate the talented midfielder went and treated him self to... yep, you've guessed it, a BMW.

So what are we to make of all this?
Is there anyone out there in the land of football with a bit of imagination? We need to know the real truth behind the mystery. Do you get 50% off at your local BMW dealer when you make it into the big-time? Please, someone show us a Mondeo or a Vectra. We'll even forgive a Porsche or a Ferrari!

KINNEAR v OLSEN
THE HEAVYWEIGHT BOUT

Who says the spirit has gone out of football? It's nice when a new gaffer comes in and the departing boss still wants to help out. The transition at Wimbledon following the arrival of Egil Olsen looked to be going smoothly when Joe Kinnear said he would be glad to stay on for a while. In fact, it showed Big Joe up to be a sound geezer. **"I've decided the club will have the best chance of surviving in the Premiership next season if I stay on to oversee Olsen's introduction,"** he said. **"It would have been easy to walk away but the owners were desperate for me to hang about."** What a nice gesture, you might think? But as usual madness set in at Selhurst Park and Egil went berserk when he heard of this kind offer. **"Kinnear is not going to be around the team at all. I think he will understand that."** Be that way then!

DETECTIVE CARRAGHER INVESTIGATES!

Shock horror! England under-21 captain Jamie Carragher has revealed the real reason why former coach Peter Taylor got the bullet in early 1999. It's all a bit hush, hush, but here is the startling exclusive revelation from undercover agent Carragher. Speaking from his hide-out and wearing a pair of dark glasses, Carragher whispered to Route 1: **"He only left because he was part of the Glenn Hoddle set-up. We basically qualified for the tournament through Peter Taylor being the coach and he had a great record. With his record he should have been kept on but it's always the way when you're linked to a previous management."** Genius, Jamie! Absolutely brilliant. Not a lot gets past you, does it mate?

CRAIG BURLEY CELTIC

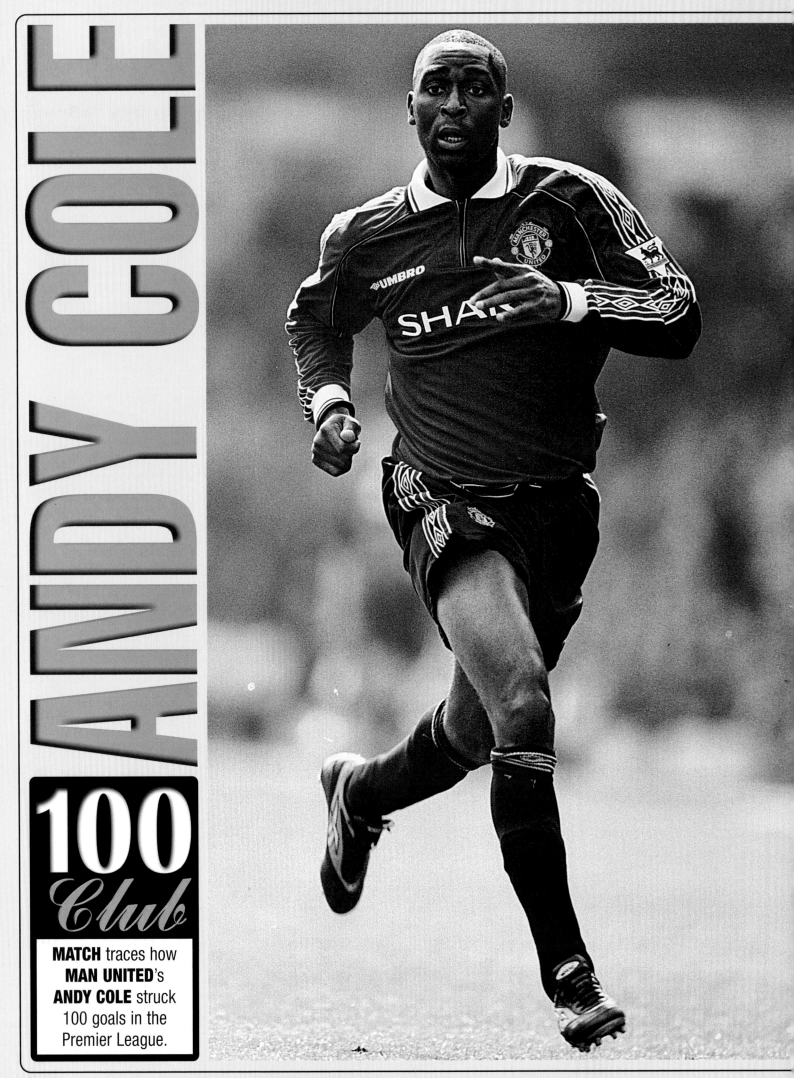

ANDY COLE

100 Club

MATCH traces how **MAN UNITED**'s **ANDY COLE** struck 100 goals in the Premier League.

A 26 MINUTE HAT-TRICK AGAINST LIVERPOOL just three months into his first Premier League season set the tone for a remarkable upturn in fortune for a man who, before Kevin Keegan signed him for Newcastle was heading for lower division obscurity. An instant hit on Tyneside, Cole rapidly became recognised as one of the top marksmen around.

A move to Man.United in January '95 put Cole under the spotlight and though he started slowly, he was soon scoring regularly and soon became one of just five players to score 100 Premier League goals.

Give Coley the slightest sniff of goal and he'll shoot.

WHERE DID HE COME FROM?

Andy Cole started out at Arsenal but could not force his way into the reckoning after Ian Wright established himself as the top man at Highbury. A successful loan spell at Bristol City brought about a permanent move to The Robins, before Kevin Keegan swooped to sign him for Newcastle. Then came the much talked about £7 million deal to Old Trafford.

STRENGTHS?

A quick and elusive striker, with lightening pace to match, he's at his best when he has to shoot on impulse. An excellent poacher in and around the penalty box, Cole gets himself into goalscoring positions with alarming regularity.

WEAKNESSES?

It's becoming a bit of a cliché but Cole really does need more than one chance to score a goal. His first touch, control and distribution have also been known to let him down, particularly on the big stage.

STRIKE PARTNERSHIPS?

The relationship he struck up with Dwight Yorke was crucial to Man. United's enormous success last season as the pair bagged a total of 35 league goals between them. Andy also established a terrific rapport with Peter Beardsley, from whom he learned a lot, in the exciting Newcastle team under Kevin Keegan.

BEST GOAL?

With Newcastle flying at the top of the table in September 1994, the visit of Chelsea was a real test for Keegan's team but a screaming shot by Cole on his weaker left side from the edge of the area was a real corker and set Newcastle on course for a crucial win.

FINEST MOMENT?

Having received so much criticism for his last-gasp miss at West Ham that would have clinched the title for United at the end of 1994-95, it was fitting that he should score the goal against Tottenham that retrieved the championship last season.

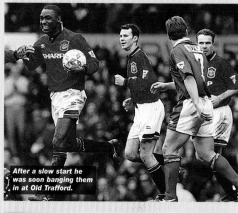

Andy had an explosive effect on Tyneside.

After a slow start he was soon banging them in at Old Trafford.

BEFORE THE PREMIERSHIP

1991-92	Fulham	**3 goals**	Division 3
1991-92	Bristol City (loan)	**8 goals**	Division 2
1992-93	Bristol City	**12 goals**	*Division 1
1992-93	Newcastle	**12 goals**	*Division 1

*Denotes Division One after the formation of the Premier League.

COLE'S PREMIERSHIP 100

NEWCASTLE UNITED

Manchester United	1-1	*August 21 1993*

1 70 mins Collected a pass from Papavisiliou's in the Man. United box and flicked the ball past goalkeeper Schmeichel as he came off his line.

Blackburn Rovers	1-1	*August 29 1993*

2 60 mins Cole latched on to a through-ball from Beresford to score left-footed from close range.

Ipswich Town	1-1	*August 31 1993*

3 47 mins Picked up a searching through-ball from Lee Clark and cracked his shot past Craig Forrest.

Sheffield Wednesday	4-2	*September 13 1993*

4 21 mins First to react after Allen's shot came back off 'keeper Woods.

5 76 mins Mathie did the hard work down the right for Lee to knock the ball to Cole who scored from ten yards.

West Ham United	2-0	*September 25 1993*

6 51 mins Beardsley superbly dummied a Malcolm Allen cross leaving Cole to knock it in.

7 84 mins Cole ran on to a Lee Clark through ball, saw off Mike Marsh and hammered the ball in.

Aston Villa	2-0	*October 2 1993*

8 80 mins Scored at the second attempt following a pass from Beardsley.

Southampton	1-2	*October 24 1993*

9 72 mins Downward far-post header from Mathie's left-wing cross.

Wimbledon	4-0	*October 30 1993*

10 60 mins Was the first to react after Lee Clark's shot rebounded off Segers.

Oldham Athletic	3-1	*November 8 1993*

11 53 mins Chipped the ball home after running on to a Peter Beardsley flick.

12 81 mins Curled shot from 18 yards after his persistence created an opening from Sellars' initial pass.

Liverpool	3-0	*November 21 1993*

13 4 mins Sellars sent Lee down the left for Cole to move in front of Grobbelaar and score.

14 15 mins Beardsley sent Sellars down the left for Cole to go in where it hurts and poke the ball in.

15 30 mins Sellars took a Lee pass and picked out Cole to complete a hat-trick.

Sheffield United	4-0	*November 24 1993*

16 70 mins Mike Hooper booted the ball half the length of the field to Beardsley to provide Cole with the chance to score in a flash.

Manchester United	1-1	*December 11 1993*

17 71 mins Beardsley sent Lee down the right and his cross was nodded in by Cole from six yards.

Everton	2-0	*December 18 1993*

18 14 mins 'Keeper Hooper's giant kick downfield was touched into Cole's path by Beardsley and Cole finished explosively.

Leeds United	1-1	*December 22 1993*

19 85 mins Had his back to goal when he received the ball from Bracewell, but he made space to lash the ball home from 20-yards.

Manchester City	2-0	*January 1 1994*

20 28 mins Scott Sellars crossed to the far post where Peter Beardsley nodded the ball for Cole to score with a header.

21 45 mins Cole beat the offside trap following a Lee Clark pass to calmly slide the ball past the helpless City 'keeper Tony Coton.

Norwich City	2-1	*January 4 1994*

22 79 mins Raced on to a through ball and rounded 'keeper Bryan Gunn before slotting home the winner.

Southampton	1-2	*January 22 1994*

23 38 mins A right-wing cross from Robinson was half-hit home by Cole.

Coventry City	4-0	*February 23 1994*

24 49 mins Atherton dropped a back-pass short to leave Cole with a straightforward chance which he tucked away with ease.

25 70 mins A Fox shot came off the 'keeper, to leave Cole a rebound to tap-in.

26 77 mins Beardsley dribbled the ball into the box for Cole to move in and slot home.

The Newcastle fans idolised him and were stunned when he joined Man. United.

His all round game has improved under Alex Ferguson.

Cole's goals took Newcastle to the top of the table.

Sheffield Wednesday	1-0	March 5 1994

27 | **88 mins** Rifled home a fierce shot after Newcastle's free-kick had been cleared.

West Ham United	4-2	March 19 1994

28 | **69 mins** Prodded home a cross after good work on the flank by Fox.

Ipswich Town	2-0	March 23 1994

29 | **73 mins** Chris Holland crossed the ball in from the right for Cole to nod in.

Norwich City	3-0	March 29 1994

30 | **37 mins** Sellars' corner fell to Peacock and then Fox, who both had a shot, before Cole volleyed home.

Leeds United	1-1	April 1 1994

31 | **3 mins** Fox played the ball to Lee whose cross was hit by goalwards by Scott Sellars. Lukic saved and Cole pounced to score from the rebound.

Liverpool	2-0	April 16 1994

32 | **56 mins** Cole finished off a quick counter-attack involving Lee and Fox.

Aston Villa	5-1	April 27 1994

33 | **41 mins** Ran on to a Sellars through ball, rounded Spink and slipped the ball into the empty net.

Arsenal	2-0	May 7 1994

34 | **46 mins** Beardsley wriggled into the penalty area and when Miller saved his shot Cole knocked in the rebound.

Leicester City	3-1	August 20 1994

35 | **51 mins** A Beardsley pass from the left was rammed in by Cole from eight yards.

Coventry City	4-0	August 24 1994

36 | **73 mins** Swapped passes with Fox and got the run of the ball before scoring with a left-foot shot.

Southampton	5-1	August 27 1994

37 | **40 mins** Another excellent cross came in from Fox for Cole to turn and score.

38 | **73 mins** A Francis Benali mistake presented Cole with an easy chance which he took comfortably.

Chelsea	4-2	September 10 1994

39 | **7 mins** A left-foot shot which screamed in from the edge of the area.

40 | **66 mins** Cole swapped passes with Lee before shooting with his right foot.

Aston Villa	2-0	October 1 1994

41 | **83 mins** Converted a right-wing cross from Newcastle newcomer Paul Kitson.

Sheffield Wednesday	2-1	October 22 1994

42 | **37 mins** With Pressman well out of his area, Cole had the easiest of chances turning in a Sellars cross.

Ipswich Town	1-1	November 26 1994

43 | **86 mins** Took a pass from Beresford, sidestepped Williams and rifled in a right-foot shot.

MANCHESTER UNITED

Aston Villa	1-0	February 4 1995

44 | **17 mins** Hooked the ball in from close range after Pallister headed down Giggs' corner at the far post.

Manchester City	3-0	February 11 1995

45 | **77 mins** A simple tap-in from six yards after Giggs turned on McClair's superb through-ball.

Ipswich Town	9-0	March 4 1995

46 | **23 mins** A clipped ball in from six yards out after Ryan Giggs supplied a low cross into the Ipswich box from the left byeline.

47 | **36 mins** A Simple tap-in after Mark Hughes' spectacular overhead kick rebounded to Cole off Ipswich bar.

48 | **52 mins** Got a touch before Ipswich defender Yallop's header went into his own net.

How Andy Cole scored his first 100 Premiership goals!

Goal Total 2 4 4 3 2 3 8 1 1 3 8 3 5 7 4 2 2 2 2 2 2 2 1 1 8 7 1 5 7

Number of Goals Scored Per Game — y-axis: 0, 3, 6, 9, 12

Teams (x-axis): Arsenal, Aston Villa, Barnsley, Blackburn Rovers, Bolton Wanderers, Chelsea, Coventry City, Crystal Palace, Derby County, Everton, Ipswich Town, Leeds United, Leicester City, Liverpool, Manchester City, Manchester United, Middlesborough, Newcastle United, Norwich City, Nottingham Forest, Oldham Athletic, Queens Park Rangers, Sheffield Wednesday, Southampton, Tottenham Hotspur, West Ham United, Wimbledon

---

49 **64 mins** Hammered ball in from ten yards after taking a McClair pass from left side of the box.

50 **88 mins** Fired the ball in from six yards after Ince headed on Giggs' corner.

Leicester City 4-0 April 15 1995
51 **45 mins** Tap-in on the line from an offside-looking position from a left-wing cross.

52 **52 mins** A goalmouth scramble ending up with Cole being given the credit for the goal.

Coventry City 3-2 May 1 1995
53 **55 mins** Pressley slipped and lost possession allowing Cole to score.

54 **79 mins** A weak back-header from Richardson exposed Gould and Cole raced through.

Southampton 2-1 May 10 1995
55 **21 mins** A shot from six yards after Charlton and Benali failed to clear McClair's cross from the left.

Wimbledon 3-1 August 26 1995
56 **59 mins** Cole netted a shot into the far corner after a pass from Paul Scholes, turning Reeves inside-out in the box before scoring.

Middlesbrough 2-0 October 28 1995
57 **87 mins** A left foot shot from 12 yards after racing on to a Cantona flick, the ball going in off Walsh's legs.

Southampton 4-1 November 18 1995
58 **69 mins** Cole finished off a far-post header from Beckham's corner.

Leeds United 1-3 December 24 1995
59 **30 mins** Fired home after Butt had dispossessed Speed at the edge of the box.

Newcastle United 2-0 December 27 1995
60 **44 mins** A right-foot shot from the right side of the penalty area after Ryan Giggs passed following a run from inside his own half.

Queens Park Rangers 2-1 December 30 1995
61 **44 mins** Far-post header from rebound after 'keeper Sommer tipped Prunier's header from Giggs' corner.

Tottenham Hotspur 1-4 January 1 1996
62 **36 mins** Neville's cross was met by Cole who slid the ball in from three yards.

Wimbledon 4-2 February 3 1996
63 **43 mins** Scored with a far-post header following a good cross from Irwin.

The QPR defence feels the force of Andy Cole's striking power.

Bolton Wanderers 6-0 February 25 1996
64 **70 mins** Collected McClair's pass, turned Coleman and placed a left-footer low past Keith Branagan.

Manchester City 3-2 April 6 1996
65 **41 mins** A Left-foot shot from 12-yards out after a neat one-two with Eric Cantona on the edge of the City box.

Middlesbrough 3-0 May 5 1996
66 **80 mins** Cracked in a swerving left foot drive from 25-yards out.

Nottingham Forest 4-0 December 26 1996
67 **74 mins** Cole showed his talent against a very poor Forest defence to grab United's the fourth of the day.

Wimbledon 2-1 January 29 1997
68 **82 mins** A right foot tap-in from four yards after Sullivan saved, but could not hold, Solskjaer's shot from Beckham's right-wing cross.

Arsenal 2-1 February 19 1997
69 **19 mins** Cole pounced on a goalkeeping error and stroked the ball in from a tight angle.

Coventry City 3-1 March 1 1997
70 **5 mins** Right-foot shot ten-yards out from Giggs' left-wing cross which went in off Jess.

Sheffield Wednesday 2-0 March 15 1997
71 **20 mins** Cole hit a left-footed shot from six-yards out on left side of the Wednesday box after running onto Cantona's ball.

Blackburn Rovers 3-2 April 12 1997
72 **32 mins** Took Cantona's pass to hit a low left-foot shot across the goalkeeper from ten yards.

Liverpool 3-1 April 19 1997
73 **63 mins** Met Gary Neville's looping high cross and headed into an unguarded net with James flapping.

Coventry City 3-0 August 30 1997
74 **1 min** Collected a short pass from Sheringham before scoring with a deflected shot from 20 yards.

Derby County 2-2 October 18 1997
75 **85 mins** Gary Pallister's ball into the area broke to substitute Cole who scored with a low right-foot shot from ten yards.

Barnsley 7-0 October 25 1997
76 **17 mins** Intercepted Sheridan's backpass and ran clear to shoot home right-footed from 12 yards.

77 **18 mins** Cole struck a right-foot shot from just outside the penalty area as he ran on to a through-ball from Ole Gunnar Solskjaer.

78 **44 mins** Cole collected Ryan Giggs' pass on the left-side of the box to score with a right-footed effort from ten yards.

Sheffield Wednesday 6-1 November 1 1997
79 **19 mins** Scored with a lucky attempt which came off his right shin when the ball rebounded out to him off a Wednesday defender.

80 **38 mins** Headed home powerfully from six yards-out after Beckham's powerful cross from the right took a slight deflection off Petter Rudi.

Wimbledon 5-2 November 22 1997
81 **85 mins** Blasted past Sullivan after another sweeping move across the pitch.

Liverpool 3-1 December 6 1997
82 **51 mins** Seized on a mistake by Kvarme and checked inside before hitting a right-foot shot in from 12 yards.

83 **74 mins** Scored having been left with a simple tap-in after Teddy Sheringham had flicked on Giggs' corner to outfox the Liverpool defence.

Newcastle United 1-0 December 21 1997
84 **67 mins** Beckham's precision right-foot cross picked out Cole who headed the ball low past Shaka Hislop from eight yards.

Everton 2-0 December 26 1997
85 **34 mins** A magnificent right foot chip from 20 yards after Butt laid the ball into his path.

Bolton Wanderers 1-1 February 7 1998
86 **84 mins** Cole headed the ball home from ten yards after Branagan had pushed away a Gary Neville cross from the right flank.

Blackburn Rovers 3-1 April 6 1998
87 **56 mins** Collected Beckham's pass on the right to cut inside and score left-footed from 15 yards.

Crystal Palace 3-0 April 27 1998
88 **84 mins** Scholes headed a rebound across the goal for the waiting Cole to stab home from just inches away.

Barnsley 2-0 May 10 1998
89 **5 mins** Cole picked up a deflected cross from Sheringham and spun sweetly before rifling home a splendid shot.

Southampton 3-0 October 3 1998
90 **59 mins** Jesper Blomqvist ran from halfway before delivering a pass for Cole to score with his left foot from 12-yards out.

Wimbledon 1-0 October 17 1998
91 **18 mins** A crisp low right-footed shot from the edge of the Wimbledon box as he beat the offside trap and turned Perry to connect with Beckham's precision pass.

92 **87 mins** Raced on to Cruyff's through-ball on the right side of The Dons' penalty area before scoring with a low right-footed shot from 12 yards.

Everton 4-1 October 31 1998
93 **59 mins** Turned on the 18-yard box and smashed the ball left-footed into the far corner of the net.

Sheffield Wednesday 1-3 November 21 1998
94 **29 mins** A one-two with Yorke before rounding the 'keeper and stabbing home from eight yards.

Chelsea 1-1 December 16 1998
95 **45 mins** Nicky Butt's first-time shot hit Cole before falling nicely for him to swivel and fire home a low right-footed shot, in off the right-hand post from 16 yards.

West Ham United 4-1 January 10 1999
96 **40 mins** Cole turned home the rebound with a right-footed volley from eight yards, after Nicky Butt's 25-yard shot had struck the post and fallen nicely for the striker.

97 **68 mins** Steered home a low right-footed shot on the left side of the box, beyond Hislop.

Leicester City 6-2 January 16 1999
98 **48 mins** Chased Giggs' ball down the left before scoring with a low, left-footed shot from six yards.

99 **61 mins** Yorke turned Steve Walsh and found his strike partner free out on the right-hand side, and Cole's angled shot from 12 yards gave Leicester 'keeper Keller no chance.

Nottingham Forest 8-1 February 6 1999
100 **7 mins** Cole held the ball on the edge of the area and, as 'keeper Beasant came out, Cole jinxed round him and drove it home into the right-hand corner of the net.

SINCE JOINING THE 100 CLUB

1998-99 Man. United   **6 goals** Premiership

Beckham provides Cole and Yorke with plenty of ammunition.

KEY HOME GAME   AWAY GAME

HOW DID YOU SCORE?

Think you're a soccer expert? There are 200 fantastic footy quiz questions in the Annual – fill in your answers on Page 108 and see how well you scored.

Shezza played the super sub role to perfection last season.

fourth XI

The right substitution can change a game, but how much do you know about football's super subs?

1 Which substitute netted twice for Crystal Palace in the FA Cup final against Manchester United in 1990?

2 Which substitute scored four goals in just 11 minutes for Manchester United against Nottingham Forest in 1998-99.

3 Which sub scored a wonder goal for Manchester United in the dramatic FA Cup semi-final win against Arsenal?

4 Which Aston Villa reserve striker scored twice after coming off the bench against Stromsgodset in the UEFA Cup in 1998-99?

5 Which substitute netted for England against Romania in the 1998 World Cup in France?

6 Who scored the opener for Manchester United in the 1999 FA Cup final only three minutes after coming off the bench?

7 Which sub scored the winning goal in the 1998 European Cup Winners' Cup final, a minute after coming off the bench?

8 Which player has made an amazing 116 substitute appearances for Wimbledon over the past eight years?

9 Which substitute scored the winning goal for Tottenham in the 1999 Worthington Cup final?

10 Which substitute came on and netted twice for Liverpool in their 1989 FA Cup final victory over Everton?

11 Which Everton substitute came on and scored two goals in the same game?

THE WORLD CHAMPIONS quiz

How much do you remember about France's 1998 World Cup winning side?

1 Who did Thierry Henry leave leave Monaco for?

2 Who did Zinedine Zidane get sent off against?

3 Who scored France's first goal of the 1998 tournament?

4 Laurent Blanc was sent off for a foul on who in the semis?

5 Lillian Thuram plays his club football for which Serie A side?

6 Which manager steered France to World Cup glory?

7 Who was France's goalscorer in the semi-final?

8 Who replaced Laurent Blanc in the Final against Brazil?

9 Which two players scored in the World Cup Final?

10 Which French striker failed to score a goal at France '98?

11 Which player was sent off against Brazil in the final?

12 Who were the two French 'keepers that didn't play?

former clubs

Name their teams before, joining the Anfield outfit?

1 stephane henchoz
switzerland

2 jamie redknapp
england

3 vegard heggem
norway

4 sander westerveld
holland

5 karlheinz riedle
germany

CIVVY STREET

Can you name this top footy star without his kit on?

GUESS THE YEAR

In what year were these players born?

1 Darren Huckerby
Coventry City

2 Steve Guppy
Leicester City

3 Paul Gascoigne
Middlesbrough

4 David Ginola
Tottenham

5 Steve Stone
Aston Villa

NAME THE CLUB!

Whose recent league record is this?

Premiership

POSITION / SEASON

'94 17th, '95 15th, '96 6th, '97 15th, '98 17th, '99 14th

patrick vieira quiz

Five tough tacklin' questions about the Arsenal midfielder?

1 In which country was Patrick born?

2 At which French club did he begin his professional football career?

3 At which Italian Serie A outfit did Patrick spend one season before he joined Arsenal?

4 How much did he cost Arsene Wenger to take to Arsenal in 1996?

5 How many appearances did Patrick make for France at the 1998 World Cup Finals?

NWANKWO KANU ARSENAL

GREAT BRITAIN UNITED?

GARY NEVILLE
Right-back

WHY? There's not a lot of competition in this position, but Gary Neville is easily experienced enough for the role. Already an established England international and highly successful club player, the quick, hard-tackling full-back also likes to push forward down the flank where he could link up in the British side with club team-mate David Beckham. Gary has been touted as a future England captain because of his ability to motivate his team-mates.

ALSO IN THE FRAME

Wes Brown: England

RYAN GIGGS
Left midfield

WHY? Ryan is one reason why the debate about a Great Britain team is ongoing. Trapped in an international side that is, quite frankly, not on his level, he would slot in ideally on the left-wing of a British team. With a steady defence behind him, Ryan would be given licence to thrill and torment the opposition with his mesmerising skill. The strikers would relish having his supply coming in from the left flank and, having achieved nothing with Wales, he would be hungrier than ever to turn on the style.

ALSO IN THE FRAME

Allan Johnston: Scotland

SOL CAMPBELL
Centre-back

WHY? In many ways Sol is from the old school of defending – he will look for any way possible to stop the opposition from scoring. But he's also much more than that. He's adapted to the new breed of international striker and his determination is complimented by strength, pace and agility. He can also add much-needed power to midfield by bringing the ball out of defence and he's not afraid to shoot either. A rock-solid defender whose leadership qualities are important to any team he plays in.

ALSO IN THE FRAME

Jonathan Woodgate: England

GRAEME LE SAUX
Left-back

WHY? This is arguably the most difficult spot to fill in the team because of the lack of quality left-footed players around today. Stuart Pearce would have made this position his own a few years back, but we've plumped for Le Saux to give the team the flexibility to adopt a wing-back system if necessary. His overlapping and pinpoint crossing would be a vital element of an attacking ploy that would provide plenty of ammunition for the head of Duncan Ferguson.

ALSO IN THE FRAME

Callum Davidson: Scotland

DAVID BECKHAM
Right midfield

WHY? How can you have a Great Britain XI without including the man himself? David is probably the best footballer in Britain right now. An outstanding player with a wonderful range of passing and tremendous shooting ability, he would be a key addition to any team anywhere in the world. His outstanding crosses would be tailor-made for the head of Ferguson and the predatory instincts of Michael Owen. Becks can be equally effective running things from a central midfield position if required.

ALSO IN THE FRAME

Keith Gillespie: Northern Ireland

TONY ADAMS
Centre-back (captain)

WHY? He might be in the twilight of his career, but Tony would provide the inspiration and experience to help the team gel together straight away. Another magnificent leader whose strength and courage have shone through on many an occasion, you can also rely on him to look out for the younger players in the side. When Great Britain win everything in sight on the world stage they will need someone who is used to picking up a trophy or two, so Big Tone would be the right man for the job!

ALSO IN THE FRAME
Colin Hendry: Scotland

DUNCAN FERGUSON
Striker

WHY? Probably the most controversial selection of the whole XI. At international level, you need variation in your attacking style so we've gone for the combination of 'Little and Large'. Many European sides can't deal with the old fashioned British forward and big Dunc is certainly that, so with the right service, not only would he have the aerial presence to score his fair share of goals but he would act as a target man and provide the nippy Michael Owen with plenty of chances. Dunc is also a lot better on the deck than a many people give him credit for.

ALSO IN THE FRAME
Teddy Sheringham: England

DAVID SEAMAN
Goalkeeper

WHY? If you're looking to build a Great Britain XI you have to start by getting a world-class keeper. There can be only one real choice for the position – David Seaman. He is vastly experienced, can organise the men in front of him and is still the man you want on your side if a game comes down to penalties. He may not be getting any younger and other 'keepers may be getting better, but for now there is no-one in Britain who can take the gloves away from one of England's most popular players.

ALSO IN THE FRAME
Paul Jones: Wales

PAUL LAMBERT
Central midfield

WHY? A rare commodity in the Scottish game – Paul is a European Cup winner! During his time with Borussia Dortmund, he played with and against some of the very best players in the world. A tough-tackling, combative midfielder, Paul is the perfect holding player who can fill any gaps left when Le Saux and Neville bomb forward. But destruction is not just the name of his game, Paul can also strike a mean shot from distance and weigh in with the odd goal.

ALSO IN THE FRAME
Barry Ferguson: Scotland

NEIL LENNON
Central midfield

WHY? In a similar midfield role to the one played by David Batty and Paul Ince for England, Lennon would add further grit and determination to the heart of the side with his energetic no-nonsense style. He's also got a great engine, which is so important when you are competing on the world stage. Tiredness can cost a goal late on in the game, but Neil will keep going for 90 minutes and beyond if need be. A tidy player who rarely gives the ball away he reads the game superbly and links up well with his team-mates. His presence would give Giggs and Beckham scope to push forward.

ALSO IN THE FRAME
Paul Scholes: England

MICHAEL OWEN
Striker

WHY? It's a straight choice between Owen and Alan Shearer for the role of lead striker. Although the Newcastle man is a proven goalscorer, there's no doubt that he's not as quick as he once was. The criticism aimed at Shearer is that he's only in the England team on reputation. So, lets shake it up a bit! Owen is younger, much quicker and is deadly when running at people, particularly in the box. With Beckham, Giggs and Ferguson around him, he should bag a hat-trick in every game. Regarded by Brazilian legend Pele as the best player in England, he comes highly recommended.

ALSO IN THE FRAME
Alan Shearer: England

Gillespie could earn a place on the subs bench if he plays at his best.

GREAT BRITAIN

HERE MATCH ASSESSES THE ARGUMENTS FOR AND AGAINST THE INTRODUCTION OF A UNITED GREAT BRITAIN TEAM...

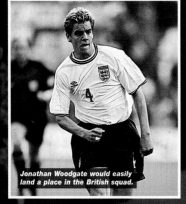
Colin Hendry would be great cover for Campbell and Adams.

SPORTS MINISTER TONY BANKS suggested last season that the four nations which make up Great Britain should join together their most talented footballers into one team – for the plain reason of achieving more success on the world stage. While in some quarters the move was welcomed, there was an uproar as English, Welsh, Scottish and Irish fans protested that they wanted to keep their own country's identity – and that meant Tony Banks keeping his hands off their treasured football teams. Here are the arguments on the matter.

AGAINST... ENGLAND RULE!
The current population of Great Britain is 59 million, but over 49 million of those people live in England, so it's likely that they would form the core of any British team because they are easily the biggest nation. Only 5.1 million live in Scotland, 2.9m in Northern Ireland and just 1.7m in Wales. The odds are stacked in favour of England and the other countries wouldn't like having to support so many English players.

5.1 million
1.7 million
49.3 million

FOR... DOMESTIC FOOTBALL!
The argument in favour of a British Super League would be solved once and for all. A clash between Rangers and Man. United, or Celtic and Arsenal would then be seen as good for the international team. Football in Scotland is seen as fairly predictable at the moment so a whole new interest would be generated. It would allow Scottish clubs to pit their wits against a supposedly higher standard of opposition and improve their chances in Europe.

Jonathan Woodgate would easily land a place in the British squad.

AGAINST... NO MORE BANTER!
Part of the thrill of international competition is seeing how England get on compared to, say Scotland. You would lose that tension, friendly rivalry and banter between the supporters that can make a one-off game extra special. Who will forget the time England went head-to-head with the Scottish at Wembley during Euro '96? If the Great Britain XI becomes a reality, you'll never see that kind of excitement in a game again.

FOR... UNITING THE NATION!
Having a united team would bring about a feeling of respect and unity across the nation. Football has a great way of uniting the masses and it would be great to see a sea of English, Welsh, Scottish and Irish fans actually singing together – without any trouble!

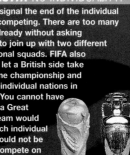

AGAINST... FAN TROUBLE!
But let's be realistic, after all the problems created by a minority of British supporters abroad over the years, would it really be a good move to let the fans from different countries stand next to each? If a player from one country is having a bad game would fans from the other countries pick up on that and start trouble? It would probably make little difference to most of fans but the disruptive minority always have to be borne in mind.

With a shortage of talented left-backs, Callum Davidson gets the nod.

FOR... A BIGGER TALENT POOL!
Obviously, having a Great Britain side would allow the manager to select from a wider range of talent. It would be easier to cope with injury and suspension to key players at crucial times if there were more players. It would make the team a stronger force and there would certainly be no hiding behind any excuses after a heavy defeat – the reserves would be queuing up for the next game!

AGAINST... NO INDIVIDUALITY!
It would signal the end of the individual nations competing. There are too many games already without asking a player to join up with two different international squads. FIFA also wouldn't let a British side take part in one championship and then the individual nations in another. You cannot have both, so a Great Britain team would mean each individual nation would not be able to compete on the world stage in their own right. Bummer!

FOR... MORE SUCCESS!
Back in the 1980s all the home nations were relatively strong. At the 1982 World Cup in Spain, Northern Ireland were one of the tournament's surprise packages, but they haven't even qualified for a major tournament since 1986. Wales haven't qualified for the final stages for many years and Scotland – while they have a good qualification record – usually struggle to progress beyond the opening phase.

Wes Brown could step in if club-mate Gary Neville was unavailable.

AGAINST...REPRESENTATION!

The question would arise about whether you would limit the number of players from each country to make sure the Great Britain team is fairly represented. Check out this dilemma: if England had to pick a maximum of three from Campbell, Le Saux, Neville, Beckham and Owen, who would miss out? It would be a nightmare for the manager. And if you were forced to choose the same number from Wales, who would they be? Giggs and, er...you kind of get the picture, don't you?

FOR... POOLING FINANCES!
With a single Football Association body in charge of the national team, the financial resources of each country could be pooled together to put the backing behind one side. This would mean the development of a better youth system to bring on young talent and more modern stadia. It would also strengthen any bid to host the World Cup or European Championships in the future. A bid by Great Britain would surely carry greater weight with FIFA.

THE VERDICT

The prospect of a Great Britain team has its advantages, but there are probably even more disadvantages. While it would be fantastic to see Giggsy and even Paul Lambert play alongside Becks and Seaman, we wouldn't want to see our countries' individual honour and tradition blown away. Maybe one day a Great Britain side could take part in a special tour or competition during the pre-season – just like The British Lions do in rugby union – but it couldn't go much further than that. It may be an exciting prospect, but it just wouldn't work.

Would Alan Shearer have to sit on the bench?

Winger Allan Johnston wouldn't get into the team past Ryan Giggs.

Paul Scholes would have to get used to being a supersub again.

Paul Jones of Southampton has a tough job to oust David Seaman.

Sheringham's presence would keep Duncan Ferguson on his toes.

SIR ALEX FERGUSON
The gaffer

WHY? He's got all the credentials to manage any international side having won everything there is to win at club level. Sir Alex is the most successful manager in the history of the British domestic game. He is the only person to have guided both English and Scottish clubs to triumph in Europe – and in all three domestic trophies. At Manchester United, he's won the title five times, the FA Cup on four occasions, the League Cup once, the European Cup Winners' Cup and best of all, the European Cup. He is respected around the world and would be able to handle the blood-thirsty British media.

ALSO IN THE FRAME

Terry Venables: England

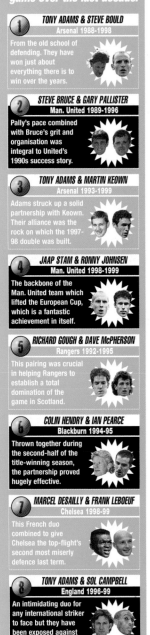

TOP 10

The greatest defensive partnerships in the British game over the last decade.

1 TONY ADAMS & STEVE BOULD
Arsenal 1988-1998
From the old school of defending. They have won just about everything there is to win over the years.

2 STEVE BRUCE & GARY PALLISTER
Man. United 1989-1996
Pally's pace combined with Bruce's grit and organisation was integral to United's 1990s success story.

3 TONY ADAMS & MARTIN KEOWN
Arsenal 1993-1999
Adams struck up a solid partnership with Keown. Their alliance was the rock on which the 1997-98 double was built.

4 JAAP STAM & RONNY JOHNSEN
Man. United 1998-1999
The backbone of the Man. United team which lifted the European Cup, which is a fantastic achievement in itself.

5 RICHARD GOUGH & DAVE McPHERSON
Rangers 1992-1995
This pairing was crucial in helping Rangers to establish a total domination of the game in Scotland.

6 COLIN HENDRY & IAN PEARCE
Blackburn 1994-95
Thrown together during the second-half of the title-winning season, the partnership proved hugely effective.

7 MARCEL DESAILLY & FRANK LEBOEUF
Chelsea 1998-99
This French duo combined to give Chelsea the top-flight's second most miserly defence last term.

8 TONY ADAMS & SOL CAMPBELL
England 1996-99
An intimidating duo for any international striker to face but they have been exposed against pace on occasion.

9 UGO EHIOGU & GARETH SOUTHGATE
Aston Villa 1995-99
A combination of the no-nonsense Ehiogu and the cultured Southgate works wonders for Villa.

10 DEAN BLACKWELL & CHRIS PERRY
Wimbledon 1995-99
The partnership of Blackwell and Perry spoiled many a day out for the top-flight's more fancied teams.

Back to school with...

...Jody Morris

"We used to get up to some tricks with these."

"That's not the prize for coming top in science is it?"

Hurray! PE next – time for a game of footy.

Ah, the playground, where Jody netted 973 times one term.

For most of us, once our school days are over you'd have to grab us by the hair before we'd ever set foot in those buildings of torture again. However, it seems that Premier League footballers are a nice lot and are quite happy to trace the steps of their early days. Route 1 caught up with three top stars as they went back to school.

"I was no angel at school and there were a few jokes going on," Chelsea midfielder Jody Morris reveals. **"We were a bit disruptive and we used to get up to loads of tricks with bunsen burners! I enjoyed school but I never liked science."** That sounds fair enough and don't leave out maths either!

West Ham star Frank Lampard reckons physics was the worst though. **"I hated physics. I could never understand it and I would always get sent out of the class for talking with my mates at the back of the room, instead of listening to what the teacher was saying!"** You can just imagine him doing that now in training with Rio Ferdinand, while Harry Redknapp talks tactics!

Martin Keown also invited Route 1 along when he went back to visit his old school in Oxford. **"Some of my old teachers are still here, believe it or not and it's great to see them and some other familiar faces,"** he says. **"One of my PE teachers helped me a lot when I was younger and I don't ever forget that."** And guess what? Route 1 even managed to get away from all those schools without having to do any homework! Fantastic!

...Frank Lampard

"I'd rather be reading MATCH than physics books."

Frank always found time for his fave footy mag.

...Martin Keown

"Blimey! This history multiple choice is hard."

Twenty questions on the Arsenal back-four had Martin stumped.

Brazilian nut

There's always a down side
when you're a foreigner looking to make it in the Premiership. Language can be the most difficult barrier, as you try to get to know your new buddies. It's not just on the pitch either – you miss out on all dressing-room banter. Since arriving at Wednesday, Brazilian defender Emerson Thome has become a cult hero to the Hillsborough faithful and is hugely grateful to his team-mates for teaching him about English culture – including how to pronounce swear words! **"I did not understand what some of the bad words are but now I know them all,"** he joked. **"Sometimes players on the other team will say something because they think I don't know what they mean, but I say 'Hey, no!'."** Yeah, listen up Roy Keane, David Batty or anyone else who thinks they're hard. Don't mess with Emerson Thome okay?

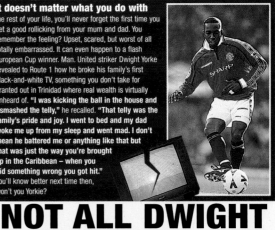

It doesn't matter what you do with
the rest of your life, you'll never forget the first time you get a good rollicking from your mum and dad. You remember the feeling? Upset, scared, but worst of all totally embarrassed. It can even happen to a flash European Cup winner. Man. United striker Dwight Yorke revealed to Route 1 how he broke his family's first black-and-white TV, something you don't take for granted out in Trinidad where real wealth is virtually unheard of. **"I was kicking the ball in the house and I smashed the telly,"** he recalled. **"That telly was the family's pride and joy. I went to bed and my dad woke me up from my sleep and went mad. I don't mean he battered me or anything like that but that was just the way you're brought up in the Caribbean – when you did something wrong you got hit."** You'll know better next time then, won't you Yorkie?

NOT ALL DWIGHT

SOL CAMPBELL TOTTENHAM

> ## "I HAD THE 'HORNY' SONG MONTHS BEFORE IT WAS IN THE CHARTS!"

LEE HENDRIE

Club: Aston Villa

Position: Midfielder

Any faves? Any soul artist

Lee says: "I can tell you now that you won't find any albums by Phil Collins in my collection! I have some massive speakers on my music system and the sound comes out very loud so I'm not sure that the neighbours like me that much! I've got a decent set of CDs, but the stuff I go for is quite mellow. I like quite a bit of soul music."

MICHAEL BALL

Club: Everton

Position: Left-back

Any faves? Michael Jackson

Michael says: "I keep all my best CDs in my car because I'm always listening to them when I'm travelling. I'm into soul and dance. My first record was something by Michael Jackson back in the 1980s around the time that he did 'Thriller'. I went to see him on his 'Bad' tour in 1988 at Aintree Racecourse. I'm a big fan of his and I like the old Jackson Five stuff. I don't like heavy metal like my team-mate Craig Short does – it really isn't my sort of thing."

MY KINDA MUSIC!

MATCH takes a look inside the music collections of some of the top footballers in the country to find out what tunes they listen to.

FOOTBALLERS HAVE GOT AS MUCH PASSION FOR MUSIC AS THEY HAVE FOR PLAYING A ROUND OF golf these days. As well as strutting their stuff to the very latest dance tracks in London, Liverpool or Manchester's trendiest clubs, they play it loud in their cars, on the team bus on the way to matches and sometimes even in the dressing-room before a game – if their managers let them!

Then there are the cool players who like to pump up the soul music when they're driving home from training. Maybe it's the relaxing sound they like after running about on a wet pitch all morning!

Recently there's also been a new generation of music-loving players who have turned to DJ-ing as their favourite hobby. Sunderland striker Danny Dichio is famed for spinning his records and Middlesbrough's Dean Gordon earned some rave reviews when he played his first set at a north-east nightclub at the end of last season. MATCH checks out what music the players love to listen to.

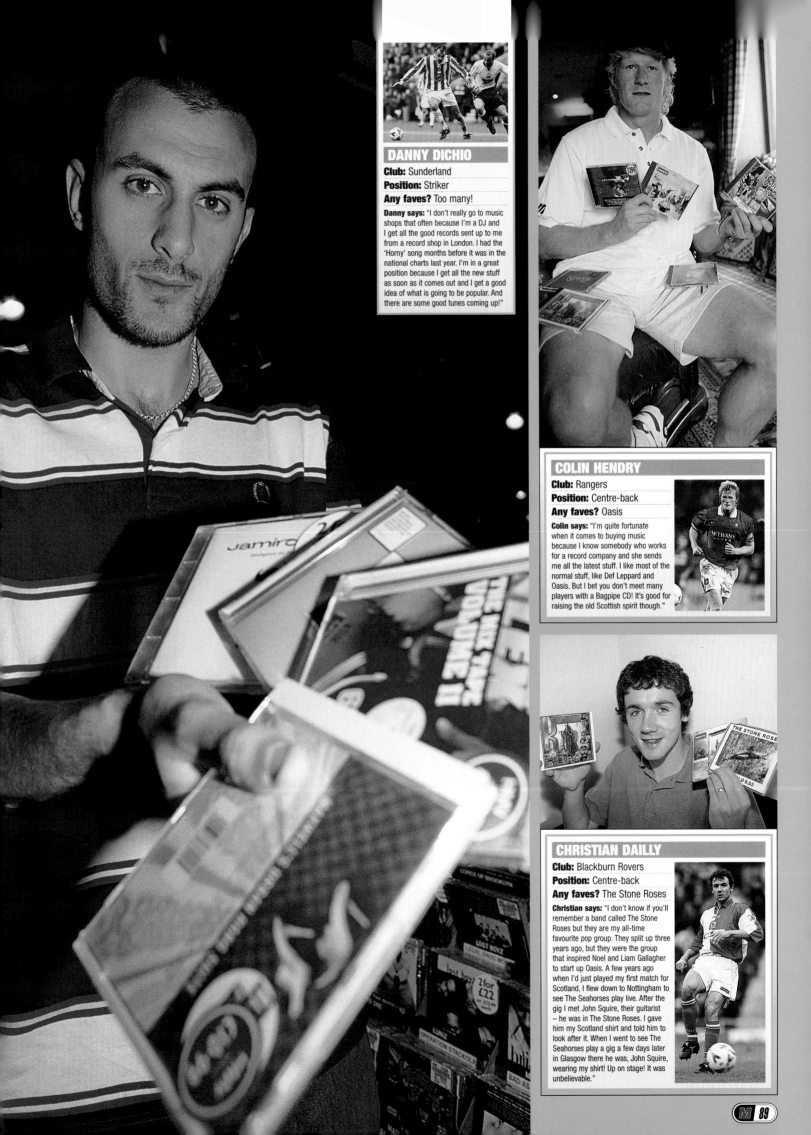

DANNY DICHIO

Club: Sunderland

Position: Striker

Any faves? Too many!

Danny says: "I don't really go to music shops that often because I'm a DJ and I get all the good records sent up to me from a record shop in London. I had the 'Horny' song months before it was in the national charts last year. I'm in a great position because I get all the new stuff as soon as it comes out and I get a good idea of what is going to be popular. And there are some good tunes coming up!"

COLIN HENDRY

Club: Rangers

Position: Centre-back

Any faves? Oasis

Colin says: "I'm quite fortunate when it comes to buying music because I know somebody who works for a record company and she sends me all the latest stuff. I like most of the normal stuff, like Def Leppard and Oasis. But I bet you don't meet many players with a Bagpipe CD! It's good for raising the old Scottish spirit though."

CHRISTIAN DAILLY

Club: Blackburn Rovers

Position: Centre-back

Any faves? The Stone Roses

Christian says: "I don't know if you'll remember a band called The Stone Roses but they are my all-time favourite pop group. They split up three years ago, but they were the group that inspired Noel and Liam Gallagher to start up Oasis. A few years ago when I'd just played my first match for Scotland, I flew down to Nottingham to see The Seahorses play live. After the gig I met John Squire, their guitarist – he was in The Stone Roses. I gave him my Scotland shirt and told him to look after it. When I went to see The Seahorses play a gig a few days later in Glasgow there he was, John Squire, wearing my shirt! Up on stage! It was unbelievable."

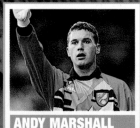

ANDY MARSHALL

Club: Norwich City

Position: Goalkeeper

Any faves? Will Smith

Andy says: "My favourite albums are mostly by Blackstreet, LL Cool J, Will Smith, Deborah Cox and other artists like that. I'm into all sorts of music, but my favourite types are definitely soul and swing. Norwich is a really quiet and relaxed place and it is miles away from anywhere so I can get away with playing my music really loud! When I come home from training, I just sit down in my house, relax and listen to some music on my stereo. It's not a bad life, eh?"

KEVIN PRESSMAN

Club: Sheffield Wednesday

Position: Goalkeeper

Any faves? Prince

Kevin says: "I went to see Prince at the Sheffield Arena and Orchestral Manoeuvres in the Dark, which I really enjoyed. I've also been out to buy 'Old Boys Reunion' and 'The Best Soul Seven' and both have been good to chill out to. I have never had a chance with the music on the team coach though, Peter Atherton is in charge so I don't get a look in."

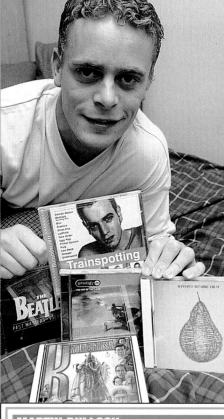

ROB SAVAGE

Club: Leicester City

Position: Midfielder

Any faves? Ministry Of Sound

Rob says: "I like my music and I buy a fair bit of stuff. My music collection is mainly made up of dance CDs, Ministry Of Sound annuals and clubbing guides. I've been to Ibiza and I really enjoyed the scene out there. I'm a bit mad about going to nightclubs and I spend a lot of time on the dance floor. Out of all the lads at Leicester, I would have to say that I'm by far the best dancer. To be honest there's not much competition there!"

MARTIN BULLOCK

Club: Barnsley

Position: Midfielder

Any faves? Oasis

Martin Says: "I'm not into any one type of music to be honest. I've got all sorts of different CDs, which I keep in my room. The collection includes such groups as Oasis, The Prodigy, Kula Shaker and The Beatles. See there's quite a range of different sounds there. I've only ever been to a couple of gigs so far and tend to have to make do with listening to my favourite bands on the radio. I've always got that on in my car when I'm driving to the training ground and back. I couldn't do without it!"

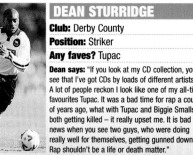

DEAN STURRIDGE

Club: Derby County

Position: Striker

Any faves? Tupac

Dean says: "If you look at my CD collection, you'll see that I've got CDs by loads of different artists. A lot of people reckon I look like one of my all-time favourites Tupac. It was a bad time for rap a couple of years ago, what with Tupac and Biggie Smalls both getting killed – it really upset me. It is bad news when you see two guys, who were doing really well for themselves, getting gunned down. Rap shouldn't be a life or death matter."

KEITH GILLESPIE

Club: Blackburn Rovers

Position: Winger

Any faves? Any chart music

Keith says: "I have quite a good hi-fi system, but I don't spend a lot of time at home really and when I do I'm usually watching the TV. I listen to music a lot when I'm driving to training in my car, so I keep my collection of CDs in there most of the time. I don't have any particular favourites, I just tend to hear something I like on the radio on my way in to training and then buy it later on!"

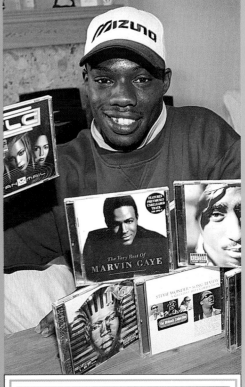

GEORGE NDAH

Club: Swindon Town

Position: Striker

Any faves? Stevie Wonder

George says: "My sound system is definitely one of my most treasured possessions. I couldn't be without my music, it's a very important part of my life and my family's too. I've had my stereo for about a year now and it's been great. I pump it up loud, but my neighbours don't mind – they pump theirs up too. I listen to mainly soul music. I've got the TLC album, which is good, Whitney Houston's latest, a record called 'NAS' and loads of albums by the legendary Stevie Wonder and Marvin Gaye. And there's one of Tupac's old albums in my collection too."

GARY ROWETT

Club: Birmingham City

Position: Centre-back

Any faves? Oasis

Gary says: "I've been playing the guitar for about 18 months now. My wife bought it for me as a birthday present after I heard my good pal Christian Dailly playing a few songs on his guitar round his house. He's very good at playing, but unfortunately I haven't managed to get anywhere near that standard yet! I can only play a few chords at the moment. But I do enjoy playing whenever I get the chance, especially Oasis songs because they're not too hard to play."

Peter Beagrie celebrates Bradford's promotion.

fifth XI

How much do you remember about the promotion battles and relegation dog-fights from the 1990s?

1 Which team did Sunderland lose against to confirm their relegation in 1990-91?

2 What was so dramatic about Oldham Athletic beating Sheffield Wednesday to clinch the old Second Division championship in 1990-91?

3 Which already relegated club did Luton Town lose against and as a result get relegated in 1991-92?

4 Why were Crystal Palace so devastated when they lost top-flight status in 1992-93?

5 On the last day of the 1993-94 season, how many teams were still involved in the battle for top-flight survival?

6 Everton came back from 2-0 down to beat Wimbledon 3-2 and stay up that year, but who scored the match-winner?

7 What was unusual about Blackburn's 2-1 defeat at Liverpool in 1994-95?

8 In 1996-97, the bottom two clubs in the Third Division met to decide who'd stay in the Football League. Who were they?

9 Manchester City went down that season, but which three teams survived on the last day?

10 Bradford City won promotion to the Premiership in 1998-99 with a 3-2 victory at Wolves, but which three players scored for them that day?

11 How many times has the Premier League title been decided on the final day of the season during the 1990s?

THE mega rangers quiz

How much do you really know about the 1998-99 Scottish treble winners?

THE early years

1 In what year was Rangers Association Football Club founded?

2 In which year did they win their first trophy?

3 Name the first team Rangers played at Ibrox Park in 1887.

4 Rangers played in the 1886-87 English Cup. Who put them out?

5 How many points did Rangers drop in winning the 1888-89 title?

STATISTICS

11 What is Rangers' record defeat and who was it against?

12 The Gers biggest win was in 1934? What was the score?

13 Which former player, played 496 games for The Gers from 1962-78?

14 What is the capacity of Ibrox to the nearest thousand?

15 Rangers record crowd of 118,567 fans was against which team?

europe

6 In which season did Rangers first take part in European competition?

7 In which year did Rangers win the European Cup Winners' Cup?

8 When did Rangers first take part in European competition?

9 Who knocked Rangers out of Europe last season?

10 At which stage did Rangers enter this season's Champions League?

THE players

16 Which ex-Hull City manager used to be an Ibrox favourite?

17 Who is Rangers' record buy and how much did he cost?

18 Who is Rangers' most capped player of all time?

19 And how many goals did he score during his lengthy Rangers career?

20 How much did The Gers pay for striker Rod Wallace?

what position?

match these players with the positions they play in?

1 ANDY MARSHALL
2 MATTHEW ETHERINGTON
3 ASHLEY WESTWOOD
4 ALAN SMITH
5 DES LINTON
6 NICKY SUMMERBEE

A Right-back
B Striker
C Left-winger
D Goalkeeper
E Centre-back
F Right-winger

connections...

What links Leicester City's Steve Guppy with Darren Huckerby of Coventry City?

former clubs

Name their teams before, joining their current club?

1 neil lennon
leicester city

2 paul merson
aston villa

3 dean gordon
middlesbrough

4 seth johnson
derby county

5 dean windass
bradford city

THE PAUL GASCOIGNE QUIZ

Gazza is one of the game's most colourful characters but how much do you really know about him?

1 Gazza released a single in 1990 and it reached number two in the charts. What was it called?

2 Who did Gazza tackle in the 1991 FA Cup semi-final when he tore his cruciate ligaments?

3 How much did Lazio pay when Paul Gascoigne joined them from Tottenham Hotspur in 1992?

4 Gazza scored a wonder goal against Scotland in Euro '96 past which 'keeper?

5 Which current Middlesbrough team-mate did Gascoigne play against when he was at Lazio in Serie A?

6 True or False? Gazza played alongside Middlesbrough boss Bryan Robson for England.

All Nations

Where are these Celtic stars from?

1 Henrik Larsson
2 Lubomir Moravcik
3 Vidar Riseth
4 Marc Rieper
5 Marko Viduka

GARETH SOUTHGATE ASTON VILLA

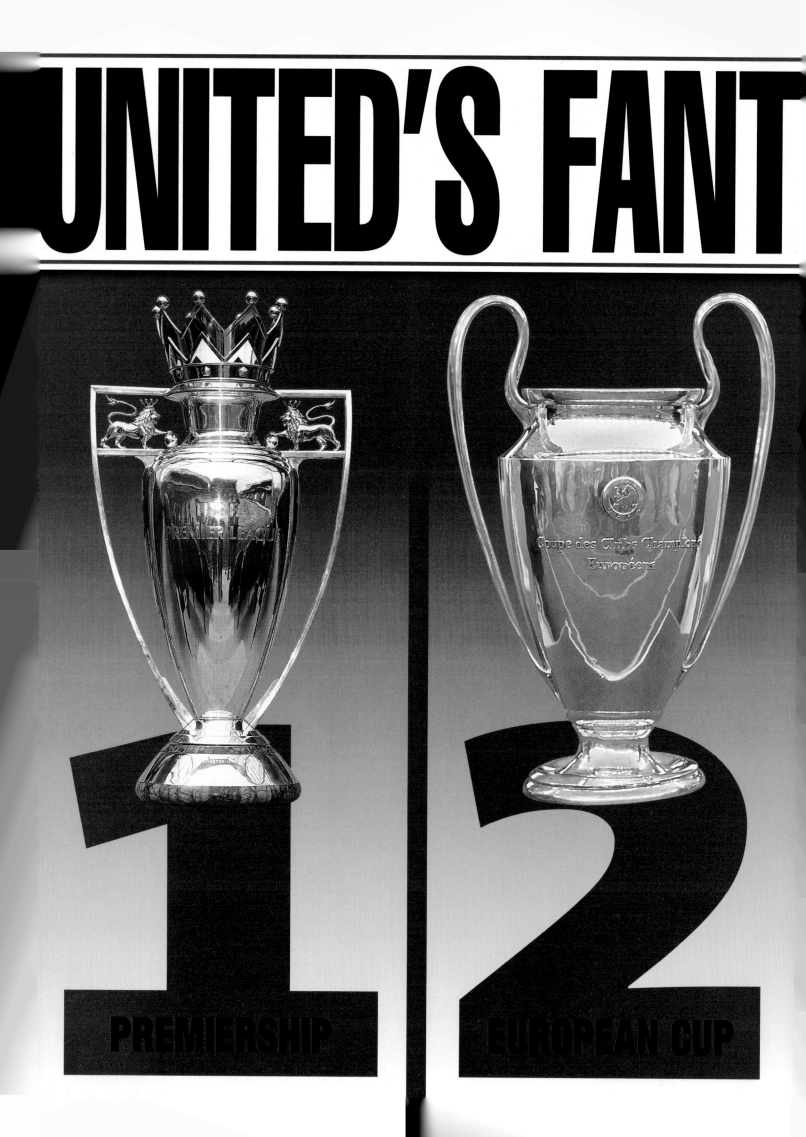

ASTIC TREBLE!

Three reasons to be cheerful. Manchester United's treble chase has been one of the most thrilling episodes in the history of soccer. It was a season of epic matches, great goals and a truly thrilling climax which provided the perfect end to a century of stunning football.

MANCHESTER UNITED HAVE WITHOUT DOUBT BEEN the team of the 1990s, but it was not until the close of the decade that they earned the right to call themselves the best club in Europe. Sir Alex Ferguson's team may have won the European Cup Winners' Cup and the Super Cup back in 1991, but the highest club honour eluded Fergie until May 1999 when his star-studded side won the European Cup.

Not only did United walk away with the coveted European prize, but they cleaned up domestically, scooping the Premier League and FA Cup double.

Their flowing, attacking style of football and steely self-belief has captured the hearts and imaginations of football fans and the British public alike.

The most nail-biting were the dying seconds of the European Cup Final when United nicked two last-gasp goals to win the trophy, after trailing so long to a goal from Bayern Munich. Only true champions can combine the spirit, confidence and luck which are required to overcome such adversity.

Over the pages that follow, MATCH looks back on the amazing history-making season, hearing the views of the players who made it all happen and giving the facts that matter on each game the team played during the campaign. And, in an exclusive interview with MATCH, Gary Neville talks of his memories of what will go down as the greatest season in the history of a great football club.

3 FA CUP

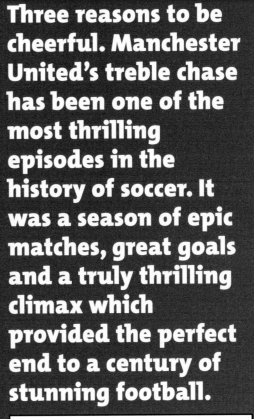

THE DREAM TREBLE!
HOW UNITED WON IT

SIR ALEX FERGUSON MASTERMIND!

What can you say about this man? A brilliant manager who thoroughly deserved the knighthood at the end of a long season. Sir Alex stuck by Jaap Stam and proved how shrewd he is in the transfer market with the purchase of Dwight Yorke. The way he handled the torment of David Beckham following his miserable time at the World Cup was great man-management. And utilising Ole Gunnar Solskjaer as a super sub showed that Sir Alex knew his squad better than anyone else. The list is endless. You've just got to take your hat off to him!

August BACK IN ACTION!

After their failure to win a single trophy the previous season, Manchester United were under pressure to win something this time out... As the players reported back for pre-season training they are introduced to their new team-mates Jaap Stam, the Dutch central defender, and Swedish winger Jesper Blomqvist... The season didn't start too well though as the double winners Arsenal beat United 3-0 in the Charity Shield at Wembley... Alex Ferguson followed up his summer spending by splashing out £12.6 million on Aston Villa striker Dwight Yorke... A 2-0 aggregate win over Polish outfit LKS Lodz saw United qualify for the group stages of the Champions League... David Beckham signed a long-term deal to keep him at United until 2003.

RYAN GIGGS "We couldn't wait to get going at the start so we could set right what went wrong the previous season. We still felt we were the team to beat and we were determined to regain the title. We've always said that winning the Premiership was our priority, but we never thought we'd be seen as a truly great side until we won the European Cup."

DWIGHT YORKE "Joining United was a dream come true. I couldn't wait to pull on the famous red shirt. I never lacked faith in my own ability, but the move made it all worthwhile. I have got a reputation for smiling, but after the move it was a permanent fixture on my face."

September SETTLING IN!

Alex Ferguson told former Barcelona striker Jordi Cruyff that he could leave Old Trafford if he could find a new team... Dwight Yorke scored his first goals for the club in the 4-1 win over newly-promoted Charlton... United revealed plans for a £30 million extension at Old Trafford. They hoped to develop the East and West Stands, adding 12,400 seats and increasing the capacity to 67,400... Ole Gunnar Solskjaer admitted he wanted to stay at United and prove himself after turning down a move to troubled Tottenham... Juventus were said to be lining up Alex Ferguson as a possible replacement for coach Marcello Lippi, whose contract expired in the summer... United slipped up to Arsenal again, this time losing 3-0 at Highbury in the league.

OLE GUNNAR SOLSKJAER "The manager told me he hadn't closed the door on me for first-team

Fergie welcomes new signing Jesper Blomqvist to Old Trafford.

Jaap Stam became the most expensive defender in the world at £10.75m!

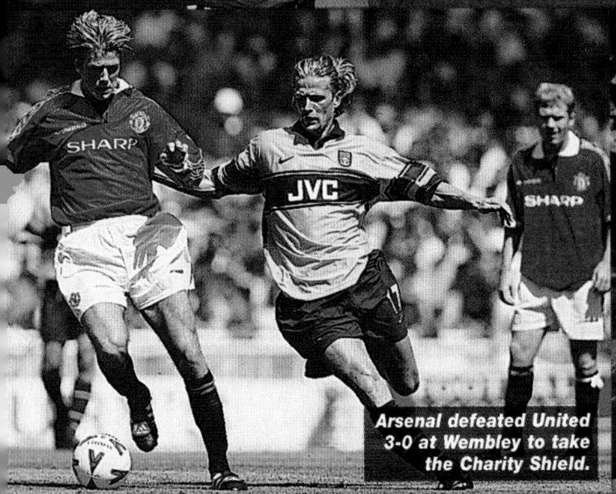

Arsenal defeated United 3-0 at Wembley to take the Charity Shield.

Giggsy was keen to erase the previous year's disappointment.

Manchester United's web expanded with the launch of MUTV.

Gary Neville returned from World Cup heartbreak.

football, so I was happy to stay at Manchester United. It is flattering when big clubs like Spurs come in for you, but, as long as our manager wants me I can see no reason to leave. I know that 1997-98 was a bad one for me, but that was largely due to injuries. Last season I felt much fitter and more confident. I wanted to repeat my success of three years ago and I enjoyed making my mark."

NICKY BUTT "We've experienced barren seasons before when we lost out on the title to Blackburn and Arsenal. But the following seasons we reclaimed the championship. That was our aim from the start of last season. Whether people liked it or not, we had a very good side and one of our strengths was that we pulled together. It hurts the team as much as the fans to lose out. But at least we could draw on that experience and that was invaluable to us last season."

October GOAL HEAVEN!

Out-of-favour striker Teddy Sheringham insisted he was happy with United even though he was not in the regular starting eleven... United hit Danish champions Brondby for six in a successful European away day... Ryan Giggs kept the Manchester United fans happy when he hinted that he may stay at Old Trafford for the remainder of his career... Everton announced that their England Under-21 defender Michael Ball was not for sale after newspapers again linked him with a move to Old Trafford.

DWIGHT YORKE "I said at the time that I wouldn't be surprised if we won everything – every competition we entered, every game we played in, finishing second was a failure in our eyes. Obviously the Champions League was the one trophy to elude United for 30 years, and we desperately wanted to get hold of that trophy. But we wanted them all – the FA Cup and Premier League trophy too. I've never experienced a team so focused on winning."

TEDDY SHERINGHAM "The way I saw it then was that wherever you go from Manchester United you go downward. I didn't want to leave. It is the biggest and best club in Europe, maybe the world. And what a place to play your football! I came to United to win trophies. Things didn't go exactly to plan, but I saw that it wasn't too late then and I was still determined to be a success here."

1 CHAMPIONS LEAGUE QUALIFIER
WEDNESDAY AUGUST 12

MANCHESTER UNITED (1) 2
LKS LODZ (0) 0
Att: 50,906
GOALS: Giggs 16, Cole 81
United made light work of this early European game. Lodz were unable to cope with the pace of Giggs and Cole and it was only a matter of time before the Welsh winger scored the first. But a second was needed to settle nerves and Cole obliged with a header nine minutes from time.
TEAM: Schmeichel 7, Neville, G 7, Irwin 7, Johnsen 7, Stam 8, Keane 8, Beckham 8, Butt 7, Cole 7, Scholes 7 (sub 82 mins Solskjaer), ***Giggs 9**. Not used: May, Sheringham, Neville, P, Cruyff, Berg, Culkin. **Referee:** A Ouzonov (BUL) 7. **Bookings** Butt (foul, 25).
MATCH RATING ★★★

2 FA PREMIERSHIP
SATURDAY AUGUST 15

MANCHESTER UNITED (0) 2
LEICESTER CITY (1) 2
Att: 55,052
GOALS: Sheringham 79, Beckham 90
A pulsating game saw Leicester run United ragged early on and take the lead. United rallied but went 2-0 down with only 14 minutes left. Sheringham scored with his first touch after coming on and Beckham equalised with a great free-kick.
TEAM: Schmeichel 6, Neville, G 7 (sub 77 mins Sheringham), Irwin 7, Johnsen 7, Stam 5 (sub 46 mins Berg 6), ***Beckham 9**, Butt 6, Cole 6, Giggs 6, Keane 6, Scholes 6. Not used: May, Neville, P, Culkin. **Referee** NS Barry 7. **Bookings** Sheringham (violent conduct, 90).
MATCH RATING ★★★★★

3 FA PREMIERSHIP
SATURDAY AUGUST 22

WEST HAM UNITED (0) 0
MANCHESTER UNITED (0) 0
Att: 26,039
Neil Ruddock and Shaka Hislop grabbed all the attention at Upton Park thanks to their rock-solid defending which left Man. United still looking for their first Premiership win of the season.
TEAM: Schmeichel 7, Neville, G 6 (sub 51 mins Neville, P 7), Irwin 7, Johnsen 7, Beckham 7, Butt 7, Cole 6 (sub 69 mins Sheringham 6), Giggs 8, ***Keane 9**, Yorke 7, Berg 8. Not used: May, Scholes, Culkin. **Referee** P Jones 7. **Bookings** Johnsen (foul, 52).
MATCH RATING ★★★

4 FA PREMIERSHIP
WEDNESDAY SEPTEMBER 9

MANCHESTER UNITED (2) 4
CHARLTON ATHLETIC (1) 1
Att: 55,147
GOALS: Solskjaer 38, 63 Yorke 45, 48
The promised demonstration by United fans against the possible £625 million takeover by Rupert Murdoch was all forgotten. In a superb performance, unbeaten Charlton took the lead but United stormed back, inspired by their new strike partnership of Yorke and Solskjaer to win easily.
TEAM: Schmeichel 7, Irwin 7 (sub 57 mins Berg 7), Johnsen 8, Stam 7, Beckham 8, Neville, P 8, Blomqvist 7, Keane 7, Scholes 7, ***Yorke 9** (sub 68 mins Sheringham 6), Solskjaer 8 (sub 68 mins Cole 6). Not used: van der Gouw, Wilson. **Referee** PA Durkin 7. **Bookings** None
MATCH RATING ★★★★★

5 CHAMPIONS LEAGUE QUALIFIER
WEDNESDAY AUGUST 26

LKS LODZ (0) 0
MANCHESTER UNITED (0) 0
Att: 8,000
United progressed to the group stages after a comfortable second leg. The Poles came close to scoring after 40 seconds when Niznik's 25 yarder dropped inches wide. But from then on United were in control.
TEAM: Schmeichel 6, Irwin 7, Neville, P 8, Johnsen 7, Stam 7, Keane 8, ***Beckham 8**, Butt 8, Sheringham 7, Scholes 7, Giggs 7 (sub 65 mins Solskjaer 7). Not used: Cole, Cruyff, Brown, May, van der Gouw. **Referee** C Graziano (ITA) 7. **Bookings** Beckham (foul, 31).
MATCH RATING ★★

6 FA PREMIERSHIP
SATURDAY SEPTEMBER 12

MANCHESTER UNITED (1) 2
COVENTRY CITY (0) 0
Att: 55,193
GOALS: Yorke 21 Johnsen 48
United did enough to beat a Coventry team who seldom troubled their opponents. Yorke scored his third goal in two games to put United ahead. The game was all but over two minutes after the interval when Ronny Johnsen scored their second.
TEAM: Schmeichel 7, Neville, G 7, ***Johnsen 8** (sub 90 mins Berg), Stam 7, Beckham 7 (sub 78 mins Blomqvist), Giggs 6 (sub 78 mins Blomqvist), Neville, P 7, Keane 7, Scholes 7, Yorke 7, Solskjaer 7. Not used: Cole, van der Gouw. **Referee** UD Rennie 5. **Bookings** Beckham (foul, 62); Yorke (dissent, 62).
MATCH RATING ★★★

7 CHAMPIONS LEAGUE GROUP D
WEDNESDAY SEPTEMBER 16

MANCHESTER UNITED (2) 3
BARCELONA (0) 3
Att: 53,601
GOALS: Giggs 17, Scholes 24, Beckham 64
Two up at half time, United conceded a point to an inspired Barcelona. It was in midfield that United lost it in the second half as Keane tired. For the last 20 minutes United played with ten men after Butt's dismissal for handling a goalbound shot.
TEAM: Schmeichel 6, Neville, G 6, Irwin 6 (sub 79 mins Neville, P 6), Stam 7, ***Beckham 9**, Giggs 8 (sub 84 mins Blomqvist), Keane 5, Scholes 6, Yorke 7, Solskjaer 6 (sub 55 mins Butt 6), Berg 6. Not used: van der Gouw, May, Cole, Sheringham. **Referee** S Brasci (ITA) 6. **Bookings** None. **Sending Off** Butt (handball, 70).
MATCH RATING ★★★★

8 FA PREMIERSHIP
SUNDAY SEPTEMBER 20

ARSENAL (2) 3
MANCHESTER UNITED (0) 0
Att: 38,142
Arsenal re-established themselves as favourites for the title with their fourth victory over United in under a year. Two first-half goals gave The Gunners a cushion and any hopes of a United comeback faded with the dismissal of Butt for a foul on the goal-bound Patrick Vieira.
TEAM: ***Schmeichel 7**, Neville, G 6, Irwin 6, Stam 6, Beckham 7, Butt 6, Giggs 6, Blomqvist 5, Keane 6, Yorke 5, Berg 6. Not used: Neville, P, Cruyff, van der Gouw, Scholes, Solskjaer. **Referee** GP Barber 6. **Bookings** Keane (foul, 8), Neville, G, (foul, 43), Scholes (foul, 57). **Sending Off** Butt (foul, 61).
MATCH RATING ★★★★

9 FA PREMIERSHIP
THURSDAY SEPTEMBER 24

MANCHESTER UNITED (1) 2
LIVERPOOL (0) 0
Att: 55,181
GOALS: Irwin 19 penalty, Scholes 79
It was vintage Manchester United following the debacle at Highbury just four days earlier, as The Red Devils dominated the first half, taking the lead through a Denis Irwin penalty. Liverpool came into the game more after the break but United appeared to get a second wind and finished by far the stronger with Scholes' tremendous strike securing the points. Gary Neville was a outstanding at the back alongside Jaap Stam in a very passionate game.
TEAM: Schmeichel 8, ***Neville G 10,** Irwin 8, Stam 9, Beckham 6, Giggs 6, Neville, P 8, Keane 9, Scholes 9 (sub 88 mins Butt), Yorke 6, Solskjaer 7(sub 69 mins Cole 7). Not used: Blomqvist, van der Gouw, Berg. **Referee** SJ Lodge 6. **Bookings** Giggs (foul, 24), Neville, P, (foul, 34), Stam (foul, 77), Scholes (foul, 79)
MATCH RATING ★★★★★

10 CHAMPIONS LEAGUE GROUP D
WEDNESDAY SEPTEMBER 30

BAYERN MUNICH (1) 2
MANCHESTER UNITED (1) 2
Att: 53,000
GOALS: Yorke 29, Scholes 49
United again squandered Champions League points by failing to keep their concentration for 90 minutes. Much the more accomplished side, throughout the game, particularly in midfield, United had the game under control until the dying minutes when Schmeichel took leave of his senses and the Germans drew level.
TEAM: Schmeichel 6, Irwin 7, Neville, P 6, Neville, G 7, Stam 8, Keane 7, ***Scholes 9**, Beckham 8, Blomqvist 7(sub 69 mins Cruyff 7), Sheringham 7, Yorke 8. Not used: van der Gouw, Berg, May, Brown, Solskjaer, Cole
Referee M Batta (FRA) 7. **Bookings** Beckham (foul,39), Cruyff (foul, 74).
MATCH RATING ★★★★

11 FA PREMIERSHIP
SATURDAY OCTOBER 3

SOUTHAMPTON (0) 0
MANCHESTER UNITED (1) 3
Att: 15,251
GOALS: Yorke 11, Cole 59, Cruyff 74
United strolled to victory at The Dell. as Saints remained bottom of the Premiership having lost seven out of their eight matches. Southampton made a game of it for an hour but once Andy Cole had added to Dwight Yorke's opener, the match really ceased to be a meaningful contest.
TEAM: van der Gouw 6, Neville, P 7, Stam 6, Neville, G 7, Irwin 7 (sub 78 mins Brown), Beckham 6, ***Keane 8,** Butt 7, Yorke 6 (sub 72 mins Cruyff), Cole 7, Blomqvist 6 (sub 72 mins Sheringham). Not used: Berg, Solskjaer. **Referee** DR Elleray 7. **Booking** Keane (foul, 63).
MATCH RATING ★★★

12 FA PREMIERSHIP
SATURDAY OCTOBER 17

MANCHESTER UNITED (2) 5
WIMBLEDON (1) 1
Att: 55,265
GOALS: Cole18, 87, Giggs 45, Beckham 48, Yorke 53.
United turned in a five-star performance against The Dons. It could have been more but for the woodwork and goalkeeper Neil Sullivan keeping the score down. Andy Cole opened the scoring for United, but Jason Euell equalised against the run of play, before Ryan Giggs restored the advantage in first-half stoppage time. The Red Devils took total control and completely rolled over Wimbledon over after the break.
TEAM: van der Gouw 7, Neville, G 8, Stam 6, Beckham 8 (sub 58 mins Cruyff 7), Cole 8, Giggs 8 (sub 66 mins Scholes 6), Neville, P 8 (sub 73 mins Curtis), Blomqvist 8, Keane 8, Yorke 8, ***Brown 9.** Not used: Solskjaer, Berg. **Referee** GS Willard 7. **Bookings** Stam (foul, 54).
MATCH RATING ★★★★★

13 CHAMPIONS LEAGUE GROUP D
WEDNESDAY OCTOBER 21

BRONDBY (1) 2
MANCHESTER UNITED (3) 6
Att: 40,530
GOALS: Giggs 2, 21, Cole 28, Keane 55, Yorke 59, Solskjaer 62
Schmeichel made a hero's return to his former club, but despite him having to twice pick the ball out of his net, United totally demolished an awe-struck Brondby who were never in the contest. Ryan Giggs put The Reds two up after just 21 minutes and after that it was a question of how many Manchester United would score against the hopelessly outclassed Danes.
TEAM: Schmeichel 6, Brown 8, Neville, P 8, Neville, G 7, Stam 8, Keane 8, Scholes 7, Blomqvist 8, Cole 8 (sub 60 mins Solskjaer 8), Yorke 7(sub 65 mins Wilson 7), ***Giggs 9** (sub 60 mins Cruyff 7). Not used: Berg, van der Gouw, Clegg, Curtis. **Referee** VM Pereira (POR) 7. **Bookings** None.
MATCH RATING ★★★

THE DREAM TREBLE!
THE PREMIERSHIP

DWIGHT YORKE SUPER STRIKER!

United deemed that it was the lack of firepower that cost them the Premiership title. After a long chase, a £12.6 million fee was agreed for Aston Villa striker Dwight Yorke. The huge transfer fee was questioned but 29 goals told its own tale and a first ever treble was in the bag for United. If you had to pick out his most vital strike of the season, it would probably be the goal he got in the European Cup semi-final against Juventus. United had gone 2-0 down early on, but they rallied to equalise before the break and Yorke scored a brilliantly controlled header.

November END OF AN ERA!

United sealed a deal with Royal Antwerp to use the Belgian club as a feeder outfit. They agreed to loan up-and-coming players to Antwerp who in turn will give them experience in the first team... Alex Ferguson tracked Croatian international midfielder Silvio Maric, available then for a fee of around £4 million... Peter Schmeichel had an off-day as Sheffield Wednesday recorded a 3-1 win over United, ending their impressive 12 game unbeaten run... The Danish 'keeper then shocked the world when he announced his decision to quit the club at the end of the season. European clubs got out their chequebooks hoping to secure his services for the following season... Barcelona hold United to another draw in the return match at the Nou Camp – again an enthralling 3-3 tie... Young defender Wes Brown signed a new four-year deal which will net him up to £2 million... Leeds were beaten 3-2 in a thriller at Old Trafford.

PETER SCHMEICHEL "I was enjoying the game as much as ever but it was getting harder to keep pace. I need to train more than I have ever had to and in order to prepare myself properly. I need more time between games than I was getting in England. I made my decision at the start of the season because two games a week all season was just too hard. It was a very tough decision to make, because, as I always said, United is the ultimate place to play."

ALEX FERGUSON "We gave away some bad goals in Barcelona, I suppose we had to be satisfied with the draw. From the moment Yorke scored, both sides always looked like scoring. It was the sort of game that stretches coaches' nerves to the limit. We were always a threat, which is good when you face a challenge like playing in Barcelona. But to come to the Nou Camp and score three goals was a satisfying performance. Our front players were superb and they could've scored more."

December ALL CHANGE!

Assistant manager Brian Kidd announced he was leaving Old Trafford to take the vacant manager's job at Blackburn Rovers... A lacklustre 1-1 home draw with German club Bayern Munich saw United qualify for the knockout stage of the Champions League, although the fans didn't realise they'd qualified at the end of the match... Dutch

Inspirational captain Roy Keane grabbed some vital goals.

Henning Berg keeps close tabs on Inter Milan striker Ronaldo.

Beckham is as at home on the catwalks as he is on the pitch.

The 'smiling assassin' proved his doubters wrong with 29 goals.

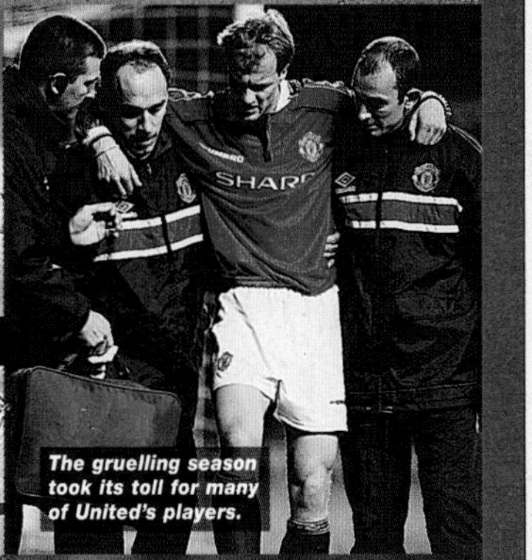

The gruelling season took its toll for many of United's players.

The work is never over for Manchester United's superstars.

A dream title-winning send off at Old Trafford for Peter Schmeichel.

international Patrick Kluivert said he wanted to play for United one day, although there was no official interest in signing him from United... Teenager Jonathan Greening was tipped by boss Alex Ferguson to break into the first team... United moved to the top of the Premiership for the first time that season following a disappointing 2-2 draw at a revitalised Tottenham... Bryan Robson's Middlesbrough recorded a superb 3-2 win at Old Trafford. It was United's first defeat at home in the league for nine months.

BRIAN KIDD "There was only one reason I left and that was in order to pursue my career as a football manager. I served a magnificent institution for over eight years as assistant manager and I would like to think that during that time I contributed in some small way to the success on the field. I think you can leave it too late and I didn't want to die wondering. My departure was entirely amicable and United had my best wishes for success in the future. I wanted them to go on to win the European Cup, but that's a chapter in my life which is now firmly closed and my devotions now are to Blackburn Rovers."

ROY KEANE "We didn't mind who we played in the quarter-finals of the European Cup to be honest. Everybody was capable of beating each other, but we knew we were capable of going all the way. It was great for the club to reach that stage for the third year in a row, but obviously we knew the quarter- and semi-finals were no good to us unless we won the trophy. We always need to win trophies, especially the European Cup – that's what counts. But when you look at the sides that qualified, there were many quality teams in there. Thankfully it wasn't us looking over our shoulders and I think a few teams wanted to avoid playing Manchester United."

January CUP FEVER!

United beat Middlesbrough 3-1 in the FA Cup and gain revenge for their home defeat a month earlier... Roy Keane reportedly threatened to quit Old Trafford unless he was given a new contract worth £40,000 a week... Cameroon international transfer target Marc Vivien Foe moved to West Ham after United pulled the plug on a £4 million deal... Dwight Yorke scored his first hat-trick for the club in the 6-2 thrashing of Leicester... In one of the most exciting games of the season, United

14 FA PREMIERSHIP
SATURDAY OCTOBER 24

DERBY COUNTY	**(0) 1**
MANCHESTER UNITED	**(0) 1**

Att: 30,867
GOAL: Cruyff 85
United were never allowed to settle and were thankful for some wayward finishing from their hosts. Only a desperate final flurry prevented them from suffering their second defeat of the season.
TEAM: Schmeichel 7, Neville, G 6 (sub 81 mins Scholes), Stam 8, Beckham 7, Butt 6 (sub 81 mins Blomqvist), Cole 7, Giggs 6 (sub 81 mins Cruyff), Neville, P 7, Keane 7, Yorke 7, ***Brown 8.** Not used: van der Gouw, Berg. **Referee** PA Durkin 7. **Bookings** Cole (dissent, 44), Neville, G (handball, 76), Beckham (foul, 90).
MATCH RATING ★★★

15 LEAGUE CUP ROUND THREE
WEDNESDAY OCTOBER 28

MANCHESTER UNITED	**(0) 2**
BURY	**(0) 0**

AET (90 mins 0-0)
Att: 52,495
GOALS: Solskjaer 106, Nevland 115
In a test of endurance both sides slugged it out in dreadful weather. United fielded a side more suited to a reserve match and found defence-minded Bury a tough nut to crack.
TEAM: van der Gouw 7, May 6, Neville, P 8, ***Curtis 9**, Cruyff 7, Solskjaer 7, Berg 6, Clegg 7 (sub 70 mins Scholes 6). Mulryne 7 (sub 46 mins Nevland 7), Wilson (sub 70 mins Scholes 6), Greening 7. Not used: Neville, G, Cooke. **Referee** KW Burge 8 **Bookings** May (foul, 84).
MATCH RATING ★

16 FA PREMIERSHIP
SATURDAY OCTOBER 31

EVERTON	**(1) 1**
MANCHESTER UNITED	**(2) 4**

Att: 40,079
GOALS: Yorke 14, Short 23 (og), Cole 59, Blomqvist 64
United's unbeaten October run continued with a 4-1 win at Goodison. Goals from Yorke and an own goal from Short shattered Everton's resistance and a Ferguson headed goal provided little consolation. Once United had extended their lead through Cole, Everton never recovered and their defence was constantly run ragged by a United team who added a fourth through Blomqvist.
TEAM: Schmeichel 6, Neville, G 7, Stam 6, Beckham 6, Cole 7, Neville, P 6, (sub 67 mins Irwin 6), ***Blomqvist 9,** Keane 8, Scholes 7, Yorke, Brown 7. Not used: Cruyff, van der Gouw, Solskjaer, Berg. **Referee** P Jones 5. **Bookings** Keane (foul, 8), Neville, G, (foul, 43), Scholes (foul, 57).
MATCH RATING ★★★★

17 CHAMPIONS LEAGUE GROUP D
WEDNESDAY NOVEMBER 4

MANCHESTER UNITED	**(4) 5**
BRONDBY	**(0) 0**

Att: 53,250
GOALS: Beckham 7, Cole 13, Neville, P 16, Yorke 28, Scholes 62.
Before kick-off the Brondby players watched as United warmed up by peppering shots at goal and little changed when the game started. Alex Ferguson rested key players, although United should have doubled this scoreline.
TEAM: Schmeichel 7, Irwin 7, Neville, G 7, Stam 8, Neville, P 7 (sub 32 mins Brown 7), ***Beckham 9**, Scholes 7, Keane 7, Blomqvist 8 (sub 46 mins Cruyff 6), Yorke 9, Cole 8 (sub 55 mins Solskjaer 6). Not used: van der Gouw, Butt, Johnsen, Curtis. **Referee** L Michel (SVK) 7. **Bookings** None.
MATCH RATING ★★★★

18 FA PREMIERSHIP
SUNDAY NOVEMBER 8

MANCHESTER UNITED	**(0) 0**
NEWCASTLE UNITED	**(0) 0**

Att: 55,174
The Magpies never allowed United to settle into their passing game as The Red Devils' goal glut ground to a halt. Too many of Fergie's men were below par after their latest European adventure, but credit must go to Newcastle players for their tremendous workrate.
TEAM: Schmeichel 7, ***Neville, G 9,** Irwin 8, Stam 8, Beckham 5, Cole 5, Blomqvist 5 (sub 88 mins Solskjaer), Keane 6, Scholes 6, Yorke 4, Brown 6 (sub 58 mins Johnsen 6 (sub 83 mins Butt)). Not used: Cruyff, van der Gouw. **Referee** SW Dunn 6. **Bookings** Stam 33 (foul, 33), Blomqvist (foul, 54), Beckham (foul, 61).
MATCH RATING ★

19 LEAGUE CUP ROUND FOUR
WEDNESDAY NOVEMBER 11

MANCHESTER UNITED	**(0) 2**
NOTTINGHAM FOREST	**(0) 1**

Att: 37,337
GOALS: Solskjaer 57, 60
Ole Gunnar Solskjaer scored both of United's goals in the space of three minutes having been put through by Jordi Cruyff on both occasions. Steve Stone was rewarded for a fine game with a superb strike for Villa.
TEAM: van der Gouw 7, Clegg 6, Curtis 6, May 6 (sub 46 mins Wallwork 6), Berg 7, Wilson 6, Greening 6, Butt 7, ***Solskjaer 8,** Cruyff 7, Mulryne 6. Not used: Notman, Nevland, Teather, Ford. **Referee** RJ Harris 7. **Bookings** Curtis (foul, 72), Mulryne (foul, 84).
MATCH RATING ★★

20 FA PREMIERSHIP
SATURDAY NOVEMBER 14

MANCHESTER UNITED	**(2) 3**
BLACKBURN ROVERS	**(0) 2**

Att: 55,198
GOALS: Scholes 31, 58, Yorke 44.
United were flattered by their 2-0 half-time lead with The Red Devils only coming to life after half an hour. When Paul Scholes made it 3-0, it looked all over but Blackburn stormed back to reduce United's advantage to one goal. United just did enough to prevent the ultimate embarrassment of throwing away the points, largely thanks to the appearance of Roy Keane to steady the side.
TEAM: Schmeichel 6, Neville, G 8, ***Stam 9**, Beckham 7, Butt 7, Cole 6, Neville, P 7, Curtis 7, Blomqvist 7 (sub 67 mins Solskjaer7), Scholes 8 (sub 63 mins Cruyff (sub 81 mins Keane)),Yorke 8. Not used: Irwin, Berg. **Referee** MD Reed 6. **Bookings** Scholes (foul, 33), Stam (foul, 45)
MATCH RATING ★★★★★

21 FA PREMIERSHIP
SATURDAY NOVEMBER 21

SHEFFIELD WEDNESDAY	**(1) 3**
MANCHESTER UNITED	**(1) 1**

Att: 39,475
GOAL: Cole 29
Dejected United left Hillsborough after another defeat thanks to a couple of blunders and the marksmanship of Niclas Alexandersson. The Old Trafford giants have won just one of their last nine matches at Wednesday and never looked like improving their record as the hard-working Owls refused to be over-awed by the Manchester millionaires and battled hard for 90 minutes
TEAM: Schmeichel 6, Neville, G 6, Irwin 7 (sub 65 mins Brown 6), Stam 7, Beckham 6, ***Cole 8,** Neville, P 6, Blomqvist 6 (sub 83mins Butt 6), Keane 6, (sub 83 mins Solskjaer), Scholes 6, Yorke 6. Not used: van der Gouw, Berg. **Referee** D Elleray 7. **Booking** Scholes (unsporting behaviour, 45).
MATCH RATING ★★★★

22 CHAMPIONS LEAGUE GROUP D
WEDNESDAY NOVEMBER 25

BARCELONA	**(1) 3**
MANCHESTER UNITED	**(1) 3**

Att: 67,648
GOALS: Yorke 25, Cole 53, Yorke 68.
A treat was dished up at the Nou Camp as Barcelona, realising only victory would suffice, attempted to outscore United. Six goals, defensive errors and chances galore saw the points shared, with Schmeichel both hero and villain.
TEAM: Schmeichel 9, Neville, G 8, Irwin 6, Stam 7, Beckham 8 (sub 81 mins Butt), Brown 7, Blomqvist 7, Keane 7, Cole 8, ***Yorke 9**, Scholes 7. Not used: van der Gouw, Neville, P, Solskjaer, Berg, Curtis, Wilson. **Referee** G Benko (AUT) 7. **Bookings** Blomqvist (unsporting behaviour, 14), Irwin (foul, 47), Keane (foul, 43), Scholes (foul, 50).
MATCH RATING ★★★★★

23 FA PREMIERSHIP
SUNDAY NOVEMBER 29

MANCHESTER UNITED	**(1) 3**
LEEDS UNITED	**(1) 2**

Att: 55,172
GOALS: Solskjaer 45, Keane 46, Butt 77.
A pulsating Roses clash saw the action swing from end to end with attacks well on top against two less-than-convincing defences. The Yorkshiremen lost Nigel Martyn at half-time after he was injured making a brilliant save to keep out Nicky Butt's 28th-minute header, and Ryan Giggs made a welcome return as a substitute.
TEAM: Schmeichel 6, Neville, G 6, ***Stam 9** (sub 77 mins Berg), Butt 7, Cole 7 (sub 65 mins Giggs 6), Neville, P 5, Keane 7, Scholes 7 (sub 72 mins Sheringham), Yorke 7, Solskjaer 7, Brown 6. Not used: van der Gouw, Curtis. **Referee** G Poll 6. **Booking** Neville, P (foul, 71).
MATCH RATING ★★★★★

24 LEAGUE CUP QUARTER-FINAL
WEDNESDAY DECEMBER 2

TOTTENHAM HOTSPUR	**(0) 3**
MANCHESTER UNITED	**(0) 1**

Att: 35, 702
GOAL: Sheringham 70
David Ginola was again the inspiration as Spurs marched to just one step away from Wembley. Armstrong showed exquisite finishing with his goals and Ginola got a deserved late killer strike.
TEAM: van der Gouw 7, Johnsen 6, Butt 6 (sub 71 mins Notman), ***Sheringham 8,** Giggs 7, Neville, P 7, Curtis 6 (sub 87 mins Beckham), Solskjaer 7, Clegg 6, Berg 6, Greening 6 (sub 87mins Blomqvist). Not used: Culkin, Wallwork. **Referee** P Jones 7. **Bookings** None
MATCH RATING ★★★★

25 FA PREMIERSHIP
SATURDAY DECEMBER 5

ASTON VILLA	**(0) 1**
MANCHESTER UNITED	**(0) 1**

Att: 39,241
GOAL: Scholes 47
Premiership leaders Aston Villa had the slight edge throughout this match at Villa Park, but United held firm to take home a point. Villa should have been two ahead before the interval but The Red Devils opened the scoring themselves just after the break, before live-wire Villa striker Julian Joachim hit a fortunate but deserved equaliser.
TEAM: Schmeichel 6, ***Brown 8,** Stam 6, Neville, G 6, Irwin 6, Beckham 5, Keane 7, Blomqvist 6 (sub 46 mins Giggs 6), Scholes 7, Cole 6 (sub 70 mins Butt 6), Yorke 6. Not used: Johnsen, Sheringham, van der Gouw. **Referee** MA Riley 6. **Bookings** Neville, G (foul, 62), Yorke (dissent, 76), Irwin (foul, 77).
MATCH RATING ★★★

26 CHAMPIONS LEAGUE GROUP D
WEDNESDAY DECEMBER 9

MANCHESTER UNITED	**(1) 1**
BAYERN MUNICH	**(0) 1**

Att: 54,434
GOAL: Keane 43
United moved into the quarter-finals of the European Cup as one of the two best runners-up from the league stages. They took the lead with a superb Keane goal before half-time, but Bayern equalised in the second half. Jaap Stam was again outstanding in defence for United and Samuel Kuffour held firm Bayern Munich's shaky back-line.
TEAM: Schmeichel 6, Neville, G 6, Irwin 6 (sub 46 mins Johnsen 7), *Stam 9, Beckham 8, Cole 7, Giggs 7, Keane 7, Scholes 8, Yorke 7 (sub 64 mins Butt 6), Brown 6. Not used: van der Gouw, Sheringham, Neville, P, Blomqvist, Berg. **Referee** D Jol (HOL) 7. **Bookings** None.
MATCH RATING ★★★★

THE DREAM TREBLE!
THE FA CUP

ROY KEANE NATURAL LEADER!

'Captain Fantastic', Roy was an inspirational figure throughout the whole campaign and was unlucky to not to feature more prominently in the crucial final 11 days of the season because of injury and suspension. Keane missed out on both the FA and European Cup Finals. If there is one player that United really miss when he's not in the starting line-up, it is Keane. It would be impossible to pick out one defining moment from his year, but he played the captain's role to pull a goal back for United against Juventus when they looked dead and buried.

made an amazing comeback when Yorke and Solskjaer dramatically snatched two goals in the last two minutes of the FA Cup fourth round epic to beat their old rivals Liverpool after trailing for 86 minutes to a Michael Owen goal.

OLE GUNNAR SOLSKJAER "How did I feel after my goal against Liverpool? Happy, excited, all sorts of emotions went through my mind. I love scoring goals, there is no better feeling. But to come on and score the winner in injury time was nice. With a few minutes left it looked like we might even go out of the competition, but then Dwight popped up to bring us level and my goal won the tie."

RYAN GIGGS "Individually, we had better players than we'd ever had, so it was up to us to turn it into a team performance. It is always hard when you bring in two or three players in the summer because it takes them a while to blend in. I always thought the best team I'd played in was the 1994 team, but I knew that potentially the 1999 side could be better."

February ON TOP FORM!

Dwight Yorke hit the best form of his career half way during the season. His double in the 8-1 caning of Nottingham Forest took his goal tally to nine in six days... Ole Gunnar Solskjaer set a United record in the same game, scoring four goals in 11 minutes after appearing again as a substitute.... Andy Cole netted his 100th Premier League goal in the drubbing and equalled David Herd's 37-year-old record after scoring in six successive games... Steve McClaren was named new assistant manager in succession to Brian Kidd after the hot favourite for the job, Preston's David Moyes, ruled himself out... David Beckham said that the way United were playing they had nothing to fear from any team... But despite that confidence Arsenal held them to a 1-1 draw at Old Trafford in the top-of-the-table clash.

OLE GUNNAR SOLSKJAER "It's not just about how well you perform, it's about how you fit in and how good an understanding you have with your partner. Andy Cole and Dwight Yorke have a good relationship on and off the pitch and that helps. It's a case of taking your chances when they come. Andy and Dwight worked brilliantly together and they were the first-choice strikers by right."

DAVID BECKHAM "There was a great deal of belief at this club and the desire to win could never

The greatest goal of all time? Giggs' wonder strike to beat Arsenal.

Scmeichs announced he was quitting and the search for a replacement began.

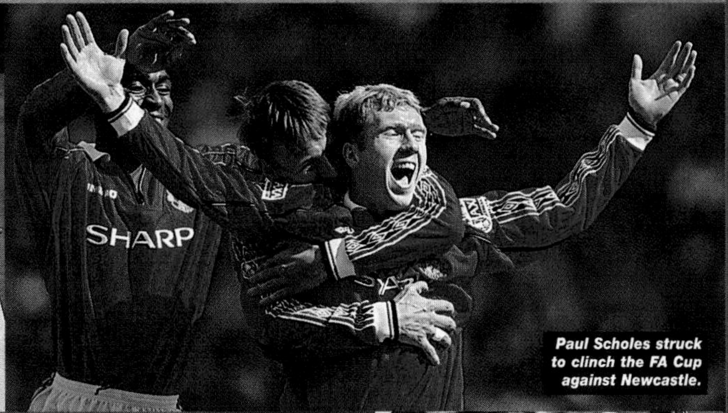

Paul Scholes struck to clinch the FA Cup against Newcastle.

Fergie with his super strikeforce of Andy Cole and Dwight Yorke.

FA Cup glory. Double sealed. Two down, one to go...

be faulted. We weren't just concentrating on one competition, we wanted to win the European Cup, the FA Cup and the league championship title. It was hard but I believed we could do it."

March MILAN MAULED!

Dwight Yorke netted twice as United took a 2-0 lead in the quarter-final first leg against Inter Milan... He repeated the feat by scoring twice as United progressed through to the FA Cup semi-finals at the expense of Chelsea... England star David Beckham scored his first league goal for six months in United's 3-1 win over Everton... Alex Ferguson shipped Jordi Cruyff out on loan to Celta Vigo for the rest of the season and Terry Cooke joined Manchester City... A 1-1 draw with Inter Milan in the second leg was enough to see United into the Champions League semi-finals.

ALEX FERGUSON "If you are to win competitions like that you have to beat big Italian teams along the way. It was a massive step forward for our club to come here and go through against an Italian side in their own back yard. We had lucky moments but we rode our luck and had chances to finish them off. It was the nature of this club to always make it as difficult for ourselves and the fans. I think I needed a triple bypass after that."

JAAP STAM "It was not us saying that we were favourite – it was other people who watched us in the competition who said it. But we just concentrated on our game like we always do. There was no team we would have rather have faced in the next round than Juventus. Whoever we played was going to be good so it didn't matter. It was just up to us to play to our strengths and we waited to see what happened."

April TRIUMPH IN TURIN!

Roy Keane told MATCH that winning the treble would be an impossible dream... After drawing 0-0 in the first FA Cup semi-final game with Arsenal, Man. United and Arsenal played out the best match of the season in the FA Cup semi-final replay at Villa Park. United played most of the game with just ten men, but managed to weather a barrage of Arsenal attacks to win the game 2-1 with Ryan Giggs scoring a wonder goal in extra time to put them through... United reach the Champions League Final after beating Juventus

27 FA PREMIERSHIP
SATURDAY DECEMBER 12

TOTTENHAM HOTSPUR (2) 2
MANCHESTER UNITED (0) 2
Att: 36,079
GOALS: **Solskjaer 10, 17**
Sol Campbell emerged as an unlikely hero for Spurs with two excellent late headed goals. United were electric at the start, stunning the home side with two strikes from Solskjaer but they were forced to make changes after Gary Neville's dismissal.
TEAM: Schmeichel 7, Neville, G 6, Johnsen 7, Stam 8, Beckham 8 , Butt 7, Sheringham 7 (sub 74 mins Cole), Giggs 8 (sub 87mins Blomqvist), Neville, P 7, Keane 8, ***Solskjaer 8** (sub 46 mins Berg 7). Not used: van der Gouw, Cruyff. **Referee** UD Rennie 8. **Bookings** Butt (foul, 9), Sheringham (dissent, 27), Neville G (foul, 29), Neville P, (foul, 33), Beckham (foul, 65), Johnsen (foul, 69).
MATCH RATING ★★★★

28 FA PREMIERSHIP
WEDNESDAY DECEMBER 16

MANCHESTER UNITED (1)1
CHELSEA (0)1
Att: 55,159
GOAL: **Cole 45**
A draw proved a fair outcome, with these two championship contenders producing some excellent technical football in a game that was more fascinating than exciting.
TEAM: Schmeichel 6, Neville, G 6, Irwin 7, ***Stam 9**, Butt 7, Cole 7, Blomqvist 5 (sub 77 mins Giggs), Keane 6, Scholes 8 (sub 85 mins Sheringham), Brown 8, Yorke 5 (sub 61 mins Beckham 5). Not used: Johnsen, Neville, P. **Referee** GP Barber 4. **Bookings** Brown (foul, 49), Neville, G (foul, 54).
MATCH RATING ★★★★

29 FA PREMIERSHIP
SATURDAY DECEMBER 19

MANCHESTER UNITED (0) 2
MIDDLESBROUGH (2) 3
Att: 55,152
GOALS: **Butt 62, Scholes 70**
A pulsating game saw United come back from the dead and almost snatch a point. The Red Devils were beaten by Boro at Old Trafford for the first time in 69 years. Ricard and Gordon scored before half-time and it appeared all over when Deane added another just before the hour, but United stormed back with Butt and Scholes reducing arrears, but to no avail.
TEAM: Schmeichel 5, Neville, P 5 (sub 78 mins Solskjaer), Irwin 5, Johnsen 5, Neville, G 5, Butt 7, Beckham 5 (sub 64 mins ***Scholes 8**), Keane 5, Giggs 6, Cole 7, Sheringham 6. Not used: Brown, Blomqvist, van der Gouw. **Referee** GS Willard 7. **Booking** Beckham (foul, 60).
MATCH RATING ★★★★

30 FA PREMIERSHIP
SATURDAY DECEMBER 26

MANCHESTER UNITED (1) 3
NOTTINGHAM FOREST (0) 0
Att: 55,216
GOALS: **Johnsen 28, 60, Giggs 62**
This defeat made it 16 games without a win for Forest. Ronny Johnsen opened the scoring and added another in the second half. But Forest were dead and buried by the time Ryan Giggs added a third. It was United's first win in seven games and first clean sheet in 12.
TEAM: Schmeichel 7, Irwin 7, ***Johnsen 9,** Beckham 7, Butt 7, Sheringham 7, Giggs 7 (sub 75 mins Blomqvist), Neville, P 7, Keane 7 (sub 69 mins Greening 7), Scholes 7 (sub 63 mins Solskjaer 7), Berg 7. Not used: van der Gouw, Brown. **Referee** JT Winter 7. **Bookings** Neville, P (foul, 29).
MATCH RATING ★★★

31 FA PREMIERSHIP
TUESDAY DECEMBER 29

CHELSEA (0) 0
MANCHESTER UNITED (0) 0
Att: 34,741
Manchester United's remarkable league record against Chelsea at Stamford Bridge continued. Chelsea dominated the first-half, with Norwegian striker Flo missing six chances. However, United consolidated in the second period.
TEAM: ***Schmeichel 8,** Neville, G 7, Irwin 7, Johnsen 7, Stam 7, Beckham 7, Butt 7, Cole 7, Giggs 7, Keane 7, Scholes 7 (sub 61 mins Sheringham 6). Not used: Neville, P, Blomqvist, van der Gouw, Berg. **Referee** MA Riley 7. **Booking** Cole (foul, 50).
MATCH RATING ★★★★★

32 FA CUP ROUND THREE
SATURDAY JANUARY 3

MANCHESTER UNITED (0) 3
MIDDLESBROUGH (0) 1
Att: 52,232
GOALS: **Cole 68, Irwin 82, Giggs 90**
United set up a mouth-watering fourth round home tie against Liverpool after an excellent second-half performance accounted for Middlesbrough. Townsend's early second-half goal put Boro ahead against the run of play. However, The Red Devils surged forward and Cole deservedly levelled. A controversial Irwin penalty decided the contest and Giggs' glorious third was the icing on the cake.
TEAM: Schmeichel 6, Brown 7 (sub 75 mins Neville, P), Irwin 8, ***Stam 9**, Berg 8, Giggs 7, Keane 8, Butt 8, Blomqvist 5 (sub 73 mins Solskjaer), Cole 8 (sub 84 mins Sheringham), Yorke 7. Not used: van der Gouw, Cruyff. **Referee** GP Barber 7. **Bookings** none.
MATCH RATING ★★★★★

33 FA PREMIERSHIP
SUNDAY JANUARY 10

MANCHESTER UNITED (2) 4
WEST HAM UNITED (0) 1
Att: 55,180
GOALS: **Yorke 10, Cole 40, 68, Solskjaer 80**
A power cut delayed kick-off at Old Trafford for 45 minutes but when play finally started, United proved light years ahead of The Hammers who barely mounted an assault on the United goal throughout the whole game. The Yorke and Cole double act was unstoppable and a late Solskjaer strike saw United home.
TEAM: van der Gouw 7, Irwin 8, Berg 8, Brown 8, (sub 77 mins Johnsen), Blomqvist 7, Keane 8 (sub 83 mins Cruyff), Butt 8 (sub 77 mins Solskjaer), ***Yorke 8,** Cole 7, Stam 8, Giggs 6. Not used: Culkin, Beckham. **Referee** MD Reed 7. **Bookings** None.
MATCH RATING ★★★★★

34 FA PREMIERSHIP
SATURDAY JANUARY 16

LEICESTER CITY (1) 2
MANCHESTER UNITED (1) 6
Att: 22,596
GOALS: **Yorke 10, 63, 84, Cole 49, 61, Stam 90**
Alex Ferguson's Red Devils were in irresistible form as they hit a plucky Leicester side for six, which included a hat-trick for in-form Dwight Yorke. Martin O'Neill had to make do with a team stripped of defensive linchpins Elliott, Sinclair and Impey, and star striker Heskey. United took just ten minutes to get into their stride.
TEAM: Schmeichel 7, Irwin 7, Brown 7 (sub 46 mins Neville, P 7), Berg 7, Stam 7, Keane 6, Beckham 7, Giggs 7, Blomqvist 8, Cole 8, ***Yorke 8.** Not used: van der Gouw, Johnsen, Scholes, Solskjaer. **Referee** SW Dunn 6. **Bookings** Keane (unsporting behaviour, 18), Blomqvist (foul, 74).
MATCH RATING ★★★★

35 FA CUP ROUND FOUR
SUNDAY JANUARY 24

MANCHESTER UNITED (0) 2
LIVERPOOL (0) 1
Att: 54, 591
GOALS: **Yorke 89, Solskjaer 90**
United pulled off a dramatic smash-and-grab raid after staring down the barrel of FA Cup elimination for most of the game. Two goals in two minutes at the end saw them overturn the two-goal advantage that Liverpool had held since their first attack.
TEAM: Schmeichel 6, Neville, G 6, Irwin 6 (sub 81 mins Solskjaer) Stam 7, Berg 7 (sub 81 mins Johnsen), Beckham 6 Butt 5 (sub 68 mins Scholes 7), Giggs 6, ***Keane 9**, Cole 6, Yorke 8. Not used: van der Gouw, Neville, P. **Referee** G Poll 7. **Bookings** Keane (foul, 68), Giggs (foul, 77), Scholes (foul, 90).
MATCH RATING ★★★★

36 FA PREMIERSHIP
SUNDAY JANUARY 31

CHARLTON (0) 0
MANCHESTER UNITED (0) 1
Att: 20,043
GOAL: **Yorke 89.**
United took advantage of results elsewhere to move to the top of the table following this narrow victory over struggling Charlton at The Valley. Yet it was a cruel blow for The Addicks who battled brilliantly and looked like gaining a deserved point until Dwight Yorke's last-minute winner.
TEAM: Schmeichel 6, Neville, G 6, Irwin 7, ***Stam 8,** Beckham 6 (sub 70 mins Solskjaer 6), Cole 6, Giggs 7, Keane 7, Yorke 6, Butt 6 (sub 82 mins Scholes), Berg 6. Not used: Johnsen, Neville, P, van der Gouw. **Referee** GS Willard 7. **Bookings** None.
MATCH RATING ★★★

37 FA PREMIERSHIP
WEDNESDAY FEBRUARY 3

MANCHESTER UNITED (0) 1
DERBY COUNTY (0) 0
Att: 55,174
GOAL: **Yorke 65**
Dwight Yorke's 19th goal of the season settled a game in which Derby proved a tough nut to crack for United's prolific strikeforce. The Rams' defence, superbly marshalled by Spencer Prior, kept United at bay until midway through the second half. United have now won six games on the trot to keep up their unbeaten record in 1999.
TEAM: Schmeichel 7, Neville, G 7, Irwin 7, Johnsen 7, ***Stam 9,** Butt 8, Keane 7, Giggs (sub 11 mins Blomqvist 7), Yorke 8, Scholes 8, Solskjaer 7. Not used: Neville, P, Cole, May, Beckham. **Referee** SJ Lodge 7. **Bookings** None.
MATCH RATING ★★★

38 FA PREMIERSHIP
SATURDAY FEBRUARY 6

NOTTINGHAM FOREST (1) 1
MANCHESTER UNITED (2) 8
Att: 30,025
GOALS: **Yorke 2, 67, Cole 7, 50 Solskjaer 80, 88, 90, 90**
After Forest's first win of 1999 against Everton, they could have done with a morale-boosting victory but instead they were utterly humiliated. Although United took an early lead, Forest countered well and were level terms seven minutes, before Cole replied to recapture the lead The second half was a different story as United took Forest apart with their quality of play.
TEAM: Schmeichel 8, Neville, G 7, Johnsen 7, Stam 7, Neville, P 6, ***Beckham 9,** Keane 7 (sub 72 mins Solskjaer), Scholes 7, Blomqvist 6 (sub 86 mins Butt), Cole 8, Yorke 8 (sub 72 mins Curtis). Not used: van der Gouw, May. **Referee** PE Alcock 5. **Bookings** Keane (foul, 37), Neville, P (foul, 81).
MATCH RATING ★★★★★

39 FA CUP ROUND FIVE
SATURDAY FEBRUARY 14

MAN UNITED (1) 1
FULHAM (0) 0
Att: 54,798
GOAL: **Cole 26**
Cole's 18th goal of the season decided a game which was never out of Fulham's reach. United started slowly but seemed well in control after Cole's opener. However, Keegan's Fulham stepped up a gear after the break and Salako missed a glorious opportunity to level.
TEAM: Schmeichel 7, Neville, G 7, Irwin 7 (sub 46 mins Greening 6), Stam 7, Beckham 6, Butt 7, ***Cole 8** (sub 88 mins Johnsen), Neville, P 7, Yorke 7, Solskjaer 6 (sub 68 mins Blomqvist 6), Berg 6. Not used: van der Gouw, May. **Referee** JT Winter 5. **Bookings** None
MATCH RATING ★★★

TEDDY SHERINGHAM GOAL HERO!

What a turn around for Teddy? He sparked a miraculous return at the end of the season after looking like he was on the way out of United. Out-of-form and out-of-luck on the injury front, things weren't going trell for him. Then just nine minutes into the FA Cup Final, he stepped off the bench and immediately opened the scoring. And with United entering injury time a goal down in the European Cup Final his vital touch got them level. Two minutes later he climbed to flick on a corner for Ole Gunnar Solskjaer to net the winner. Wow!

4-3 on aggregate in the semi-final. They looked dead and buried in the second leg, going 2-0 down in Turin, but Roy Keane rallied his troops to spark yet another sensational comeback with goals from Keane himself, Yorke and Cole. However, there was a downside as he and Paul Scholes were ruled out of the Final through suspension...

ROY KEANE "I still thought that to win all three major trophies, especially when it was the European Cup, FA Cup and the Premier League would take a miracle, but I suppose you should never say never. We were just taking each game as it came and were waiting to see what we'd have at the end of the season. But saying that, if I was a betting man I would have put a lot of money on it happening."

RONNY JOHNSEN "It was a little bit of magic from Ryan Giggs and that won us the game. We worked hard even after Roy Keane was sent off because we still thought we'd be able to get through and we did. It was an unbelievable game for us. The fans really got behind us and it was a really exciting game to watch and to play in. I have to say that we were a bit lucky as well. They also had some good chances but Giggsy pulled out the magic for us when it really mattered. It was a really great goal that won a really great game. "

May WINNING THE FINALS!

As the league season approached its climax, the old enemy, Liverpool, came back from a two goal deficit to hold United to a draw in a nail-biting encounter at the start of the month... Dutch goalkeeper Edwin van der Saar announced that he would love a move from Ajax to Old Trafford as Peter Schmeichel's replacement... United's draw at Ewood Park condemned former favourite Brian Kidd's Blackburn to relegation... Arsenal slipped up at Leeds, which meant that United went into the final day a point ahead of the 1998 champions... It takes another comeback, but United's 2-1 win over Spurs takes the Premier League title to Old Trafford for the fifth time in seven seasons and Arsenal ended up with nothing...

TEDDY SHERINGHAM "We could have ended up with nothing with a week of the season left to go and that would have been devastating, but once we got one trophy – the Premier League title – it calmed us down a little bit."

United became the only English club to achieve the League and Cup double on three occasions with a 2-0 win over Newcastle in the FA Cup Final. Man of the match Teddy Sheringham

Solskjaer strikes in injury time to cap an amazing comeback.

Over the moon. Peter Schmeichel leaves United on a high.

The crowd were stunned as United grabbed victory from the jaws of defeat.

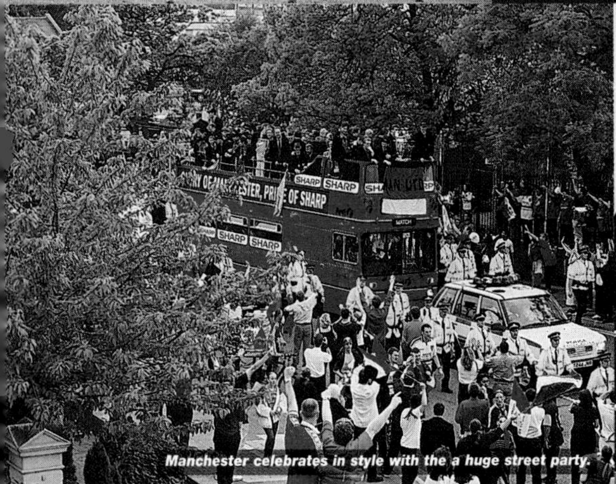

Manchester celebrates in style with the a huge street party.

It's all smiles as the team celebrate their stunning achievement.

scored the first goal just 90 seconds after coming on for the injured captain Roy Keane. Paul Scholes added a second to kill off any faint hopes Newcastle fans may have had.

PHIL NEVILLE "I was surprised by the reaction of people going into this game. It was as if they didn't think the FA Cup was important to us. That was nonsense. We were desperate to win the double again. Winning the double was our main aim at the start of the season."

DWIGHT YORKE "From the start of the season I maintained that we could go all the way and win the treble. If ever a club deserved to re-write the history books, this club did. We could not contemplate what it was like to lose. We didn't have to deal with that feeling and winning was just inbuilt in our side."

With the almost the whole of Britain behind them, Alex Ferguson's men went into the European Cup Final at Barcelona's Nou Camp Stadium. Early on United went behind to a Bayern free-kick. As time drew on, it looked like this was one match where they wouldn't make a comeback. Then supersub Teddy Sheringham popped up to equalise in injury time. The Bayern fans looked sick, but it got worse for them as Ole Gunnar Solskjaer snatched a last-gasp winner moments later… United returned to Manchester the next day for an open-top bus parade around the city to show off their three trophies and the city held one of the biggest parties it has ever had.

TEDDY SHERINGHAM "It was a brilliant week. Up to that point in my career all I had to show was a Division Two winners medal with Millwall, but after that all those people who kept singing those stupid songs about me had to shut-up. If they want to see my medals, now they can."

OLE GUNNAR SOLSKJAER "I had said earlier that it would be my night. I don't know why. I just woke up in the middle of the night and I got the feeling I would score the winning goal. I wouldn't swap it for anything. It means when people talk about the European Cup, they will remember this goal as much as I do."

DAVID BECKHAM "It was nice that Paul Scholes and Roy Keane came out at the end. It was hard for them and it must have been nice to hear the fans chanting their names because they deserved a great deal of credit. Without Roy Keane in Italy, I'm not sure that we would have beaten Juventus. And Scholesy was brilliant for us all season!"

40 FA PREMIERSHIP
WEDNESDAY FEBRUARY 17

MANCHESTER UNITED (0) 1
ARSENAL (0) 1
Att: 55,171
GOAL: Cole 60
United remain top of the table but failed to lay their recent Arsenal bogey to rest. The Red Devils blew a golden first-half opportunity when Dwight Yorke missed a penalty. Nicolas Anelka's early second-half strike was cancelled out by Andy Cole as United's 100 per cent start to 1999 ended.
TEAM: Schmeichel 6, Neville, G 7, ***Neville, P 8,** Johnsen 6, Stam 6, Beckham 7, Keane 6, Butt 5 (sub 78 mins Giggs), Cole 7, Yorke 5, Blomqvist 5 (sub 62 mins Scholes 6). Not used: van der Gouw, Solskjaer, Brown. **Referee** GS Willard 7. **Bookings** Yorke (foul, 33), Keane (foul, 53).
MATCH RATING ★★★★★

41 FA PREMIERSHIP
SATURDAY FEBRUARY 20

COVENTRY CITY (0) 0
MANCHESTER UNITED (0) 1
Att: 22,596
GOAL: Giggs 78
Ryan Giggs scored the goal which separated the teams but Manchester United had a late scare when Coventry almost grabbed a stoppage-time equaliser. Giggs gave the league leaders the advantage late on in the game, but in the last few seconds Coventry striker Darren Huckerby got the ball around Peter Schmeichel only to see Henning Berg scramble it away before it could cross the goal-line.
TEAM: Schmeichel 7, Neville, G 7, Irwin 6, Johnsen 6, Stam 7 (sub 46 mins Berg 6), ***Beckham 8,** Giggs 7, Keane 7, Scholes 6, Cole 5 (sub 73 mins Solskjaer), Yorke 6 (sub 85 mins Neville, P). Not used: Blomqvist, van der Gouw. **Referee** DJ Gallagher 6. **Bookings** Scholes (foul, 12), Stam (foul, 20), Cole (foul, 44).
MATCH RATING ★★★

42 FA PREMIERSHIP
SATURDAY FEBRUARY 27

MANCHESTER UNITED (0) 2
SOUTHAMPTON (0) 1
Att: 55,316
GOALS: Keane 79, Yorke 83
United limbered up for their Champions League clash against Inter Milan with an expected victory, but it was hardly the pre-European preparation Alex Ferguson was hoping for. The Red Devils were a pale shadow of the side which has looked so exciting all season and only late goals from captain Roy Keane and Dwight Yorke spared their blushes.
TEAM: Schmeichel 7, Neville, G 7, ***Neville, P 8** (sub 78 mins Irwin), Johnsen 7, Berg 7, Beckham 8, Scholes 5, Butt 5 (sub 46 mins Keane 7), Solskjaer 5 (sub 68 mins Cole 6), Giggs 4, Yorke 6. Not used: Brown, Blomqvist. **Referee** P Jones 6. **Bookings** None.
MATCH RATING ★★

43 EUROPEAN CHAMPIONS CUP QUARTER-FINAL FIRST LEG
WEDNESDAY MARCH 3

MANCHESTER UNITED (2) 2
INTER MILAN (0) 0
Att: 54,430
GOALS: Yorke 6, 45
A five-star performance saw United outclass Inter Milan. Dwight Yorke took his goals tally to 23 for the season with two headers. Peter Schmeichel made magnificent saves from Zamorano and Ventola. United's defence was outstanding throughout, with Henning Berg making an unbelievable clearance off his line from Colonnese in stoppage time.
TEAM: Schmeichel 8, Neville, G 8, Irwin 8, Johnsen 7 (sub 46 mins Berg 8), Stam 8, ***Beckham 9,** Cole 8, Giggs 8, Keane 8, Scholes 7 (sub 69 mins Butt 7), Yorke 8. Not used: van der Gouw, Neville, P, Blomqvist, Solskjaer, Brown. **Referee** H Krug (GER) 6. **Bookings** Keane (unsporting behaviour, 26), Irwin (foul, 38), Scholes (foul, 48).
MATCH RATING ★★★★★

44 FA CUP QUARTER-FINAL
SUNDAY MARCH 7

MANCHESTER UNITED (0) 0
CHELSEA (0) 0
Att: 54,587
A much-awaited FA Cup tie failed to live up to expectations and ended goalless. Chelsea produced a brave rearguard performance after Di Matteo was sent off before half-time. Ferguson left Yorke and Cole out of the starting line-up but was eventually forced to throw them into the fray.
TEAM: Schmeichel 7, ***Neville, G 9,** Irwin 7, Berg 8, Brown 8, Neville, P 7 (sub 73 mins Yorke), Beckham 7, Keane 7, Blomqvist 6 (sub 82 mins Cole), Scholes 8, Solskjaer 6 (sub 82 mins Sheringham). Not used: van der Gouw, Curtis. **Referee** PA Durkin 4. **Bookings** Keane (dissent, 10), Scholes (foul, 43), Scholes (foul, 43). **Sending-off** Scholes (second bookable offence, 86)
MATCH RATING ★★

45 FA CUP QUARTER-FINAL REPLAY
WEDNESDAY MARCH 10

CHELSEA (0) 0
MANCHESTER UNITED (1) 2
Att: 33,075
GOALS: Yorke 4, 59
Sunday's draw was ominous for The Blues because in 59 previous encounters against Manchester United at Stamford Bridge, Chelsea had won just 16 to United's 29. Gianluca Vialli's unbeaten home record fell to United who had just three shots on target all game but scored twice through Yorke to keep their hopes of an unprecedented treble alive.
TEAM: ***Schmeichel 8,** Neville, G 7, Irwin 7, Stam 7, Beckham 7, Cole 7 (sub 72 mins Neville, P), Giggs 7 (sub 76 mins Blomqvist), Keane 7, Scholes 7, Yorke 8 (sub 85 mins Solskjaer), Berg 7. Not used: van der Gouw, Brown. **Referee** PA Durkin 8. **Booking** Yorke (unsporting behaviour, 67)
MATCH RATING ★★★

46 FA PREMIERSHIP
SATURDAY MARCH 13

NEWCASTLE (1) 1
MANCHESTER UNITED (1) 2
Att: 36,776
GOALS: Cole 24, 50
Two-goal Andy Cole sunk his former club without a trace as United ran out easy winners, more so than the scoreline suggests. Cole's brace took Alex Ferguson's men's unbeaten run in the Premiership to 11 games. What made it all the more pleasing for Ferguson was that his side came from behind, after Solano had given The Magpies the lead direct from a free-kick.
TEAM: Schmeichel 6 (sub 46 mins van der Gouw 7), Neville, G 8, Irwin 8, Berg 8, Stam 8, Beckham 7, Keane 8, Scholes 7 (sub 86 mins Neville, P), Giggs 7 (sub 74 mins Johnsen), ***Cole 9,** Yorke 7. Not used: Solskjaer, Blomqvist. **Referee** DR Elleray 7. **Booking** Irwin (dissent, 69).
MATCH RATING ★★★★

47 EUROPEAN CHAMPIONS CUP QUARTER-FINAL SECOND LEG
WEDNESDAY MARCH 17

INTER MILAN (0) 1
MANCHESTER UNITED (0) 1
Att: 79,528
GOAL: Scholes 88
United weathered all-out Inter pressure and lived dangerously in a whirlwind opening spell, surviving Zanetti's drive against the post. An amazing backs-to-the-wall display then saw United hold firm before silencing the home support in the dying minutes when Paul Scholes struck to score the equaliser and secure United's passage into the next round.
TEAM: Schmeichel 8, ***Berg 9,** Irwin 7, Stam 8, Johnsen 8 (sub 77 mins Scholes), Keane 7, Beckham 8, Cole 7, Yorke 7, Neville, G 7, Giggs 7 (sub 82 mins Neville, P). Not used: van der Gouw, Blomqvist, Sheringham, Solskjaer, Brown. **Referee** G Veissiere (FRA) 9. **Bookings** Johnsen (unsporting behaviour, 36), Neville, P (foul, 90).
MATCH RATING ★★★★

48 FA PREMIERSHIP
SUNDAY MARCH 21

MANCHESTER UNITED (0) 3
EVERTON (0) 1
Att: 55,182
GOALS: Solskjaer 54, Neville, G 63, Beckham 67
Manchester United appeared to be suffering post-Inter syndrome during an appalling first half. However, they came to life ten minutes after the interval when Solskjaer scored his 16th goal in as many appearances this season. Gary Neville notched only his second senior goal before Beckham produced a trademark free-kick to kill off Everton.
TEAM: Schmeichel 7, Neville, G 8, Neville, P 7, ***Stam 9,** Berg 8, Beckham 7 (sub 71 mins Greening), Butt 6, Johnsen 6, Solskjaer 7 (sub 90 mins Curtis), Cole 6 (sub 71 mins Sheringham), Yorke 8. Not used: van der Gouw, Brown. **Referee** MA Riley 7. **Bookings** None.
MATCH RATING ★★★★

49 FA PREMIERSHIP
SATURDAY APRIL 3

WIMBLEDON (1) 1
MANCHESTER UNITED (1) 1
Att: 26,121
GOAL: Beckham 44
Wimbledon managed a backs-to-the-wall performance for much of the second half to break a three-game losing streak. United time and again stormed in to dangerous territory in the closing stages. Only a string of magnificent saves from Neil Sullivan saved the point for The Dons, particularly when he diverted a stinging shot from Jesper Blomqvist with his foot.
TEAM: Schmeichel 6, Neville, G 7, Irwin 6, Johnsen 7, Beckham 7, Cole 7, Blomqvist 6 (sub 72 mins Solskjaer), Keane 7, ***Scholes 8,** Yorke 8, Berg 7. Not used: Butt, Giggs, Neville, P, van der Gouw. **Referee** GP Barber 8. **Booking** Berg (foul, 15).
MATCH RATING ★★★★

50 EUROPEAN CHAMPIONS CUP SEMI-FINAL FIRST LEG
WEDNESDAY APRIL 7

MANCHESTER UNITED (0) 1
JUVENTUS (1) 1
Att: 54,487
GOAL: Giggs 90
Ryan Giggs gave United a lifeline for the second leg in Turin when he fired the equaliser more than a minute into stoppage time. United had been fortunate to keep the Italians to a single-goal half-time lead, after Antonio Conte had struck. Yet Old Trafford came to life in the last five minutes when Teddy Sheringham had a goal disallowed for offside and Paul Scholes directed a point-blank header at Angelo Peruzzi.
TEAM: Schmeichel 7, Neville, G 5, Irwin 6, Stam 7, Beckham 7, Cole 6, Giggs 8, ***Keane 9,** Scholes 6, Yorke 5 (sub 79 mins Sheringham), Berg 5 (sub 46 mins Johnsen 7). Not used: van der Gouw, Butt, Neville, P, Blomqvist, Solskjaer. **Referee** MD Vega (SPA) 6. **Bookings** None
MATCH RATING ★★★★

51 FA CUP SEMI-FINAL
SUNDAY APRIL 11

MANCHESTER UNITED (0) 0
ARSENAL (0) 0
After extra-time
Att: 39,217
The two top teams in the Premiership fought out a goalless draw at Villa Park. The Red Devils had a first-half goal by Keane disallowed while The Gunners had to battle bravely in extra-time after Vivas was sent off for a second yellow card.
TEAM: Schmeichel 7, Neville, G 7, Johnsen 7, ***Stam 8,** Irwin 6, Beckham 7, Butt 7, Keane 7, Giggs 6 (sub 99 mins Solskjaer 6), Cole 6 (sub 113 mins Scholes), Yorke 6. Not used: Blomqvist, van der Gouw. **Referee** DR Elleray 6. **Bookings** Neville, G, (dissent, 2): Irwin (dissent, 40).
MATCH RATING ★★★

THE DREAM TREBLE!

GARY NEVILLE

"These moments will affect me for the rest of my life."

GARY NEVILLE tells **MATCH** about **MAN. UNITED**'s greatest ever season.

GARY NEVILLE HAS DONE IT ALL. EVER SINCE HE forced his way into the first team, back in 1994, the Man. United full-back has won three Premier League titles, three FA Cups and one European Cup. He has been a model of consistency and his partnership with David Beckham down the right flank has been a thorn in the side of many unfortunate opponents.

His England career has been almost as spectacular since he burst onto the scene in Euro '96, suffering the heartbreak of losing on penalties against Germany in the semi-final and then again against Argentina in the World Cup in France last year. Gary Neville is already a Manchester United legend. And he's only 24 years old! Gary spoke to MATCH about what winning the treble means to him personally and reflected on what has been the most amazing season in Manchester United's prestigious history.

WHAT DID WINNING THE EUROPEAN CUP MEAN TO YOU?

"There are no words which can explain what winning the European Cup means to a Man. United player or fan. Words understate how important this was. We went around Manchester and we saw grown men screaming with their veins popping out of their heads and kids were crying. These moments will affect me for the rest of my life and the memories will stay with me forever."

DID YOU EVER THINK YOU COULD REALLY ACHIEVE THE TREBLE?

"No, at the start of the season we'd have taken any trophy and there is no way we thought we would win all three – although you do set out to win every trophy you can and every game. I don't know who wrote the script for us, but it was a dream season. You are always going to get difficult games when you need something – like against Arsenal in the FA Cup, Juventus and Bayern Munich in Europe – we've just been able to produce the unbelievable at the right time."

DID WINNING NOTHING IN 1997-98 HELP TO MOTIVATE YOU?

"Sometimes you look back and think that some things give you a necessary kick up the backside. Winning nothing the previous season was nasty, but it gave us the kick we needed to win everything. We had to remember how devastated we were and take that with us into the future. No great team has won trophies without feeling the devastation of defeat as well."

IT WAS A BIT OF A BUMPY RIDE GETTING THERE WASN'T IT?

"In the FA Cup there was strong competition because we played Liverpool, Arsenal, Chelsea and Middlesbrough. We drew the so-called 'Group Of Death' in the Champions League and people said we couldn't get through. We got through then met Inter Milan, Juventus and Bayern again. People can't say we've had it easy. We've played the best teams in every competition and we've won the lot."

YOU SEEMED TO LEAVE EVERYTHING TO THE VERY LAST MINUTE!

"I don't think Man. United fans – and any fans in general – will ever be entertained as much in terms of the way we won everything. Obviously Liverpool have won a treble and teams abroad have done it, but not in the same way. Most people get one or two really exciting games in their career, but we've had five or six this season."

YOU'VE NOW ACHIEVED MORE THAN UNITED LEGENDS ROBSON, BRUCE AND CANTONA...

"It's a great honour to win the European Cup, but the

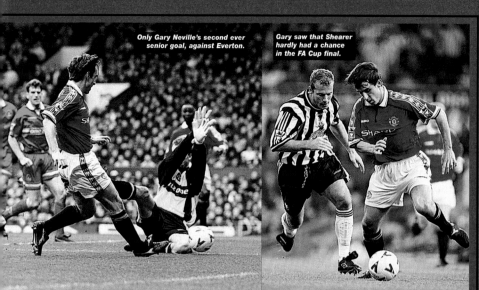

Only Gary Neville's second ever senior goal, against Everton.

Gary saw that Shearer hardly had a chance in the FA Cup final.

Victory in the Stadium Delle Alpi, Turin.

Michael Owen watches Gary break away.

Gary and younger brother Phil with the FA Cup.

The trophy aloft, United have fulfilled the impossible dream.

Celebrations after the final whistle blows in the final.

...egends who have come before us set the platform. We weren't under as much pressure to win the European Cup as players like Eric Cantona and Bryan Robson were under to win the first title in 1992-93. That year was the greatest moment for me as a Manchester United fan and it surpassed any title I have won – until now."

HAVE MANCHESTER UNITED SEALED THEIR STATUS AS A GREAT TEAM NOW?

"Yes we have. This team has shown that it is one of the best teams in Europe. Everything at this club is special though. I have never played to much less than a full house and whatever games you play in at United, the atmosphere is tremendous. That is one of the things which helps the players to be motivated for every game."

HOW HAPPY ARE YOU ALL FOR ALEX FERGUSON TO HAVE FULFILLED HIS GREAT AMBITION?

"I think everyone's delighted for the manager because all the players at the club realise that he has given them an opportunity – especially the youngsters. For us to be playing in the youth team five years ago and now winning the European Cup under his management is unbelievable – he has done so much for all of our careers. People said he would never be recognised as a truly great manager until he won the European Cup – now he has, he's up there and there will never be another manager like him."

---

52 FA CUP SEMI-FINAL REPLAY
WEDNESDAY APRIL 14

MANCHESTER UNITED	(1) 2
ARSENAL	(0) 1

AET (90mins 1-1). Att: 30, 223
GOALS: Beckham 17, Giggs 109.
A brilliant extra-time goal by substitute Ryan Giggs enabled ten-man United to win their tenth successive semi-final. Irf the last ever FA Cup semi-final replay, The Gunners went behind to a Beckham special but levelled through Bergkamp's deflected effort in the second half. High drama saw an Anelka 'goal' disallowed, Keane sent off and Schmeichel save a last-gasp Bergkamp penalty before Giggs' strike.
TEAM: Schmeichel 7, Neville, G 6, Johnsen 6, Stam 6, Neville, P 6, Keane 7, Blomqvist 6 (sub 62 mins Giggs 7), Sheringham 6 (sub 75 mins Scholes 6), Solskjaer 6 (sub 91 mins Yorke 6). Not used: Irwin, van der Gouw. **Referee** DR Elleray 7. **Bookings** Stam (foul, 27), Keane (foul, 33), Beckham (foul, 34). **Sending-off:** Keane (second bookable offence, 73).
MATCH RATING ★★★★★

53 FA PREMIERSHIP
SATURDAY APRIL 17

MANCHESTER UNITED	(2) 3
SHEFFIELD WEDNESDAY	(0) 0

Att: 55,270
GOALS: Solskjaer 35, Sheringham 44, Scholes 62.
United won at a canter with the perfect warm-up for their European Champions Cup semi-final second leg against Juventus. Solskjaer put United ahead with a simple goal and Sheringham doubled the lead with a superb effort in the closing seconds of the first half. Scholes completed the scoring, with Alex Ferguson making three substitutions soon after, which included a first league outing for David May.
TEAM: van der Gouw 7, Neville, G 7, Neville, P 7, Stam 7 (sub 63 mins May 6), Brown 7, *Scholes 9, Keane 7 (sub 63 mins Greening 6), Butt 8, Solskjaer 8, Sheringham 8, Blomqvist 7 (sub 75 mins Irwin). Not used: Yorke, Beckham. **Referee** NS Barry 8. **Bookings** None
MATCH RATING ★★★

54 EUROPEAN CHAMPIONS CUP SEMI-FINAL SECOND LEG
WEDNESDAY APRIL 21

JUVENTUS	(2) 2
MANCHESTER UNITED	(2) 3

Att: 64,500
GOALS: Keane 24, Yorke 34, Cole 84
On a spellbinding night, United at last progressed to within touching distance of the European Cup. Even a two-goal deficit failed to break their resolve and in a breathtaking fight-back, United scored three and struck the woodwork twice. A Roy Keane yellow card means he misses the final, while Paul Scholes also misses out after his booking.
TEAM: Schmeichel 9, Neville, G 8, Irwin 9, Johnsen 9, *Stam 9, Beckham 8, Keane 9, Butt 8, Blomqvist 7 (sub 68 mins Scholes 7), Yorke 8, Cole 9. Not used: van der Gouw, May, Sheringham, Neville, P, Solskjaer, Brown. **Referee** U Meier (SUI) 7. **Bookings** Keane (foul, 33); Scholes (foul, 76).
MATCH RATING ★★★★★

55 FA PREMIERSHIP
SUNDAY APRIL 25

LEEDS UNITED	(1) 1
MANCHESTER UNITED	(0) 1

Att: 40,255
GOAL: Cole 56
For the second time in a week United showed the resilience of champions, fighting back to take a hard-earned point. David O'Leary's young Leeds side, with seven of the starting line-up aged 22 or under, again gave notice that they will be a team to be reckoned with in the future with a fine display. The Red Devils, drained from their win in Turin, grafted through a game when at one time they looked like being overwhelmed and almost stole the points late on, but Yorke fluffed a chance.
TEAM: Schmeichel 7, Neville, G 7, May 6, Brown 6, Irwin 6 (sub 71 mins Neville, P), Beckham 6 (sub 84 mins Scholes), Butt 7, *Keane 8, Blomqvist 7 (sub 77 mins Sheringham), Yorke 7, Cole 7. Not used: van der Gouw, Curtis. **Referee** DJ Gallagher 7. **Bookings** May (foul, 9), Butt (foul, 35), Keane (foul, 73).
MATCH RATING ★★★★

56 FA PREMIERSHIP
SATURDAY MAY 1

MANCHESTER UNITED	(1) 2
ASTON VILLA	(1) 1

Att: 55,189
GOALS: Watson 20 own goal, Beckham 46
United went ahead thanks to an own-goal by Steve Watson but they relaxed and allowed Aston Villa back into the match when Julian Joachim equalised. Beckham set Old Trafford alight though, when he scored from one of his amazing free-kicks a minute after the interval to recapture the lead. The result should have been put beyond doubt when United were awarded a penalty but Irwin's kick was saved by Oakes.
TEAM: Schmeichel 7, Neville, G 7, Irwin 6, May 7 (sub 79 mins Brown), Johnsen 9, *Beckham 9, Butt 6, Scholes 7, Sheringham 7, Yorke 7, Blomqvist 6 (sub 63 mins Neville, P 7). Not used: van der Gouw, Wilson, Greening. **Referee** KW Burge 7. **Bookings** None
MATCH RATING ★★★★

57 FA PREMIERSHIP
WEDNESDAY MAY 5

LIVERPOOL	(0) 2
MANCHESTER UNITED	(1) 2

Att: 44,702
GOALS: Yorke 22, Irwin 57 (pen)
Another comeback saw Gerard Houllier's Liverpool put a massive dent in United's championship aspirations. Former United skipper Paul Ince gleefully slid home the equaliser with minutes remaining. United appeared home and dry through Yorke's 28th goal of the season and Irwin's

58 FA PREMIERSHIP
SUNDAY MAY 9

MIDDLESBROUGH	(0) 0
MANCHESTER UNITED	(1) 1

Att: 34,665
GOAL: Yorke 45
A disputed 29th goal of the season by the prolific Dwight Yorke took United back to the top of the table. Both Sheringham and Yorke looked offside as they played head-tennis across the six-yard box before the leading scorer nodded home in first-half stoppage time. But justice was done because what looked like a perfectly legitimate Teddy Sheringham's strike was ruled out earlier in the game.
TEAM: Schmeichel 6, Neville, G 6, May 6, *Stam 8, Irwin 7, Beckham 7, Keane 6 (sub 25 mins Butt 7), Scholes 7 (sub 90 mins Neville, P), Blomqvist 6 (sub 66 mins Cole 7), Yorke 7, Sheringham 7. Not used: van der Gouw, Brown. **Referee** GP Barber 5. **Bookings** Scholes (foul, 6), Sheringham (foul, 72), Neville, G (foul, 87).
MATCH RATING ★★★

59 FA PREMIERSHIP
WEDNESDAY MAY 12

BLACKBURN ROVERS	(0) 0
MANCHESTER UNITED	(0) 0

Att: 30,436
One point was insufficient to keep Blackburn Rovers in the Premiership, temporarily at least, but it gives United a slight advantage in the championship race. A fairly dour contest saw few genuine scoring chances created by either side, but The Red Devils will be disappointed with the manner in which they failed to capitalise on having the bulk of attacking possession during the game, especially in the first half. Giggs struck a post and was thwarted by goalkeeper Filan, but Ashley Ward squandered a great chance for Rovers to steal the game late on.
TEAM: Schmeichel 7, Neville, G 7, Johnsen 7, Stam 7 (sub 46 mins May 7), Irwin 6, *Beckham 8, Butt 7, Neville, P 6 (sub 75 mins Scholes), Giggs 7, Yorke 7, Cole 6 (sub 71 mins Sheringham). Not used: Solskjaer, van der Gouw. **Referee** MD Reed 7. **Bookings** Butt (foul, 51), Beckham (foul, 90).
MATCH RATING ★★

60 FA PREMIERSHIP
SUNDAY MAY 16

MANCHESTER UNITED	(1) 2
TOTTENHAM HOTSPUR	(1) 1

Att: 55,189
GOALS: Beckham 42, Cole 48
Old Trafford went wild as Manchester United celebrated the first leg of their treasured treble by clinching the Premiership title in front of their own fans at Old Trafford. The Red Devils had to come from behind after Les Ferdinand's shock goal gave Spurs the lead. United scored twice and created many more good chances. But Spurs threatened to spoil the party on a number of occasions.
TEAM: Schmeichel 7, Neville, G 8, Irwin 8, May 7, Johnsen 7, Keane 8, *Beckham 8, Sheringham 6 (sub 46 mins Cole 8), Giggs 7 (sub 78 mins Neville, P), Scholes 7 (sub 70 mins Butt 7), Yorke 8. Not used: van der Gouw, Solskjaer. **Referee** G Poll 7. **Bookings** Sheringham (foul, 27).
MATCH RATING ★★★★★

61 FA CUP FINAL
SATURDAY MAY 22

MANCHESTER UNITED	(1) 2
NEWCASTLE UNITED	(0) 0

Att: 79,101
GOALS: Sheringham 11, Scholes 53
Man. United made it three doubles in six years and moved to within one step of a momentous treble, but Newcastle provided poor opposition in a final that was far from a classic. Fate was on the side of United, who lost skipper Roy Keane after just eight minutes through injury, only for his replacement Teddy Sheringham to score just 80 seconds after coming on. In the second half, Sheringham turned creator as he set up Scholes for a decisive second, shortly after half-time.
TEAM: Schmeichel 7, Neville, G 7, Neville, P 6, May 8, Johnsen 7, Keane (sub 9 mins *Sheringham 8), Beckham 7, Scholes 7 (sub 77 mins Stam), Giggs 8, Cole 7 (sub 61 mins Yorke 7), Solskjaer 7. Not used: van der Gouw, Blomqvist. **Referee** P Jones 8. **Bookings** None
MATCH RATING ★★

62 EUROPEAN CUP FINAL
WEDNESDAY MAY 26

BAYERN MUNICH	(1) 1
MANCHESTER UNITED	(0) 2

Att: 90,000
GOALS: Sheringham 89, Solskjaer 90
Extraordinary scenes in the Nou Camp saw United clinch an amazing victory – and an historic trophy treble – from the jaws of defeat with two late goals. A nightmare start saw the departing Peter Schmeichel at fault from Basler's early free-kick which put the Germans ahead, but The Red Devils dug deeper than ever to rescue a seemingly lost cause. Substitutes Sheringham and Solskjaer snatched the history-making strikes on a night of celebration in Barcelona.
TEAM: Schmeichel 7, Neville, G 7, Irwin 7, Stam 8, Johnsen 7, *Beckham 8, Butt 7, Blomqvist 6 (sub 67 mins Sheringham 8), Cole 6 (sub 81 mins Solskjaer 8), Yorke 6. Not used: van der Gouw, May, Neville, P, Greening, Brown. **Referee** P Collina (ITA) 8. **Bookings** None
MATCH RATING ★★★★

John's room is a shrine to The Sky Blues and he goes to nearly all their home games.

MANCHESTER CITY F.C.

M.C.F.C.

JUNIOR BLUES

A TYPICAL WEEKEND

FRIDAY
3PM: LEAVE SCHOOL AND DRIVE TO BELFAST.

5PM: SET SAIL ON FERRY TO STRANRAER.

7PM: DRIVE TO MANCHESTER. ARRIVE AT MANCHESTER LATE AT NIGHT AND STAY AT NANA'S HOUSE.

SATURDAY
3PM: KICK-OFF AT MAINE ROAD AND ANOTHER THREE POINTS HOPEFULLY!

6PM: FISH AND CHIPS.

7PM: DRIVE TO STRANRAER AND ARRIVE AT THE PORT 'SLEEP' FOR A WHILE IN THE CAR UNTIL 4.30AM.

SUNDAY
5AM: FERRY BACK TO BELFAST.

8AM: ARRIVE HOME AND DO MY HOMEWORK.

8PM: BED AND FINALLY SOME PROPER SLEEP!

FAN OF THE YEAR!

MATCH goes in search for the most footy mad readers on the planet!

John's family spend between £200 and £350 twice a month on City.

JOHN CATCHES A FEW HOURS SLEEP ON THE FERRY!

Name: John McDermott

Age: 14 years old

Occupation: schoolboy

There are thousands and thousands of loyal fans across the country who follow their teams through thick and thin, through the ups and the downs. Whether you support Manchester United or Kingstonian it doesn't matter, it's all about getting involved in football that counts. So, although every football fan is special, the MATCH Fan Of The Year had to offer something more, something that made them unique.

So how about a fan who takes a four hour ferry ride across the Irish Sea and a ten hour car journey to watch all his team's home games? And remember after the game he has to then go all the way back again. It's almost unbelievable, but that's the trip that Manchester City season ticket holder John McDermott makes with his parents every other Saturday.

John has lived in Millisle in Northern Ireland for the past eight years, but couldn't live without seeing his beloved City and he saw all but one of City's games at Maine Road last season. "I only missed the other home game with Walsall because it was moved from a Bank Holiday to a school day at short notice," John says.

The 14 year old sits in the Main Stand, he is a Junior Blues member, he tries to covert his Irish mates by taking them to games, and he owns far too many City videos, shirts, souvenirs and magazines to mention. John's even made extended trips to Manchester, which allowed him to go to City's training ground and get the autographs of his fave footy stars – ranging from Shaun Goater to Richard Edghill.

It sets John and his family back between £200 to £350 per match and hours of seemingly endless travelling, but when there's 90 minutes of pure excitement (and three points sometimes!) it's all worth it.

All around the WORLD

Check out these **MATCH** readers in exotic places.

Ryan Scott of Strathaven in Scotland took his copy of MATCH to the 'Countdown To Extinction' exhibition at the Animal Kingdom, **FLORIDA**.

MATCH received this holiday snap from **EGYPT**, where **Andrew Brinkhurst** of Macclesfield took his magazine on holiday.

What a way to read MATCH! **Robert Johnson** of Solihull was in The **THE ALGARVE** when he had his picture taken with the nation's top footy mag.

Sir Alex and the lads are big armchair footy fans – like most Man. United supporters.

the essential MATCH guide to becoming a...

MAN. UNITED COUCH POTATO

1 A telly! As you never go to games to see United play, you won't see them at all without one, unless your living room window looks out over the pitch at Old Trafford!

2 A very large sofa to seat all of your mates – Manchester may be a million miles away but you're all Red through and through!

3 A tray of Man. United party snacks for your mates, including some Stam-Burgers, a packet of Giggsy Crisps, a bottle of Coley Cola, and a Beckham Bar – the chew with a kick!

4 A full Manchester United squad list so you don't embarrass yourself in front of your mates by asking "Who's that?" when you see a close-up of Denis Irwin!

5 A stop watch, so you can tell exactly how much stoppage time has been played if you're losing!

6 A copy of '100 fantastic Facts About Man. United', in case one of your mates tries to catch you out with a trick question during the game!

7 A box of Kleenex in case Teddy Sheringham is lined-up to take a penalty!

8 A good book in case the only way to see the Reds tonight is by watching MUTV big match between United reserves and Coventry Reserves!

9 A 'Know Your team' poster, showing all of United's current playing kits – that way you will be able to tell which team to cheer for!

10 Alan Hansen and Jimmy Hill – if you've got them with you on your sofa, you won't have to listen to that mingin' ITV Champions League team summing up the game!

11 A video recorder and a collection of United championship, FA Cup and European Cup Final videos, just in case they lose a game or something less than brilliant happens, one day!

David Pearson of Ware, Hertfordshire, visited **VENICE** with his copy of MATCH. Someone saw the shirt and shouted 'Gianluca Vialli' at him!

Daniel Johnson lives in **PAPUA NEW GUINEA** and his friend in England sends him MATCH each week! He even goes snorkelling with the mag!

Jean-Luc Bragard from Stockport took his copy of MATCH to **URAGUAY** to the Centanario Stadium where the first World Cup Final was held.

POTENTIAL VIRUS ALERT!

The Manchester United virus: your PC gets a virus where the memory forgets everything before 1993.
The Dwight Yorke virus: everything in your computer goes goofy.
The Beckham virus: the lights on your PC are on, but nothing works.
The Roy Keane virus: throws you out of windows.
★ *Richard Thomas, Wrexham*

POSITION OF THE WEEK

Boy: "Mum, I've been picked for the school football team."
Mum: "Brilliant dear. What position do you play?"
Boy: "My teacher says I'm one of the drawbacks!"
★ *Edward Elgood, Winford, Somerset*

COLE'S NO JOKE

Andy Cole is ill, so Alex Ferguson goes to the supermarket for him, here he bumps into Gerard Houllier.
"Hello Alex, what are you doing here?" asks Gerard.
"I'm getting a bag of potatoes for Andy Cole," says Alex.
"Sounds like a fair swap to me!"
★ *Ally McCrae, e-mail*

CUP BLUES

Walter Smith got a phone call early one morning from the fire station. The fireman says: "Walter, Walter there's been a fire at Goodison!"
Walter shouts: "Save the cups!"
The fireman adds: "Don't worry – it hasn't spread to the canteen!"
★ *Jon Yates, Liverpool*

PLAYING CHICKEN

A chicken is playing football. He's having a great match scoring six goals. Later on, the chicken goes to take a throw-in and the ref comes up to him and says: "You're having a cracking match!"
"Thanks ref. I think it's all the extra-training I put in this week," says the chicken.
The ref says: "What's your job mate?" "I'm a lawyer," says the chicken. Suddenly the ref sends him off and all of his outraged team-mates run after him to ask why?
"Because he was a professional foul." he says.
★ *Peter Woolley, e-mail*

SEND YOUR JOKES OR PUNS TO: Jokes On You, MATCH Magazine, Bretton Court, Bretton, Peterborough, PE3 8DZ

THE FINAL WHISTLE ANSWERS

There are a grand total of 200 points available if, by some miracle, you managed to answer every question on all five Final Whistle pages correctly. Check out how many answers you got right below, add up your tally and then find out in the below just what kind of footballer you are!

171-200
YOU'RE WORLD FOOTBALLER OF THE YEAR!

Congratulations! There's not much that you don't know about football – in fact you're the type of person the nickname 'Statto' was made up for! It's very impressive, it has to be said. Do you have a life outside of football?

141-170
YOU'RE PLAYER OF THE YEAR!

Well done! You certainly know your stuff, but you haven't got your head stuck in a footy stats book all day long. You like to keep up-to-date with all the very latest news and you know the game inside out!

111-140
YOU'RE A FIVE MILLION POUND MAN

An impressive score. You know more about football than most people do, but your mates don't necessarily turn to you when they're stuck on the very toughest footy questions. Still, you can be pretty pleased with that effort.

81-110
YOU'RE A REGULAR STARTER

That's not bad. You have a better than average knowledge of football, but you don't have to know every statistic to enjoy your football – just the players' name will do for you! A decent enough try.

61-80
YOU'RE ON A WEEKLY CONTRACT

You're okay, but your knowledge is nothing special. You may be able to talk footy with your mates up to a point, but it won't be in any great detail. Keep up with the footy news and who plays for who in the future.

41-61
YOU'RE AVAILABLE ON A FREE TRANSFER

Hmmm. You'd better keep reading MATCH every week to keep yourself up to date with what's going on in the world of footy and maybe you'll do a little bit better next year. You're a real part-time supporter!

under 40
YOU'D BETTER TAKE EARLY RETIREMENT MATE!

Oh dear. What can we say? Football's not really your game is it? Perhaps you prefer to watch an enthralling game of tiddlywinks or even go trainspotting than watch the world's greatest game. We sympathise.

Final Whistle One — page 20

FIRST XI

1.
2.
3.
4.
5.
6.
7.
8.
9.
10.
11.

1. Andy Cole; 2. Graeme Le Saux; 3. Michael Owen; 4. David Seaman; 5. Chris Sutton; 6. David Beckham; 7. Tony Adams; 8. Alan Shearer; 9. Paul Gascoigne; 10. Nigel Martyn; 11. Teddy Sheringham.

CIVVY STREET

1.

Frank Lampard.

WHO PLAYS WHERE

1.   6.
2.   7.
3.   8.
4.   9.
5.

1: C; 2: A; 3: D; 4: E; 5: B; 6: I; 7: F; 8: G; 9: H.

WHAT WAS THE RESULT

1.   4.
2.   5.
3.   6.

1. 4-0; 2. 1-0; 3. 1-2; 4. 2-0; 5. 0-3; 6. 0-1.

1-0

1.
2.
3.
4.
5.

1. Dwight Yorke; 2. Marc Overmars; 3. Robbie Earle; 4. Brian Deane; 5. Steffen Iversen.

GUESS THE PLAYER

1.

Alan Shearer.

Final Whistle Two — page 48

SECOND XI

1.
2.
3.
4.
5.

6.
7.
8.
9.
10.
11.

1. Lee Chapman; 2. True; 3. £1.2 million from Leeds; 4. John Gorman; 5. Three; 6. True. 5th; 7. Andy Linighan; 8. John Gorman; 9. Nottingham Forest (Three times);10. 92 by Man. United in 1993-94; 11. 13th in 1990.

THE ANFIELD QUIZ

1.
2.
3.
4.
5.
6.
7.
8.
9.
10.
11.
12.

1. 1992; 2. Stanley Park; 3. You'll Never Walk Alone; 4. 1994; 5. This is Anfield; 6. False. Goodison Park has though; 7. Stromgodset; 8. Boxing and tennis matches; 9. Victims of the Hillsborough disaster; 10. Aintree racecourse; 11. France v Holland; 12. 45,000.

CONNECTIONS

1.

Both have missed a penalty in an FA Cup semi-final.

FORMER CLUBS

1.
2.
3.
4.
5.

1. Crystal Palace; 2. Monaco; 3. Juventus; 4. Coventry; 5. Leicester City.

SOL CAMPBELL QUIZ

1.
2.
3.
4.
5.

1. Sulzeer; 2. True; 3. 1999 Worthington Cup; 4. Eight; 5. Hungary (May 18,1996).

NAME THE CLUB

Manchester City.

GUESS THE YEAR

1.   2.
3.   4.

MY TOTAL OUT OF 200

5 ☐

1. 1965. 2. 1972. 3. 1973. 4. 1969. 5. 1972.

Final Whistle Three — page 62

THIRD XI
1
2
3
4
5
6
7
8
9
10
11

1. Christian Vieri. 2. Jaap Stam. 3. Alan Shearer. 4. Juninho. 5. Christian Vieri. 6. Chris Sutton. 7. Gianluca Vialli. 8. Dwight Yorke. 9. Ronaldo. 10. Denilson. 11. Christian Vieri.

CLUB NICKNAMES
1   4
2   5
3

1. B. 2. D. 3. E. 4. A. 5. C.

WHOSE NUMBER?
1
2
3
4
5

1. Alan Shearer. 2. Dion Dublin. 3. Paul Kitson. 4. Andy Cole. 5. Robbie Fowler.

2-1
1
2
3
4
5

1. Cadamarteri. 2. Flo. 3. Solskjaer. 4. Smith. 5. Giggs.

CONNECTIONS
1

They both played for Arsenal.

WHAT'S GOING ON?
1
2
3
4
5

1. Newcastle. 2. Bradford. 3. Middlesbrough. 4. Arsenal; 5. Nott'm Forest.

WHO'S MISSING?
1

Woodgate and Fowler.

ALL NATIONS
1
2
3
4
5

1. French. 2. Italian. 3. French. 4. Finnish. 5. Nigerian.

Final Whistle Four — page 80

FOURTH XI
1
2
3
4
5
6
7
8
9
10
11

1. Ian Wright. 2. Ole Gunnar Solskjaer. 3. Ryan Giggs. 4. Darius Vassell. 5. Michael Owen. 6. Teddy Sheringham; 7. Gianfranco Zola. 8. Andy Clarke. 9. Allan Nielsen. 10. Ian Rush. 11. Stuart McCall.

WORLD CHAMPIONS QUIZ
1
2
3
4
5
6
7
8
9
10
11
12

1. Juventus. 2. Saudi Arabia. 3. Christophe Dugarry. 4. Slaven Bilic. 5. Parma. 6. Aime Jacquet. 7. Lilian Thuram. 8. Frank Leboeuf. 9. Zinedine Zidane and Manu Petit. 10. Stephane Guivar'ch. 11. Marcel Desailly. 12. Bernard Lama and Lionel Charbonnier.

FORMER CLUBS
1
2
3
4
5

1. Blackburn. 2. Bournemouth. 3. Rosenborg. 4. Vitesse Arnhem. 5. Borussia Dortmund.

PATRICK VIEIRA QUIZ
1
2
3
4
5

1. Senegal. 2. Cannes. 3. AC Milan. 4. £3.5 million; 5. Two.

CIVVY STREET
1

John Aloisi.

GUESS THE YEAR
1   2
3   4
5

1. 1976. 2. 1969. 3. 1967. 4. 1967. 5. 1971

NAME THE CLUB
1

Everton.

Final Whistle Five — page 92

FIFTH XI
1
2
3
4
5
6
7
8
9
10
11

1. Manchester City. 2. They scored an injury-time winner to deny West Ham first place; 3. Notts County. 4. They went down on goal difference. 5. Five; 6. Graham Stuart; 7. They also won the championship; 8. Hereford and Brighton; 9. Southampton, Coventry and Sheffield Wednesday. 10. Beagrie, Mills, Blake; 11. Twice.

RANGERS MEGA QUIZ
1
2
3
4
5
6
7
8
9
10
11
12
13
14
15
16
17
18
19
20

1. 1873. 2. 1879 The Glasgow Charity Cup; 3. Preston. 9. Aston Villa; 5. None; 6. 1956-57; 7. 1972; 8. Third; 9. Parma; 10. Qualifying round; 11. 2-10 v Airdrie; 12. 14-2; 13. John Greig; 14. 51,000; 15. Celtic; 16. Mark Hateley; 17. Kanchelskis, who cost £5.5m; 18. Ally McCoist – he won 59 caps for Scotland; 19. 250; 20. Nothing.

CONNECTIONS
1

They were both signed and sold by Kevin Keegan during his time at Newcastle.

FORMER CLUBS
1
2
3
4
5

1. Crewe; 2. Middlesbrough; 3. Crystal Palace; 4. Crewe; 5. Oxford.

PAUL GASCOIGNE QUIZ
1
2
3
4
5

1. Fog on the Tyne (Revisited); 2. Gary Charles. 3. £5.5 million; 4. Andy Goram; 5. Gianluca Festa; 6. True; ten times.

WHAT POSITION?
1   4
2   5
3

1. D. 2. C. 3. E. 4. B. 5. A. 6. F.

ALL NATIONS
1
2
3
4
5

1. Swedish. 2. Slovakian. 3. Norwegian. 4. Danish; 5. Australian.

MEGA CROSSWORD & MEGA WORDSPOT

Crossword Answers: Across: 1. Branch; 4. Phil; 8. Parlour; 9. Kanu; 10. Walter; 13. Robson; 15. Ross; 19. Ruddock; 20. Boyd; 21. Batson. Down: 1. Blinker; 2. Aspin; 3. Davis; 5. Hurst; 6. Lee; 7. Nolan; 11. Rushden; 12. Bondsi 14. Barry; 16. Oakes; 17. Zola; 18. Job

SON OF A TOP GUN!

Our award for Best Footballer's Son Of 1999 goes to Charlie Sheringham – who managed to get himself onto the team coach after the European Cup Final! Nice one son!

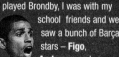

i've met a footballer, but...

Have you ever met a famous football player in an unusual place? These **MATCH** readers have!

"I've met a footballer in a weird place. I met **Michael Owen** and **Danny Murphy** in a Little Chef on the A41, in the South Wirral, last summer after the World Cup. I got their autographs on a menu!"
Thomas Astley, **Wallasey**

"The other week I was walking past my local laundry and as I had a quick glance, I could see Tottenham's **Steffen Iversen** sitting in there. As I am a Spurs fan, I nearly fainted! I rushed in there and I was talking to him just as if he was my best mate. I got his autograph, but he didn't give me any news of what was going to happen at Spurs. He did say that training under George Graham is very hard though."
Robert Burns, **London**

"I am an Arsenal fan who recently moved to Denmark. One day in Copenhagen, the day before Barcelona played Brondby, I was with my school friends and we saw a bunch of Barça stars – **Figo**, **Anderson** and **Zenden** – outside McDonald's. We called over to them but they didn't like us very much, they thought we were weirdos!"
Mark Crowdey, **Hørsholm, Denmark**

"When I was in the car going on holiday with my family, I saw **Nicky Butt** of Manchester United in his car in the next lane. He then stopped right next to our car as the traffic lights were on red! He didn't look over at at me or anything, but I did notice he had a really nice car!"
Robert Pamphlett, **Bolton**

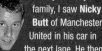

10 ESSENTIAL WAYS...

...to get into a football match absolutely free!

1 Get your school teacher to invite an official from the club to give your class a talk. Hopefully they'll bring in some free tickets. Cheeky, but good!

2 Get a job working on the turnstiles or working in the canteen. Neither are busy during the match so you can watch the game.

3 Tell your parents their house is a dump and get them to move. There's some great places in Luton and Barnet where you can watch the match from your bedroom window.

4 If you're a girl, join your local cheerleading group. You get to walk out on the pitch when you to do the entertainment at half-time. Be sure to hide your face with a pom-pom though.

5 Join your local academy – that's how Michael Owen used to get tickets to watch Liverpool. If it's good enough for him, it's good enough for us.

6 Turn up to the match early and walk around the ground. Keep your eyes peeled to the floor just in case anyone's thrown away a spare ticket.

7 Join your local branch of St John's ambulance. You can help them out at footy games, when they're on hand for emergencies.

8 Become a member of your team's supporters club and who knows, you could be chosen to present the supporters' award for Player Of The Year. It'll be on the pitch and you get a seat in the Directors' Box for the day

9 Become best friends with someone who's a season ticket holder who also happens to work night shifts. They won't be able to go to any of the evening matches, so they should hopefully give their ticket to you!

10 Join your local footy side. Nationwide league teams often run penalty shoot-out competitions at half-time and you could get your team involved. The downside is you could end up feeling like David Batty missing a penalty in front of thousands of people!

11 Enter a competition in MATCH. We're always offering free tickets to go to see important matches and all it will cost you is the price of a stamp, it's certainly worth a try!

Well, unfortunately everything has to end somewhere and you've now reached the last pages of the MATCH Annual 2000, so why don't you write in (to MATCH, Bretton Court, Bretton, Peterborough, PE3 8DZ) to tell us what you think. But before you put the annual to the back of your cupboard, remember in next year's book we will be printing photos of MATCH readers pictured on holiday or with a footballer – as long as you get the annual in the picture! So get the cameras ready.

We hope you've had a great read and have a great Year 2000!